MW01100575

GOLDEN THROAT

My journey with family in faith

A memoir by **Paul Francis Bickert**

WRITERS REPUBLIC L.L.C.
515 Summit Ave. Unit R1
Union City, NJ 07087, USA

Website: *www.writersrepublic.com*
Hotline: *1-877-656-6838*
Email: *info@writersrepublic.com*

Ordering Information:
Quantity sales. Special discounts are available on quantity purchases by corporations, associations, and others. For details, contact the publisher at the address above.

Library of Congress Control Number:		2020950902
ISBN-13:	978-1-63728-020-1	[Paperback Edition]
	978-1-63728-021-8	[Digital Edition]

Rev. date: 12/14/2020

Introduction

by Richard Joyce

Wearing the distinctive purple and white neck scarf of the 5th Nelson Wolf Cub pack, Paul walked through the snow past my childhood home and that's where we first met when we were both nine. I desperately wanted to become a Cub and especially a member of the 5th Nelson which met once a week in a classic log building. I asked Paul how to join and he told me he would call for me next Monday evening and he would take me to the meeting. Our friendship grew through that winter and after into many summers.

In Nelson children seldom watched television but spent the summer afternoons and early evenings on the streets and in the alleys near their homes playing softball, kick-the-can, red rover and hide and seek. They sometimes formed alliances and built forts in the bush and the Catholics fought mock battles against the Protestants throwing the ripened chestnuts that seemed to bounce and roll endlessly down Nelson's steep streets. At noon each day the Angeles bell rang from the nearby Cathedral of Mary Immaculate and Paul always paused whatever game it was to revere the Blessed Virgin Mary. Some of us knew the significance of the Angeles but those who did not ever questioned Paul's devotion

Ghost stories were popular as twilight set and after the daytime alliances had dissolved both Catholic and Protestant sat together terrified and spellbound by the tales. Paul and the rest of us would head home in groups only when the evening curfew horn sounded at 9:30 from the Nelson fire hall.

It was during these halcyon days in Nelson we all learned tolerance much beyond the often, strident lessons of home. When the afternoon chestnut battles ceased between the Catholic and Protestant children and when we all sat together for the twilight stories, we came to the knowledge that we all read the same comics, came from good parents or bad of any faith, that we all shared the same pleasures and that we all harboured the same fears and misgivings. We learned there that none of us held the monopoly on truth.

Paul's roots and his strong Catholicism are firmly rooted in the Canadian Prairies, but I believe it took the days and the youthful experiences in the Kootenays and the Okanagan to mellow him and to form the tolerant and resourceful adult he would become.

Paul and I lived in a part of Nelson where the older women in the neighbourhood seemed to have no interests other than hanging out the wash every Monday morning and peeking through the curtains each time a car drove by, a dog barked or a child's voice was heard. We played the game well as we walked by their houses laughing or singing and then watching how long it took the curtains to move. Fortunately, it was about this time that our lives and interests began to expand beyond the neighbourhood. The streets by our homes now became the streets downtown and the playing areas became the city parks and often the highways.

Gyro Park with its forested areas and Lakeside Park with its cottonwoods and warm beach are Nelson's two finest parks and we both spent many hours hiking through Gyro or swimming and ogling the girls at Lakeside. But it was at the City of Nelson's baseball park that Paul taught me a life's lesson. One evening when we were in grade eight, we strolled downtown hoping to find a pick-up softball game and found none, but we did hear some older teens giggling and speaking of things

I did not understand. Paul explained to me that they were talking about sex and then he enlightened me.

Paul always held a sense of wonder and adventure. He marvelled at something as ordinary as a bee pollinating a flower. He was intrigued by the size of the universe and how many stars were in the heavens. I asked him if even God knew how many bees there were, or the number of stars and Paul assured me that He did. Often, we feared the Russians would bomb us and we consoled each other with assurances that Nelson was of no importance and besides they didn't even know where it was.

We discussed these things and many others when we sometimes spent summer afternoons hitchhiking to Kaslo, Salmo or to Ainsworth Hot Springs just for something to do. When rides were slow, we often hitchhiked either way. The destination was not as important in Paul's mind as was the adventure. He was a young Jack Kerouac.

———————◆———————

When he was twelve Paul moved with his family to a residence where they lived and operated a small café, ten miles from Nelson near the West Arm of Kootenay Lake. It was there another phase of life began. Nearby was Kokanee Provincial Park with its hidden trails along Kokanee Creek. Paul and John often took me there where we marvelled at the sight of scarlet Kokanee fighting the current upstream to spawn. On hot days we waded the frigid waters of the pristine stream while Paul cautioned us about disturbing the spawning beds.

During the afternoons we picked huckleberries for Paul's mother's remarkably delicious pies which she sold in the cafe. Our charge for the berries was simply a piece of a pie with ice cream or as Paul called it "Pie a la Mode with ice cream on top." Often when we had more berries than could be used in pies, Paul's father would buy them from us for twenty-five cents a pound. To weigh the huckleberries, he held a pound of butter in one hand and a bag of berries in the other and when the two weights appeared equal, he would hand the butter and the bag to us for confirmation. There never was any dispute.

We often walked to the other side of Kokanee Park to swim in the lake and to explore the forested area nearby. In one marshy spot mosquitoes abounded and drove us nearly to distraction. I cursed the plague of insects and asked of what use they were. Paul told me of Job and his patience while John reminded me that mosquitoes too had their place in God's creation, for they were food for the Kokanee and for the birds that flew overhead.

We walked the woods and swam the beaches, but we also met people far removed from the city. The Sodlosky sisters lived not far away and they had eyes for Paul and John. Mr. Clum lived seven miles away and we bicycled there to speak with him. Mr. Clum was a gentle old man living alone in a log house surrounded by forest and by the flowers he kept. He invited us in and treated us to Coca-Cola. George Clerihew, a gentleman farmer who raised pigs lived nearby. Once Paul and John and I went there in the evening and watched a sow suckling her young. John remarked that it was too bad that these animals would soon be, slaughtered and George told us that that was the purpose of domestic animals. We learned something and understood then that that was the case.

Paul's fervent Catholic faith and his sense of quest have motivated him throughout life and often in circuitous ways. After finishing grade nine in Nelson, Paul moved to Alberta to complete high school at three schools while during that time also pursuing a career in radio broadcasting in Edmonton. Paul had an extraordinarily rich and pleasant baritone voice which served him well as a newscaster both in Alberta and again upon his return to British Columbia where he worked at stations in Kamloops and Trail. In fact, we nicknamed him "golden throat" during his tenure in Trail. Accomplishing success in broadcasting came to Paul after much work overcoming earlier difficulties with reading. After defeating those earlier demons, Paul became a successful and sought-after broadcaster remembering his most painful moment as the day he had to announce the assassination of President John F. Kennedy in November 1963.

Paul's two-way road changed direction again shortly after his time back in British Columbia taking him again to Alberta where he rekindled an old acquaintance with Marlene, a friend of a friend he had met earlier during high school days in Edmonton and now a woman he had always wanted to know better.

Marlene and Paul married and settled in Edmonton, but Paul had never forgotten the near miraculous work Nelson chiropractor Dr. Bill Murphy had performed on his sister, Janice, when she was very young. Paul has always contended that it was the dedicated approach of Dr. Murphy using chiropractic techniques to help Janice that made her life much more comfortable. He had left radio before marrying and subsequently, spent three years working for Capitol and Columbia Records. It was soon afterwards that Paul's quest continued when he left Edmonton with his wife and two-year-old daughter, Natalie, to enrol at Palmer College of Chiropractic in Davenport, Iowa.

———◆———

Paul moved to Calgary where he practiced as a chiropractor for eight years before moving on to British Columbia settling in Kelowna where he continued to practice chiropractic for another twelve years while he and Marlene raised a family of three. Paul's professionalism and dedication to his work manifested themselves during those years when he served in several capacities as a Director with the Alberta Chiropractic Association, President of the Okanagan-Kootenay Chiropractic Society as well as Representative Assembly Director and International Director for the International Chiropractic Association of Arlington, Virginia.

A concern regarding the safety of cell phone antennas led Paul to experiment with a safer system and to develop a better antenna. Marketing his improvement took much time over a long and frustrating period but in the end proved financially rewarding.

His lifelong devotion to Our Lady and his unshakable support of and faith in the Catholic Church have shaped his life in manifest ways. Paul has made pilgrimages to Lourdes, Fatima and Medjugorje. In addition, he has visited the Holy Land and travelled to Rome five times. Through faith Paul witnessed a personal miracle while at Medjugorje.

Paul lives his faith, acts his faith and contributes to it. Perhaps his crowning achievement in mirroring his devotion is his co-founding the Chiropractic for the World Foundation dedicated to working with Dominicans in Ghana in building a school and dormitory. He has travelled extensively to Ghana and to cities in North America raising funds in addition to his own extensive financial contributions to the project.

———————◆———————

The late 1960's was an exuberant and tumultuous time for all of us making the transition between youth and adulthood. Youth questioned their parents' values, their own spiritual values and those of their leaders. The music of the time often fuelled the simmering discontent. During that period Paul, too, had doubts about his faith. He briefly explored other faiths and beliefs but returned soon to his lifelong Catholicism for it was there he found the solace, the sense of contentment and the structure which provided the inner peace which has guided him throughout life. Faith lent Paul spiritual strength while Marlene provided the other supporting pillar.

From his childhood in Saskatchewan through his youth in the Okanagan, West Kootenay and Edmonton and until this day, Paul has influenced many and has been influenced by many in turn. His father's quiet honesty and his mother's resourceful and spiritual nature have guided him. The Gospels of Luke and the aestheticism of Saint Francis of Assisi have been as much an influence as has the gritty prose of Charles Dickens or the wry ironies of Somerset Maugham.

Richard Joyce

This book is dedicated to my mother, Kathleen Helen Bickert

Preface

Before my mother, Kathleen Helen Bickert, passed away at 80 years of age, she had started to assemble a series of autobiographical essays consisting of sixteen anecdotal writings. I am certain that she would have liked to write more, however; in the end, her lengthy struggle with congestive heart failure in her old age, permitted her to complete only stories about the childhood and adolescent years she lived. That journal, which she named "Keeping Memories Alive," is an important record of the period from 1922 to 1940. It documents her developmental years spent on the farm in rural Saskatchewan, a few miles from the village of Marquis located about 20 miles north of Moose Jaw. The stories provide a concise and entertaining description of her small family that came together as a result of unusual circumstances.

My mother's parents had tragically short lives. As a result, she and her three siblings were raised in three separate households providing some excellent story fodder. Strangely, as life would have it, my wife's grandmother, Matilda L'Heureux, took ill with tuberculosis and was hospitalized for eight years in a sanatorium, succumbing to the illness and leaving her children to be cared for by others, too. When Matilda died my wife's mother, Leonie was just fifteen. In addition to being motherless, Leonie, along with her five siblings, was essentially fatherless. He wandered the country looking for a means to provide for his family during the Great Depression ending up an amputee with both legs dismembered, the result of being run down by a train while he attempted to hitch a ride. Consequently, he was not able to provide for his family after the accident. The children were all separated being raised by various relatives and friends of their parents. Regrettably, the families that took in the children scorned the father as a useless beggar.

Ultimately, these similar family pasts have provided some common ground in the history of my wife's family and mine. Marlene's mother passed in June 2007 at eighty-five years. Witnessing Leonie failing with Alzheimer's and my own mother's death in 2002, at eighty, alerted me of the few short years one has, and another generation passes.

It's enjoyable to read the written records left on both sides of the family. I relish those memoirs left in "Keeping Memories Alive" and other historical accounts of my past ancestry. The LaLonde family tree provided by Ken Cannon's work and research along with the notes of the Foerster Genealogy, about the family of my grandmother, Mary Anne Foerster, wife of Michael Griffin and birth mother to my mother, a record that I found in my mother's effects after her death.

Marlene's family's stories recorded in The L'Heireux biographies and other historical documents of the Ibbotson family are a good read. One such document from her side of the family is Cheadle's "Journal of Trip Across Canada 1862-63" chronicling the efforts of Battenotte the Assiniboine (Metis) guide who assisted Lord Milton and Cheadle on their journey as the country's first trans Canada tourists. Patineaud was the correct French spelling of the name. He is the great grandfather of Marlene's Grandmother (Ibbotson) Manson, mother to her father, Alleyne Charles Ibbotson.

Seeing the growth of the family, at the age of seventy-four and the members that have already passed, I feel that my attempt to continue recording life in these memoirs honours my own mother's efforts as well as those of our other family historians. It should pass on some appreciation to future progeny of the endeavours made in building family and the experiences that members have valued. Hopefully, this journal and the reading of other documented lives, made on all sides in this family, will be enough to provide the reader entertainment and motivate future recordings of family history.

In the early chapters, much of what I write is information from conversations that I had with my mother before she died. That material was shared over the years when I became interested and inquired about my deceased relatives. These conversations were either about mom's own experience with members or recollections of accounts handed down to her about them.

I felt it equally important to include biographical chapters on the early years of my stepfather and only dad I've known, John Irven Bickert and his family in an attempt to pull together a history about the two fragmented families that I was to eventually become a part. His early ancestral Mennonite faith and after marrying my mother to raise the family in the Catholic faith, helped to encourage tolerance of what faith may exist in each of us. These biographies give deeper insight into the fabric of roots and what I feel is valuable about life's lessons to pass on to the future. Hence, it is my objective, to secondarily provide a journal of my own life in relation to the time that I came into this family.

Yes, I express my feelings about the purpose of life, marriage and family while I sit as a father living my own legacy, but if you'll bear with it, there's an importance to share a faith perspective and teach why that upholds one. Faith retrieves us from trials and temptations that bring us down. We are better off when faith, hope and love move us to be better people and to have a dependence on The Creator. Most important it gives us the spiritual roadmap on our journey to the afterlife.

I've been touched by lives spanning three different centuries coming from various Christian denominations. In my heritage are wonderful people like those of my grandparents, Bickert, Dyck, Griffin and LaLonde, who were born in the late 1800's and my own parents, who were born at the end of World War I. All today can benefit from the value of family and need to discover heritage and what cements family. Much of today's society sees no value in marriage and family, instead replacing an opportunity to raise children with domiciling pets instead.

"Golden Throat" a handle I earned in my early broadcast career is an historical and autobiographical account that can assist any reader in discovering the value of faith and family and the period of history in which I've lived.

My mother spent many hours writing essays about her life. Additionally, she was a poet writing about family and musings. Her works were an instrument to search out the meaning of life and have left a legacy. An example of this is in her poem, "I Write" published in her book of "Collected Poems."

> "I write of all the hours God was near
> Through summers lively walk with six to rear.
> And as a parent, pen my love and trust
> And so, I know I write because I must."

Kathleen Bickert was a woman I like to credit for having passed faith on to me. She loved the Mother Church of Rome and she defended it rigorously, but had an appreciation of the heritage of Christianity and the two-thousand-year work of building church, and how she viewed unity in the 'Mystical Body in Christ' as what Jesus Christ himself prayed for at The Last Supper, the night before he died. She explained, "The church searches out truth when tempered by the faith of one another growing together over the course of history. We are a people living together in God. We pray like an orchestra our individual praises." She'd say.

Aside from Mom's writing, it was easy to extract information in conversations about her life and the people she loved. When it came to fulfill my own curiosity about family, she was always willing to.

My father, while being a humble and quiet man, seldom shared stories from his youth. He was not the one I found most of the information from regarding his side. It was by questioning his other family members and from stories shared by his mother, Helen and siblings Margaret Krahn and Peter Dyck, as well as my dad's sisters Jeanne and Frances. Privately, Dad would reveal little about his past, but largely the stories

I write about are sketches from those that I recall hearing about in my youth from his mother, Helen Bickert, or from Mom.

Regretfully, I left my family home in Nelson, when I was sixteen in order to attend the Franciscan boys' school, St. Anthony's College, in Edmonton which was also a minor seminary. Although, the time I spent there for the most part was a good experience, that separation resulted in my missing out on much of what my family would have offered had I remained at home.

I believe that as people of God age, they should begin to turn love out from themselves as opposed to youth that generally have shallower love, a love at least partially turned in on itself. My richest legacy is that of the marriage I've shared with my wife Marlene for fifty-three years now. It's the most secure offering to my own children, that their mother and I have had that life together.

Marriage has allowed us to grow by transforming two incomplete people who may otherwise have been shallow lovers into a loving couple. Years with each other have taught us to learn forgiveness as 'Love's Lesson' taught by the necessary contact between God and us through our partnership with Him in forgiveness as Christians in marriage. Forgiveness came as a requirement of our love for one-another, a gift that was valued more through the stages of our struggles to be charitable toward each other. Always when forgiveness came, it was because we reached to the soul to find it. In those occasional contact moments with the Divine our marriage was saved, and biases began to fade. Like most successful marriages, ours tested the boundaries and delivered rewards that seemed to be bestowed on us for the part we played in conciliation on the road to maturing our friendship in sacramental matrimony.

My parents were principled people. They taught me how to endure the trials that life would deal. By learning to uphold my father's obliging and honest effort as a standard, prepared me as a husband and father. His self-effacing demeanour and retiring disposition were always his greatest assets in heading family. My mother was bold, forthright and yet, obliging in her association with Dad. Their own lessons in love and forgiveness resulted from personal weaknesses and strengths colliding in a continuous struggle that required a similar contact with God in the lessons they, too, learned in forgiveness. Mom's boldness and Dad's unassuming nature ultimately made for a balanced relationship.

Today, people's views are different than when I was younger. Certainly, our technological world has helped to change us and most of that change has value. Television and the Internet have opened our world up to many other societies. In contrast, when I was younger, communication from the outside world was limited. Then, people enjoyed much more domestic experience at the exclusion of the world. In the early nineteen fifties television began to open our society; however, news journalism was still affected by past biases. Personally, my protected upbringing obviously influenced what I perceived as being right or wrong. After leaving home, I became aware of a whole new perspective which exposed my mind to a considerable number of other viewpoints. Those came from maturing friendships, new acquaintances and worldly perspectives that challenged my own, most of all in marriage!

My family was Catholic. My wife's family was not. Hers had experiences with the Mother Church that were not so flattering and resulted in some notions that were different from mine. Even though her mother was born Catholic, she had been excommunicated when she married an Anglican member of the family that took her in after the loss of her own parents.

We were both from respectable and similar backgrounds; however, we like other couples, had lived in two different homes where opinions had formed, and attitudes were set. Our two separate societies from past protected environments collided in our marriage resulting in years of division, confusion and hurt, before healing of those scars began to occur. After time, we finally began to appreciate what we were each separately made of. Subsequently, we loved more in a mature appreciation of the heritage of one another's roots.

Surprisingly, Canadian society had changed with us. Our minds were broadened by a new society that was televised into every household's living room re-shaping attitudes ridding past biases while assisting every human family that wanted more.

Our personal arguments about denominational issues were then seen as futile or destructive and new attempts to respect the others' positions brought peace. Concurrently, every citizen in Canada was living in a more tolerant society as Grace transformed it.

Reading and searching the depth of one's own self is usually rewarded with the contemplative being aroused, to the wonders of the ethereal and what is beyond self and this life. Social media offers little connection to do with God and how our Creator has been explained through scripture, faith, philosophers and can be discovered in prayer by regularly talking to the Lord. In the short time we have in this physical world, I believe that it's important to discover how our eternal life might work out after we leave this physical world; however, no less, I believe that God is with us all and our journey toward him can only be quickened by our co-operation with His grace and in getting to know him. The Church was established by Christ to assist in this through the institution of the Sacraments and reading The Holy Scriptures. They were truly assembled by The Church. I would like my family to respect Baptism, Holy Matrimony and Holy Communion along with what other of the sacraments The Church dispenses.

In 1988, while on a pilgrimage throughout southern Europe, I recall how impressed I was by the frescos at the different basilicas, particularly in Italy. I don't believe there are any more profound in the world than those that are in the village of Assisi, the home village of the 12th century, Saint Francis of Assisi (b.1182 - d.1226). My middle name is Francis, so this adopted patron has always interested me. He is not my namesake, but as I understand, that was the middle name of my great grandmother, Marie Anne (Anna) Frances LaLonde. Having the name Francis has always interested me in the saint from the Province of Perugia, Italy. Another introduction to me of this twelfth century canonized mendicant, who influenced youth in his day, was that by the age sixteen, I attended St. Anthony's College, a boys' school in Edmonton run by Franciscan Friars.

The works of art at The Basilica of Saint Francis in Assisi, credited to have been painted by Giotto di Bondone, of which many were destroyed when an earthquake brought down the roof of the basilica in 1997, gave an amazing witness to the period when Francis lived. They depict his life in art and historically the age he lived in murals on walls and ceilings of the basilica freezing the moments in history and all the intricacies of the day. I am certain, that Assisi's artistic detail would be equally fascinating to any historian, not just casual observers like me. Each work displayed the event, clothing, hairdos, architecture, lighting, tools of the day, etc., telling stories of the era when Francis lived. To comprehend the beauty of the work at the basilica, one needed to view the frescoes up close and then at a distance. Close up at first glance, they detailed what one might have thought of as imperfections in the art; however, what appeared as a flaw usually was a characteristic feature of the painting, used for the purpose of highlighting something in the mural.

Perhaps the life of each person should be viewed akin to art. The closer one gets to an individual, without reflecting on the whole person and collectively what roles different individuals played in the formation of that person or what needs to be completed, imparts a shallow perspective eclipsing the real value of the individual. That holds true for family members being viewed by others in the family as well, especially those who have not known the person as have older members of the same family. It can be true for various cultures, people and religions as well.

Love, gentleness, thoughtfulness, forgiveness and investigation are necessary to understand the complexities and wholeness of any individual, society or religion. Otherwise a viewpoint is blighted.

I first want to thank my wife, Marlene for her untiring friendship, fidelity and love and for the lessons we've learned together with our children. Then, I'd like to thank our children; Natalie, Taylor and

Charity, for being patient with me while I've fumbled through rearing them cautioning them to grow themselves in truth and to discover veracity in respecting heritage of faith and life itself. I thank them for the grandchildren they've given me. I'm grateful to my son, Tad Conrad Goddard for returning to me after being raised in another family as this story of my life will reveal.

I thank my deceased parents for the loving home they provided and my siblings for their love and friendship. I thank my extended family and good friends, who know who they are. Finally, I wish to thank Richard Joyce for his untiring efforts in editing this work.

I dedicate this book to my mother, the late, Kathleen Helen Bickert, who in strength and courage, taught me that good legacy is more than persuasion or flaunting one's history, but is achieved through sharing conviction while inadequate.

Golden Throat
My Journey with family in faith
by Paul Francis Bickert
Copyright 2020

Chapter One

D ad showed me through example that strong men are seldom forceful but always dependable, faithful, humble and gentle. Several moments in my life have re-enforced the value of that model. While on my own, I learned that ambition proceeded from vanity, wisdom from humility and success was usually overrated making most of the possessions that resulted from it superfluous.

Mom taught that she liked gentle men, but deplored patsies. "Predators can devour you!" she'd warn. She could be malicious when attacking others and I presumed she was training her sons to defend themselves with good debating skills. I interpreted her boldness and dad's meekness as a reason for me to become somewhat intrepid in defying challenges. Still, I learned to retreat to my core for reflection and peace after tiring from defending my own vanity.

I guess you could say I've always been a dreamer. That characteristic would spur ambition and the subsequent goals that I set for myself, would ultimately complicate my life. In the end, I discovered that ambitions would overshadow my soul's attempt to place perspective in my life. When these vain exercises were over, I'd awake to find that the best reveries for me were those that I had in faith and family and that any distraction that I allowed from those I could live to regret. I now discipline myself with my musings and consequently, have become a less complex person, even though the debasing exercise of growth continues to be humiliating but good.

The phone rang in our Kelowna, British Columbia home and I picked up the receiver in the kitchen. It was my brother Patrick on the other end of the line.

"Paul, Mom's gone!"

"How do you mean, Pat?" I asked.

"She's gone…dead!" he replied. From Patrick I expected a joke. He was full of humour, but this time he was serious.

It was about 8:30 on the evening of June 30th, 2002. Patrick and his family had intended to have our mother and forty-eight-year old sister, Janice, over for dinner. Mom had called him prior to the meal and declined the invitation for both her and Janice, because she was not feeling well that day. In turn, Patrick suggested that he could drop in on the two of them later that evening and bring the meal to their home. Happy with that arrangement she accepted the alternate plan.

Our mother had lived for eight years in the Glenmore district's senior's community of Sandpoint off Yates Road in Kelowna. It was a development home that she had built after having another house constructed that both my parents planned prior to Dad's death in 1986. That dwelling was distant from the centre of the city and consisted of two levels that she couldn't manage in any longer.

Fourteen years earlier, she was bedridden in Kelowna General Hospital's intensive care ward for three weeks and then afterwards convalesced for months at her home as a result of a dissecting abdominal aneurysm that could have taken her life. After what seemed a full recovery, the resultant gradual deterioration of my mother's health with congestive heart failure led her to rely on a constant stream of caregivers, coming and going from her home to attend to her and Janice. Four years prior to her death, Patrick and I had assumed control of her finances along with other matters that our mother was no longer capable of managing on her own.

Janice had continued to reside with Mom after Dad's death due to my sister's cerebral palsy condition which left her both mentally and physically challenged since infancy, a result of a brain haemorrhage that occurred shortly after her birth. The mutual enjoyment of one-another's companionship since Dad's passing was facing deteriorating standards as a result of improper nutrition and a decline of basic needs that ensued in Mom's final years. With home care support declining from government cutbacks, those left assisted living in the home at a minimum.

A month before Dad's death, my parents and Janice had moved to Kelowna from Edmonton. Relocating had been with the intention of spending their retirement years closer to two of their four sons. Brothers John and Geoffrey lived in Calgary and Vancouver respectively with their wives and families, but Patrick and I were permanently residing in Kelowna along with our families. Our sister, Sherry, who had resided in Vancouver passed years earlier. Two of my deceased father's sisters lived in the neighbouring city of Vernon where remaining members of his family had continued to dwell since 1935.

After retiring from real estate sales in Edmonton, Alberta, their intention was to have a home built in Kelowna where they had recently purchased a lot to erect the retirement dwelling, but Dad's unexpected death occurred while they had taken up temporary quarters in a bonus room above the garage in my family's country home. The sudden death occurred a few days after the building lot purchase, resulting in our mother picking up and carrying on with the completion of the project on her own. Eight years later she had the second house constructed in Glenmore district when she was seventy-one. That was the home she resided in at the time of her death preferring to live independently with Janice until the end.

Since she was in her late seventies, her attitude didn't accommodate anyone who interfered with her financial matters or intruded on her privacy at home. What were obvious shortcomings in banking and bill paying were not apparent to her. I would visit and find mail piling up on the fireplace or shoved in kitchen drawers unopened. Snooping to examine the contents, I'd discover threatened caveats were about to be placed on her property for failure to pay invoices. Her memory was so poor but her determination to be independent persisted.

"I just paid that bill, Paul and I've already taken my pills!" she insisted, even though that was not the case. The bills were usually past any past due date and something had to be done. It frustrated me how a woman who was usually rational on other matters could become so absurd on her personal well being.

Janice was like a parrot. Family learned never to discuss with one another in front of her something that they didn't want repeated later. When surveying Mom's affairs I found it extremely difficult to muster the courage to snoop to determine where she was with her mail. She became aware of my meddling and obviously spoke to my sister of it when I'd leave. "Mom, he's snooping again! Tell him to go home!" Janice would complain. Mom dispensed with the remark hoping I hadn't heard it.

Serious intervention became necessary when my oldest daughter complained about Mom's vehicle nearly colliding with hers while my mother motored around the city oblivious of her own inattentive driving habits. A second near collision could have occurred with my youngest daughter as well and we all would speculate on how many near misses had happened until I finally had Mom's driver's privileges revoked through the Superintendent of Motor Vehicles.

Encountering my mother's inability to comprehend her own shortcomings as an aging senior was most difficult for me. She still had her pride and self determination and that meant that I was interfering with a person that wanted to go it alone and required that I would have to learn patience and gentleness in order to deal with her, not two of my better attributes. She didn't like that anyone would suggest that help was necessary. The obvious was embarrassing to her and was discarded as mundane while she'd provide a litany of responses that were more apparent to her. "Can't someone wash my car for me and hang my Christmas lights?" she'd remark in a perturbed manner adding, "I don't need to be treated like a child!"

The years following my father's death in 1986 were full of venturesome moments for Mom as she'd demonstrate near heroic independence landscaping her yard managing finances and travelling with or without Janice, while organizing her life to accommodate some sort of freedom from being tied to the addresses she resided. She would engage in a social life with people she met in restaurants, the Canadian Legion and church. Circumstantially, no sooner had she settled and found friends she began to deteriorate in her health. The dissecting abdominal aortic aneurism and then a series of heart attacks required numerous hospitalizations. Consequently, her social interaction slowly ended. She no longer attended the Legion to dance, nor shopped and began to miss Sunday Mass as her independence waned. I took Holy Communion to her for several months.

Younger brother, Geoff was astute enough to suggest she take up writing in order to pen her life for the sake of family, advising that her earlier work in her book of Collected Poems was refreshing and that she should write more. That suggestion took Mom out of a temporary slump as she began to assemble several essays that Geoff eventually bound into a book called, Keeping Memories Alive.

Dad was the finishing touch on my mother's character. He succeeded in bringing out what comforted me in her, because viewing Mom without him wasn't the way I was accustomed. She was far above an extended period of mourning the loss of Dad being determined to complete her life's work on her own with a great deal of focus. She was first, a mother and caregiver for Janice and then secondly, a widow living out the final period of her life's vocation. She viewed her other adult children as independent and requiring less of her.

She dated a few men. All irritated her family as grossly inadequate when compared to our father. Mom would be patient with them far too long, but eventually she'd send them on their way.

For a time, I thought that my mother was incomplete after the death of Dad. As time moved on, I understood that it was more a discomfort that I felt, in seeing Mom a single woman again. Now, I can see that her life after Dad was more a therapeutic period for her, to re-visit the single life and then, her role as a mother on life's path, walking the final steps to her eternity. The necessary redress of her own convictions needed to be completed while she lived out the remaining affirmations of her faith in front of her family. She was weaker, but determined, vulnerable while triumphant, focused, yet limited, refined, while out of form. My father broadened her personage as a woman and wife; however, she was still the one capable of completing the polish of the necessary persuasion and fervour in her family before she died. It was a labour of love in faith for her and she was graced for the task. In her last few years, she spent many hours quietly passing time reading books that centered on days past and lives lived, watching old movies on television, praying and writing her memoirs.

I was always amazed by my mother's forthrightness in matters of persuasion. Her untiring defence of the Church was frequently made in frustrated outbursts meant to defend it. I was beginning to see myself being like her and needing to clarify other misunderstandings of my faith's teachings. I often felt inadequate for the job.

It wasn't until a few weeks before Mom's passing that I began to comprehend the work that she was completing in her life. This occurred while I fumbled along in my efforts to assist as an obliging son, advocating for her in front of Social Services and supplementing her care. Near the end she remarked, "You're a good man, Paul."

I presume the remark was a consequence that I had finally learned to be gentle and patient with her, by accepting her shortcomings which in part, I understood to be a result of a failing senior's mind. Was she taking account and noticing or just feeling more for me at that time of her life? Seldom did she ever compliment any of her children to their faces.

There was something that I recognized in my mother's appearance when I last saw her alive. Her eyes began to exude a peaceful resignation in life, something I was coming to understand but lacked. She was no longer frustrated over keeping pace with the world around her and what she felt it required of her, or she of it, believing it was now better not to resonate audacious convictions as she had throughout life.

Up until the year prior to her death, I sensed a form of friction between us, a perplexing coolness over how I managed a part of my life and affairs. It was as if she harboured resentment for many years making me feel I had done something to my mother that needed to be repaired. That had ended as my story will tell.

Kathleen Bickert was the last surviving person of her Griffin family. In all, she was a good steward of the legacy she left. Her life inspires me to be proud of her and the heritage she left.

Chapter Two

There is a special splendour in South Central Saskatchewan that is peculiar only to that part of Canada. The flat open distance that seems to go on forever offers its farmers some of the best dry land grain farming in the world. In summers, locals are rewarded with the beautiful gold colour of the crops that present their perennial hues by enriching the landscape with each passing day of July and August. Complemented with an azure sky, the grain fields and the warm summer breezes make life on that open expanse boundless. Saskatchewan offers its citizens a special liberty that locals find difficult to part from. Any native who leaves this rural countryside in the Canadian Shield longs for its special quietude as the landscape enriches souls with the area's natural serenity. In addition, the long cold winters, with their relentless winds, impart peace on the hardy rural residents who are shut-in by the snow drifts which can bury telephone lines and farm buildings alike as the extended chill lingers on until late spring.

There the frigid temperatures render travel uncertain throughout much of that season; hence, lengthy preparation in anticipation of the usual six- month freeze is necessary for each family. They put up food for their homes and livestock, fill root cellars, churn butter, preserve vegetables, install storm windows, reinforce shelters, pile hay, and prepare vehicles for ploughing and winter travel. Winter presents residents with a sense of satisfaction and they anticipate the season with a certain joy that only the resilient can understand. Canadian prairie rural life is unique and demands special people to live it. The quiet on a Saskatchewan farm requires peaceful residents to endure it.

Church is the center of each small rural prairie community. The families residing in or around each village continue even today to actively attend to faith matters on Sundays. Probably, the simple life of farm communities and the fact that shopping or other distractions are not so available continues to foster time for reflection on spiritual matters. In addition, the social aspect of church provides more community involvement. That could explain why, even today, rural living encourages a life-long comfort for the spiritual part of the person being attended to.

At forty-four John LaLonde was not a talkative person and liked his peace. He had grown up on Minnesota and Saskatchewan farms and enjoyed listening to the soft breezes outdoors with the sounds of nature or the stir of farm equipment moving the soil and harvesting crops.

Born on May 18, 1892, the Marquis farmer was the third son of the four boys and two daughters that Anna Zoller and James LaLonde parented, after their marriage on July 22, 1887 in Minnesota. In the 1870's the Xavier LaLonde family moved to North Dakota and Minnesota, after leaving from the French line north of Perth, Ontario, Canada's first Capital City. They were in search of a better life promised in the more prosperous USA during a Canadian depression during that period. The LaLonde's were the descendants of Jean Luc LaLonde, who was stationed in Canada as a soldier of the King of France in what was then referred to as New France. A few years after his arrival in 1665, Jean Luc was killed by an Iroquois Indian raiding party while he, a Jesuit priest and five others constructed the Catholic Church near the early settlement, Baie D'Urfe, the ancient site of the Island of Montreal.

Jean Luc had taken an imported bride, Marie Balan (Barbary) in 1669 who gave birth to five children, three of them surviving. She had been exported to the new French colony along with many other peasant women (called Daughters of the King) brought here by the French monarch to populate the territory and to encourage troops to stay.

Centuries later, descendant, James LaLonde and his wife Anna relocated in Saskatchewan from the family's thirty-year stint in Minnesota and

North Dakota. Then, the Canadian Government was enticing ex-patriots back to Canada, with land as a bribe, offering free quarter sections to farmers that would relocate on the uninhabited prairies that were becoming targets of American annexation attempts. The US wanted to take the territory away from the Dominion. The depression that had existed in Canada since 1870 until the turn of century had lured many Canadians to the USA and later the more prosperous northern states were no longer attractive compared to the appeal of homesteaded land that the Canadian government offered.

When James and Anna LaLonde's son, John met Gladys Naylor in Marquis on the homestead, he was twenty-six years old and the pressure by his mother was heavy on him to get married. Although he was attracted to Gladys, he was not making his mother happy with his slow advances on the attractive, but too chatty kitchen help that Anna and James had hired. Gladys's amorous attempts coupled with the interference from his mother were a bit too much for John; nevertheless, he gave in and consented on his mother's persistence to marry Gladys. The whole matter was assisted by the chiding of his brothers and a wedding took place while his sceptical and silent father, James LaLonde looked on. By then, Naylor had been with the LaLonde's for one year.

After the marriage the couple struggled to get along as John's silence tormented Gladys. She could not bear a child, so totally depended on his communication which he offered her little of. Eventually the couple adopted a baby. First, the baby was taken in by the LaLonde's as a foster infant but adopted within five years with the permission of a reluctant widower, Mike Griffin, the baby's natural father. Griffin was Marquis's town constable whose wife passed two weeks after giving birth to Kathleen and her twin, Mary. Mary was adopted by the neighbouring Kennedy couple. For a few years the entertainment of having a child in the household helped Gladys until Kathleen grew to compete with Gladys for her father's attention. Then the disharmony resurfaced.

The John LaLonde family sustained its fair share of hardship during the Great Depression with financial struggles that required John seek work away from Marquis managing and living with a road crew for the duration of the Great Depression. Communication worsened with the couple during that period and Gladys grew more impatient as John's letters or cards were mostly directed to Kathleen.

On an impressive Saturday evening outing in nearby Moose Jaw, Kathleen celebrated with her Marquis friends at the Capitol theatre where the teens watched attractive Myrna Loy and handsome William Powell in "The Great Ziegfeld" motion picture. The exciting movie would win Best Motion Picture in the 1937 Ninth Academy Awards as Miss Loy sang and danced stirring audiences throughout North America while that evening leaving a lasting impression on Kathleen. For years afterwards Kathleen described the theatre scene as full of handsome cadets from Moose Jaw's airbase and how she wanted to jump to her feet and dance down the aisle in the crowded building, just as the actress did in the film. Instead, she restrained herself, content to let the thought dance in her mind. Kathleen was still not so interested in men as her twin sister, Mary, whose head kept turning away from the screen to eye reciprocating cadet glances with stares of her own. At fifteen, Mary was more developed for her age than Kathleen.

When the movie was over, John LaLonde drove the girls back home after meeting them at the Grand Hotel Cafe where the friends enjoyed Cokes after the movie. Unfortunately, the next day, the thrill of the evening's outing was ruined. In the morning, Kathleen was informed by her father that her mother had left the family while they were out the night before. LaLonde held his daughter in the center of the farmhouse kitchen while the two cried. All her mother's late-night threats spoken in anger that had reverberated through the bedroom walls over the years were no longer threats. It was autumn 1937.

The prior Sunday, during a Pancake breakfast, Gladys's announced to friends from the Catholic Women's League her intention to leave her husband. It was after Saint John's Catholic Church Sunday Mass in Marquis. The morning that her family became aware of the details, that came from a note left for John LaLonde in the farm bungalow placed on the player piano. It was found after he arrived home that night from Moose Jaw. He discovered Gladys was not asleep in the bedroom after he quietly entered the room but left the matter until morning to discuss with Kathleen.

Feeling assaulted to the core of her Catholic faith, Gladys had believed that such an event could never unfold in her life, but she was left empty in Marquis and nothing that her husband attempted to say during their prior discourses convinced her otherwise. They couldn't continue.

"Bei Mir Bist du Schoen," sung by the Andrews sisters, in a popular Artie Shaw arrangement was played over the car radio merely adding annoyance to Gladys that Saturday in her friend's departure vehicle. "Can we turn that off?" she asked the companion who was driving Gladys to Moose Jaw's train station.

For Gladys during the evening's leaving, the reflections brought more tears on the dusty gravel road to Moose Jaw. The grim circumstance made the monotonous half hour drive, seem endless while her emotional mind reviewed two significant episodes of her life as both a mother and wife. Those were of her wedding day on August 25, 1919, at Marquis, as well as the memory of the day, less than three years later, that she brought home her newly adopted infant daughter, Kathleen Helen Griffin, from Providence Hospital in Moose Jaw.

After the adoption the LaLonde's continued calling the infant Kathleen Helen, even though the birth records did not record the proper name the Griffins intended, but instead recorded the infant's name as Catherine Helen. The adoption never resulted in a legal change of name from Catherine Helen either, necessary to correct the Province's error on her birth certificate.

Mary Anne Griffin had succumbed to an infection in the womb, after the delivery of her twins. An unsanitary practice by the attending delivery physician, who was not in the habit of washing his hands after dissecting cadavers in the hospital basement, caused an infection that would kill the birth mother.

Gladys had visited her friend, Mary Anne earlier and the two had discussed the matter of taking on the babies if the birth mother succumbed. The father of the twins, Michael Griffin was Marquis's town constable. He consented to the LaLonde's taking one twin within two weeks. Gladys chose Kathleen, but soon the father was forced to give up the other twin, Mary, to the Kennedys. Subsequently, for a few years, Michael continued to work as town constable and then moved with his sons to nearby Ernford to operate the grain elevator. A housekeeper, Gertie Hanlan, assisted in caring for his sons, Patrick and John aged two and four. Later, in 1926 Michael married Gertie and then moved on to Fort William to continue as a grain elevator operator. The adoption of the twins was first permitted before his departure.

Michael Griffin was born in the Diocese of Kerry, in the Parish of Dingle, Ireland on March 28th, 1875. His father, Thomas Griffin worked with Ireland's Coast Guard and resided with his wife Hanna, born an O'Sullivan in the Irish hamlet of Doonshean. Michael immigrated to the United States after teaching Gaelic at the Christian Brothers School in Killarney, Ireland. From Dublin in 1900, he sailed to New York City on the White Star Lines and soon afterwards immigrated to Canada residing first, in Ontario and then later, on the Prairies. Before heading West, he met Mary Anne of Hesson, Ontario. She was born a Foerster on August 19, 1881 the daughter of the Peter Michael Foerster who married Suzanna Ritz, both coming to Canada from Muetzenich, Germany to reside in Hesson since the 1840's. Later, Mary Anne and Michael were already middle aged when they reconnected in Saskatchewan and married in Regina on June 19, 1917.

Now that she had left John LaLonde, what was most upsetting to Gladys was that her husband would never ask her to return. She later claimed that he felt cold and indifferent to her. Nevertheless, the grain farmer, would have his wife back within the year, but only to have her depart for good after another two years.

John and Gladys LaLonde (front) wedding with Con
McCann and Mary LaLonde, John's sister.

Chapter Three

A momentary distraction from Gladys's own gloom was the train's passage through the 'Hobo Jungle' which had formed over the years along the lakeshore bordering the entrance to North Bay's train yards. The yards and station added additional prosperity to the region for that period. There was the further intrigue that she'd possibly catch a glimpse of the famous Dionne quintuplets that had been born in nearby Corbeil, Ontario in 1934. Their birth and the construction of the train yards was a source of a boom for the city during a time that left the rest of the country suffering the effects of the Depression years. Thousands of tourists poured into the city from all over the world to see the international celebrity youngsters whose fame was the result of exploitation by the quintuplets' parents and the media.

North Bay was cold, damp and windy when Gladys de-boarded. She had grown up in the town, in a family with five siblings, two sisters and three brothers. Realizing that she needed to find work, she rushed to leave the train ahead of others permitting her time to clean up and get an interview in at one of the North Bay furriers before the day was over. Her brother that would pick her up at the train would take her to her first interview after she cleaned up at the railway station.

Prior to her departure from Marquis, news had arrived from family that there was work in that part of Ontario which was well known throughout the world for its fur harvesting. Living on adrenalin, while standing in front of the station's washroom mirror with a dampened towel in her hands, the estranged farmwife removed some of the train engine's soot from her face and then rearranged her hair.

"That'll have to do," she mumbled while examining herself."

With suitcase in her hand, she climbed into her brother's car and he drove to the manufacturing plant that was an unimpressive building on the edge of the downtown area. It housed the community's most successful operating furrier, a small business looking for experienced seamstresses to sew fur hats, vests and scarves. After an interview in the enterprise's employment office she was immediately hired on.

In North Bay, Gladys would experience several encounters with Hobo Jungle reprobates while she waited at bus stops throughout the city encouraging her to quickly find an apartment adjacent to her work, less affected by the transients. Those conditions sorely reminded her of the dignified life that John LaLonde had provided in the Marquis home she had left. Meanwhile at work, the near sweat shop conditions provided just a meagre living that was enough to make her frequently rethink her decision to leave Marquis.

Not long after settling Gladys started writing letters addressed to Kathleen, who reciprocated with letters back attempting to encourage her mother's return home. Most of the letters were destroyed by Kathleen when she'd read her mother's return responses that ignored the pleadings.

Eventually, the self recriminations and isolation made Gladys uncomfortable at Sunday Mass, so she drifted from the Church that she once was honoured to hold the Catholic Women's League president's post. By then the country was about to go to war and the emphasis in the nation was on survival, not the luxurious fur garments that she was hired to make in North Bay. Consequently, the work in North Bay fizzled out within a year and she returned to reside on the farm in Marquis, temporarily offering hope to her family, but only to leave again.

In 1939 there was ample work available in Toronto requiring military clothing preparation for what was a most certain involvement for the Dominion with the Allied forces in Europe. That offered another opportunity for Gladys to move on to Toronto to work sewing uniforms instead of continuing after she felt no improvement in Marquis with John LaLonde. At Toronto she rented a three-room apartment enhancing her standard over that in North Bay. Shortly after a stint with the military garment manufacturer she found new work doing alterations for Eaton's Department Store, a position she held for several years after the war ended.

The LaLonde's' Catholic faith did not permit divorce, so it was mutually decided by the couple to settle on legal separation as annulment was seldom sought. Ultimately, Gladys did partner with Charlie Cowperthwaite, in Toronto, prior to the war, never legally divorcing John LaLonde, but by then she gave birth to a son, Charles junior, while continuing to reside with Cowperthwaite. In the 1950's they moved to Pefferlaw and later Sutton in the Lake Simcoe area where she continued to reside until her own death in 1996 at ninety-six years. Cowperthwaite died in 1961. Charles Jr. married and continued to reside in Pefferlaw with his wife, Alice living close to his mother.

Years later, the separation by distance between Ontario and Kelowna, British Columbia where Kathleen eventually resided helped to heal the injury. Words were exchanged in letters rather than verbally and were thought out to include endearing rather than spontaneous ruinous remarks. Eventually, before her death, Kathleen preferred to dwell on the good memories of her mother, while earlier visits between the two would always erupt in accusations coming from both reopening old wounds. Age brought maturity and consideration toward one-another's feelings and both would carefully avoid discussing John LaLonde.

Writing in "Keeping Memories Alive," Kathleen's stories depicted a happier Marquis home life. During the many years of separation both mother and daughter would communicate with periodic phone calls and seasonal letters. Her mother sent crocheted doilies and unique handmade Christmas ornaments for the tree. It was a special effort that demonstrated her affection that was always reciprocated by gift packages and letters destined for Pefferlaw and Sutton.

Prior to her death, I visited Grandma LaLonde in the seniors' facility at Sutton. We lunched in a restaurant that day and there my grandmother reminded me so much of my own mother, Kathleen. The music system in the restaurant played a tune called "Old Fashioned Love" and Grandma remarked, "I would like to dance. Can we dance together?" It was ironic that the lyrics went something like this:

> "Whatever happened to old fashioned love?
> The kind that survived the good and the bad
> The kind of love that good old Mom and Dad used to
> Have...?" (Lyrics by B.J. Thomas)

She was frail and it felt like I was holding a china doll in my arms, one that would easily break. It was then that I realized, there was a period when my grandmother just wanted more love and attention in her life. When she received love, she responded well to it. Perhaps my Grandpa John LaLonde could not give her the attention and affection that she required, for whatever reason, but she had forgotten that by then. For me that day, she was a perfect grandmother on the dance floor, full of warmth and gratitude for my visit that seemed to mean so much to her. I also recognized why my mother loved to dance so much. It was because her mother once would dance with her in the Marquis home. She had taught my mother to tap, ballroom dance, sew, crochet and knit and how to make a loving home. Those all assisted her Dad in her mother's absence. Likely what Gladys LaLonde gave was her best effort under the circumstances of the day.

Through the years of her being alone without Charlie senior, her son and his family loved and cared for my grandmother. That short visit to Pefferlaw helped me to understand the dignity of everyone's life. Both grandparents shared in the marriage fracture that wounded my mother for many years. Gladys LaLonde had succeeded in the end to be a peaceful and loving woman. When my grandmother died, just a year after my visit, my mother did not attend the funeral because her own health was in crisis at the time. Mom wept for days over the death of Grandma LaLonde. The death was the result of a pneumonia complication, from a form of modern medical heroics where a month earlier a hysterectomy was performed on her at ninety-five.

Perhaps my mother's own perception of others' contributions to her life was affected by her only-child perspective until she eventually was fully exposed, throughout life, to her own larger family. A self examination, years later, when she wrote, "Keeping Memories Alive" provided perspective of the injuries of her youth as the reflections in her stories made her aware of the contribution her mother made to her childhood home.

Chapter Four

The only place colder than Saskatchewan in southern Canada is Manitoba. Along with the sub-zero winter temperatures that part of the continent is full of frozen lakes left from an Ice Age thaw and the Red River's annual flooding of the prairie landscape. Manitoba boasts of green riverbanks, endless prairie and numerous waterscapes inhabited by an abundance of waterfowl and mosquitoes. The province exudes a pioneer spirit remaining from its early days which has been fostered by the hardy outdoor lifestyle of its inhabitants braving inhospitable winters and humid bug infested summers. Its history is enriched by the followers of Louis Riel, rebelling against the establishment in Central Canada and the numerous cultures of the people who were the early inhabitants of the province.

Parts of Manitoba are populated by the followers of Swiss reformer, Huldreich Zwingli's radical Protestant group. Mennonites promoted confession of faith as the exclusive right to be "interpreted solely by individual conscience as the authority for Christian doctrinal matters," while rejecting infant baptism and inheriting the sub-title of 'Anabaptists'. They emigrated from Germany and Holland as a result of rigorous persecution in the late 18th century, moving into southern Russia where the peaceful sect eventually became regarded as subversive for their refusal to accept military service and to fight in wars. Most, then immigrated to Canada and the United States. In the early twentieth century there were over thirty thousand Mennonites residing in Canada, primarily in southern Manitoba and some in parts of Saskatchewan. These are not to be confused with their Amish cousins, who were followers of Swiss Mennonite Bishop Amman. Those settled mostly in the USA.

South of Winnipeg is the community of Winkler, a large rural farm town that prides itself on its Christian living as community, boasting of good workmanship and morals. It is the thriving Mennonite center for several small Mennonite hamlets that now dot the map around this larger rural town. Some are Morris, Steinbeck, Horndeen, Plum Coulee and Reinland.

Again, to protect the Prairies from the American annexation attempts, the Mother Country, Britain had encouraged the Dominion of Canada to take them as refugees, in order to help populate The Prairie provinces in Canada. Ironically, these new transplants were mostly conscientious objectors to any military effort that the young Commonwealth country was to eventually become engaged in.

The Mennonites came by ship to Montreal where they were again re-boarded onto ships destined to North Bay to be herded on to train livestock cars at North Bay for travel to Winnipeg, known earlier as Fort Gary. Eventually, the members of the sect were loaded on to buckboard carts and covered wagons to be pulled across the bumpy primitive roads, behind horse or oxen, to the open tundra of southern Manitoba. Each immigrant family was given provisions which consisted of a ration of salt ham and a shovel with a piece of paper that entitled them to farm the quarter section of land that they were pointed to.

In late September of 1880, Herman Dyck, his wife, Helena and son ended their trip on to the bleak prairie about seven miles south of Hoffnengsfeld (translated: field of hopefulness), the early settlement name for the town known today as Winkler. It was part of the Western Settlement of the Mennonite Reserve lands granted by Manitoba province which had entered Confederation in 1870. About 6 other Mennonite villages were erected along with Winkler dotting the map on that huge land mass. Earlier arrivals were already adapting to the area since first landing in the province in 1874 after the Russian

Government under Czar Alexander III cancelled the Mennonite exemption to conscription that had been in force since a century earlier under Catherine the Great. The Mennonite village standards developed over the years in Russia were beginning to take form in Winkler having large community barns with one main street of thatched roofed and mud hut dwellings. Herman was provided land in the Rhineland area, later known as Osterwick, a remote quarter that he was directed to by Winkler's Mennonite organizers.

The couple stood in wonderment before gathering their thoughts and then the large man commenced to dig a dwelling place that would become the family's sod hut home. Similar slightly raised prominences dotted the prairie of the day.

Dyck noticed his pocket watch fall out as he bent over to remove the first surface stone where the hut would be dug. He took the watch by the chain hanging it on the only small tree that stood on the newly acquired property. Herman anticipated having a roof over his family by that night; however, his aspirations were immediately challenged when the spade hit rock hard soil baked by that year's summer sun.

While Herman excavated the surface soil, Helena and her five-year old son, Johan collected whatever would burn for fuel to heat the family's sod dwelling, mostly buffalo paddies which were becoming scarce on the Canadian plains by then.

The thought humoured Herman who watched his family gather the animal waste in an effort to pitch in.

"Schite!" he laughed to himself breaking through to a softer sandy layer of soil toward the end of the day's work.

It took four days to dig a hole large enough for the family home. The first evening Helena prepared hot drinks from the brie of the salt ham given them, a finishing touch on the rustic meal she prepared. All added smiles to the meals goodness before camping under the stars.

The scattered population of homesteaders that had arrived earlier assisted Herman by advising and providing a few of the necessary provisions for the winter ahead. Those visits and the autumn breezes that occasionally moved sounds of chatter over the plain's aromatic grass offered the family what reassurance was needed to endure the pioneer conditions.

It wasn't long before driving winter storms arrived silencing human activity on the southern prairie as fall arrived early keeping inhabitants indoors. September frost was followed by unrelenting snow in October and the homestead became walled in by snowdrifts.

The Dyck's and the few inhabitants nearby had collected scarcely enough food before the freeze. Stores consisting of wild corn, wheat, oats, millet, rice and dried waterfowl, lay frozen on the ground in a dugout by the hut. Herman managed to trap several wild hares that he wrapped in cloth and hung on a line between posts. With goose fat he made lamp oil, while goose down, furs from rabbits and mink sufficed for bedding, boot and glove linings.

The serenity of the prairie became a part of their being as the family members began to embrace the earth and the livelihood it delivered. Their faith and trust in God provided hope and encouragement that someday circumstance would deliver them. Unfortunately, by 1883, after three arduous years on the homestead, Herman at fifty succumbed. By then, he had crafted a house with an outbuilding for the animals while managing to eke out a living, grain farming. Afterwards, eight-year old son, Johan, assisted Helena by producing crops barely enough to feed the family. He cared for his mother until 1907, when Helena died. Johan was thirty-two by then. He wasn't alone having taken a wife, Russian born Mennonite, Agatha Heide of Winkler. She had been adopted out by her parents, along with two brothers who had come to Canada with their adoptive parents after spending years living in a barn in southern Russia. Agatha worked for Helena and Herman meeting Johan who always remarked that he liked Agatha's fried eggs. That was enough to convince him that she would make a good wife.

Johan and Agatha had twelve children. The first was Helen, born August 14, 1897 and then came Agatha on February 25th, 1899, followed by John, June 12, 1901, Lizzie, February 3, 1903, Mary March 5, 1907, Jacob July 24, 1909 and Katherine on July 26, 1910. Susanna, who was born on January 7th, 1913, died of complications on Feb 23 that same year. The children kept coming. The next year came William, on April 27, 1914, followed by Peter on February 8, 1916, Margaret on March 30th, 1918, and finally Agnes on June 29, 1923.

By 1914, another new home had been constructed in Winkler where a new Marconi radio brought music to the family. Herman's Dyck's granddaughter, Helen was courting Harry Bueckert a short assertive man, slightly bent by Ricketts, a condition that resulted from malnutrition in his youth causing the softening of his long bones and leaving him with noticeably bowed legs. Harry had been doing work in neighbouring farms and particularly enjoyed the work for Osterwick, Manitoba's Johan and Agatha Dyck, Helen's parents.

Some people grace the presence of those they are around with peacefulness and encourage a special respect from them. That respect few will attempt to disrupt as it is reflected as an inner gift exuded as a genuine grace from God found present in very few. Helen Dyck possessed this gift and her quiet prairie upbringing in the small communities that she lived nurtured it. She did not have to speak a word to depict who she was. She merely had to be her quiet serene self, an unpretentious woman, who always enjoyed life. Her kind round face displayed a happy, polite, decorous disposition, which affected others that she encountered lovingly. While she worked, her silence was filled with smiles for things she was fond of. Seldom, did she use words, other than to bring the best out of any circumstance. Helen had warmth in her heart that made everyone she encountered smile.

Harry Bueckert had been doing work on Johann and Agatha's farm by then and became attracted to Helen, sporadically dating her for a year prior to their marriage in 1916.

On April 4, 1919 at home in Horndeen, Manitoba, a neighbouring town of Winkler about twenty miles northeast of Osterwick and seven miles east of Winkler, she gave birth to son, John Irven, named after his grandfather. There Harry and his brother, John had opened a small general store.

Helen's new infant son had dark brown hair and the prominent brow, characteristic of the Dyck family. Eyebrows nearly connecting across the bridge of the nose decorated the child's forehead. He too, was blessed with his mother's gift having such a quiet and peaceful nature that Harry was perturbed by it and suspected that there was something wrong with him.

"He's sure got his mother's disposition. Is that possible for my son to be like his mother?" Harry would ask. Eventually, when second child, Frances arrived, Harry was relieved that his daughter had her father's disposition.

"Now that's more like it!" Harry laughed. "She sounds more like a Buechert than that son of mine."

Gladys, who was born in Plum Coulee, came after Frances, in 1925, then Edward in 1931. For a period, the family lived in Winkler again after Harry's mother died. The family moved in with his father who was lonely after the death. In Winkler, John, who was eight and Francis at six started school together. The family then spent six years in Chortitz area, about three miles southwest of Winkler, where John quickly did seven grades to complete his education while Harry worked on Ben and Peter Bueckert's farm.

Harry and Helen had both grown up with a musical talent. He had taken up the violin and was quite popular with that ability using it to play area dances. Helen accompanied his violin with her own skills on piano and the lap harp.

Those dances were an additional source of upset for the Mennonite community causing church elders to object. While voicing their concern over Harry and Helen's music at dances, Harry and his brother, John were also attacked by the elders for their sale, from the Horndeen store, of tobacco to community residents.

In 1929, the Crash occurred causing the business to struggle, but the brothers managed with their entrepreneurial spirit and Helen's thriftiness. Both families continued to have food on the table; however, for periods the slim rations caused oldest daughter, Frances to suffer from malnutrition.

Many of the customers in the store failed to pay their accounts which made it difficult for Harry to restock shelves, so the store closed in the early thirties.

"Don't worry Helen I can still do farmhand work." Afterwards he did work for his brothers, Ben and Peter while also doing work on other area farms.

Eventually, Harry had enough of the prairie life in Manitoba and grew impatient with the cloistered Mennonite community's ways. Word from British Columbia was that the much warmer Okanagan Valley in The Interior was full of opportunity for farmers, so he decided to move his family to follow Helen's parents who had already made the move to Enderby, British Columbia.

"How's an Englishman ever going to take a man serious with a name like Bueckert?" he remarked as he grew more discontent with his Mennonite heritage. A name change was encouraged by his disgruntled brother, John, who also had moved to British Columbia a year earlier. It was early in the spring of 1935 and the family was living in Glencross, Manitoba at the time, another community just a mile southwest of Chortitz, when the thirty-nine-year-old Mennonite rebel loaded his thirty-eight-year-old wife of sixteen years and family into their 28 Ford and left Winkler. The hardships of the Depression years would not hold him back in life and if a move was necessary to improve his lot, he was prepared to do that. Harry was a stubborn industrious man who'd find ways to provide for his expanding family in any part of the country. His stubbornness had held him in Winkler area long enough while others in the family had left.

Harry believed that faith was to be lived not preached and was sick of Winkler's hypocrites feeling they were impractical about life's needs, being subservient to shallow faith gestures.

"The soul needs a heart," he would state.

Steering the vehicle south, Harry silently settled into sucking on the hand rolled cigarette that he had prepared for the trip while Helen quietly attended to young Edward. Sixteen-year-old, John Irven, thirteen-year-old Frances and ten-year-old Gladys, sat in the back seat of the automobile.

Apparently, after Helen's parents sold their farm in Winkler to follow others that had left, they purchased their Enderby residence from the town for the Depression Years' tax bill. The seventy-five dollars was left owing by a family that abandoned the residence

Helen's brother, Jack continued working in Chicago where he sold cars for a dealership. Brothers, Peter and Bill left the next year to work in Alberta. Meanwhile, Jack's decision to stay in Chicago had lasted for a couple of years before eventually moving on to California where he attempted working while the American immigration authority was 'hot on his heels.' Shortly thereafter he returned to Canada settling for a period in Olds, Alberta where he became partner in a farm implement dealership. After the Depression ended, he moved on to Lumby.

Johan Dyck and Agatha (Heide) Dyck

Harry and Helen Buechert with Frances, Gladys and John

Chapter Five

"**W**hat's this about individual conscience? They're hypocrites!" The remarks broke the silence in the vehicle, offered by Harry for the benefit of the audience riding with him. He wanted his family to understand he disapproved of the confined life they lived in Winkler.

Ignoring her father's ranting, daughter, Gladys commenced singing a song over her dad's shoulder from the back seat. The departure was supposed to be a happy occasion and she felt that it would be a long trip across the prairie if he insisted on complaining any longer about the hometown they'd just left. The young girl's mellow voice soothed him immediately and he returned a grin in the vehicle's rear- view mirror cutting his remarks short.

Gladys had learned, from her mother, that her dad could easily be distracted by music in moments when it was necessary to change his temperament. It was a subtle attribute that the girl exploited in order to mollify any annoyance around her. Siblings Francis and John smirked at each other and were content to let their sister take control of the moment.

The narrow dirt road from Winkler connected with the widened gravel segment of Manitoba Highway 10 which went north toward Winnipeg or south to North Dakota (today's highway 75) as it bisects the towns of Morris and Morden. During those years traversing North Dakota was US Route 2, an east-west paved segment that spanned 2579 miles across the northern continental United States. That highway was preferred by most Canadian Prairie residents destined for British Columbia. The road was commissioned in 1926 and split into two segments, divided in half by the roadway into southern Manitoba. Today, Interstate Highway 94 joins the Route 2 with segments remaining that have been jointly commissioned as Interstate 94 and US Route 2.

There wasn't a Trans Canada Highway in the 1930's, so travel across the Canadian plains usually involved a dip into North Dakota. In 1932 the Interprovincial Highway between Regina and Winnipeg was completed, but that was as far as it went. After Regina only substandard roads connected Saskatchewan and Alberta Communities. Prairie summer storms or heat would make those segments either too greasy or dusty for enjoyable travel.

After North Dakota the Bueckert's would go on to Spokane and then head north toward Trail, B.C. where they'd catch the Cascade highway on to Grand Forks. Afterwards they'd take the subsequent paved segments leading on to their Okanagan Valley destination via a steep decline into Osoyoos, part of today's Highway 3.

Their arrival in the Okanagan was delayed by an accident that occurred while Harry nervously manoeuvred his Ford over the Cascade segment. He lost control of the wheel on a slippery section that still had ice remaining from the spring thaw. Carelessly the inexperienced mountain driver reached into the back seat for one of the sandwiches Helen prepared earlier at the roadside. The vehicle ended down an embankment stopped by trees.

"I managed to save our sandwiches," Helen announced, while holding up the box displaying its contents attempting to humour the situation. Fortunately, the car landed upright and no one was hurt. In a few hours it was pulled back up on to the roadway and they were on their way to Vernon area again.

Harry and his teenage son, John would have a good chance of finding work around Vernon where fruit and vegetable farming were abundant.

The small city's many packing houses offered employment. Vernon was the commercial center of the Okanagan Valley. Neighbouring Kelowna and Penticton were less diversified during the period.

Harry succeeded in securing a rental home the morning after their arrival and found time to look after the second order of business on his agenda. Intent on copying his brother, John, he legally filed papers that day to assume the new Bickert name for the family. It was both brothers' final demonstration of rebellion against the Mennonite community and the religious sect they were abandoning. Harry risked spending the money before he found work but chose to solidify his relocation decision by proceeding with filing to change the family name.

"Well you're not going to be Mennonites any longer," he announced to his family on his arrival in front of them at the end of the day's affairs, "and not Bueckerts either. Our name will soon be Bickert! For good!" he continued. For Harry the moment was like converting the family to a new religion. He would continue to respect Christian values, only this time Harry's style. He had heart and soul for the Lord but ceased to formally practice his ancestral faith.

Oldest son, John, who had left school four years earlier after completing eighth grade in Manitoba, would continue to work in Vernon, rather than resume school that spring. It was a form of forced child labour resulting from domestic hardships brought on by the Depression. In Manitoba, John skipped seventh grade when twelve and advanced to finish the eighth grade. He and many boys worked to help provide for their deprived family. Most worked as hired hands on Manitoba farms. Meanwhile, his sisters, resumed their education.

Young John and his dad found employment on the hot valley hillsides picking tomatoes. Sunburnt and worn by the end of the first day's work, they were both fired, because they couldn't keep up with the imported Chinese workers that had migrated to the valley from the harsh train crew camps while building the railway lines throughout British Columbia. Manitoba farming was easier.

31

Harry and John promised each other that they would not announce the bad news to Helen until after they had found replacement work. Fortunately, the next day, after canvassing a couple of orchard operations, they were hired to prune apple trees where there was shade.

The nearby village of Armstrong was known nationwide for an annual fair that commenced in 1900. It exhibited poultry, other livestock and area goods, known today as The Interior Provincial Exposition. Harry felt confident that prized birds left behind in Winkler and shipped to the valley from Manitoba would compete successfully for prize money in Armstrong. He understood and few would be able to challenge his ability to select the best poultry stock for showings. Harry attended that autumn's exposition where he found an unsuspecting poultry exhibitor to swindle out of two prize birds.

"You know why you lost that contest and came in second? The birds had a few crooked feathers and poop on their rears." Of course, Harry had first pointed those facts out to the judges before their decision was made to select Harry's birds for the winning ribbons. As a result, he purchased the birds cheap from the disappointed man after he failed to impress the judges!

Helen's brothers, Peter and Bill were destined to move to Vernon area. They had communicated their intention to Helen's parents who occasionally received word by mail that the two were struggling on Alberta farms.

Jack, on the other hand, who had become a bit of a transient during the Depression years, managed to hold on to good employment in Alberta. In the past, he would show up in Winkler with new automobiles and proudly display those to impress locals of his successes in the States during a difficult time for Canadian Prairie folk. Usually, after a few months being home and showing off, he would end up like most other young men who tried to return to the southern Manitoba towns and eventually have empty pockets. They would then, be forced to sell the new vehicles to finance a return trip to the States where work was available. Jack's eventual success in Olds with the new business partnership selling and servicing farm machinery would keep him there while his brothers one by one headed to the Valley.

Peter remained in Alberta that fall while his brother, Bill followed his parents and sisters over to Vernon. Bill worked for awhile with his Uncle Wilhelm who had earned a steam ticket and operated road building equipment in the North Okanagan. That was a big improvement for young Bill who had ridden rail cars with his brother, Peter during the early thirties shuffling between available jobs in central Alberta. Bill did do some temporary work in Calgary, welding and steel fabricating.

Peter's continued struggles in Alberta were compensated with a meagre five-dollar monthly income which included room and board. Eventually he heard of his brother's successes with work in the Okanagan and wanted to follow but was too financially strapped. At first, he unlawfully secured a ride to British Columbia on a train boxcar, but that became disastrous. In Banff, as he lay hidden on the railcar below sheets of metal destined for the shipyards in Vancouver, he was spotted by the rail police after a group of hobos hopped over to his car, thinking Peter's car offered more security then theirs. The subsequent arrest meant that Peter would have to spend the night in the Banff Jail.

The next morning, he along with the other reprobates, were ushered into the courtroom for the trial and given a choice of sentencing. Peter opted to pay a fine in lieu of a jail term. Fortunately, he had the money that day to pay the fine, but it left his pockets nearly empty with only eighty-five cents remaining of his farm earnings. After the courtroom appearance, a friend that he had made that day talked him out of hopping another train and Peter instead caught a ride by automobile back to Calgary.

The prairie had turned cold by then, so Peter slept on the rail station's washroom floor. In the morning he again hitched a train ride, but this time north to Olds where he worked for several weeks on farms. In autumn 1937, Peter did get to the Okanagan to see his parents and family where he picked apples for four cents a box, picking fifty to sixty boxes a day.

A year after arriving in Vernon, Helen Bickert gave birth to third daughter, Norma Jeannette. The baby was bestowed with the eyes and smile of her mother. She was the last child that Helen would give birth to and she always enjoyed the closest relationship to her mother of all the siblings. Norma Jeannette later took the name Jeanne.

The agreeable and cheerful personality of the child added a refreshing, but difficult challenge to Helen who was attempting to work in order to financially assist the struggling family. For several years she worked outside the home at area canneries and packing houses. Occasionally, the work was interrupted over her preference to remain for periods of time in the home.

After a few years doing orchard work, John found work at NOCA Dairies in Vernon. NOCA was a co-operative dairy farmers business run by the North Okanagan Cattle Association, in the middle half of the Twentieth Century. That was before its operation sold out to Dairyland, an enterprise owned by Vancouver billionaire, Jimmy Pattison.

In the 1940's Harry became employed as custodian for two local schools while raising chickens commercially at the house and property on 43rd Avenue that his son, John had purchased for seven hundred and fifty dollars from savings. From the home, Harry delivered eggs and butchered poultry meat while he continued to win the prize ribbons at various expositions throughout Western Canadian communities where he would ship his birds for exhibiting.

Vernon offered its residents a quiet and humble lifestyle. Most people lived in small homes and had large families, characteristic of the day. The community's numerous churches, one theatre and several dance halls were always busy with weddings and other social events, as people entertained themselves collectively, making Vernon a great venue for musicians to perform at events. For the Harry Bickert family who were musicians, it meant that they would always have weekend work.

John would accompany his parents on the guitar and Gladys would sometimes sing. Later, Edward played guitar, too, but seldom with his parents as he preferred to perform in musical groups that were more into the swing jazz arrangements.

Music does something to people. It quietens them and puts them at peace as they express the best of their emotions through their artistry. For the Bickert's music gave them the satisfaction of gathering in their kitchen at home or at social events to enjoy hours together in harmony. There were never a lot of words but in smiles and with laughter they'd be together. Occasionally, Harry's husky melodic voice would accompany his fiddle as the small framed man would perform in harmony with his instrument. Helen was faithfully beside him playing the piano or lap harp, but she was too shy to sing.

Harry on fiddle in later years

Helen on the lap harp

Chapter Six

B y 1939 a nation that existed for less than three-quarters of a century was about to engage an enemy in Europe along with England and her allies. After years of turmoil in the world, there had been a short period where hope prevailed in Canada as peace had been won in the First World War and the Great Depression was over. The economy was re-developing normalcy and home provisions provided Canadians a more positive domestic atmosphere. From the Depression most of the country's citizens had grown to appreciate one-another more and understood the valuable fabric of family and home life. Surviving the effects of the recent horrific struggles now encouraged a form of domestic security where past trials were never anticipated again.

Few Saskatchewan residents felt that the new menace evolving in Germany was that remote to them as most understood the serious implications. It was the sacrifice of its Prairie sons and those from other rural communities that played such an important role in past Commonwealth commitments overseas. Life in smaller communities was such that work opportunities were less abundant and rural youth jumped at enlisting in the military in order to travel and be adventuresome. In Marquis, young men and women were again signing up and leaving the community to serve. They were taking heed of Churchill's warnings to member Commonwealth countries that their citizens prepare to do their part in order to obliterate the tyrant's campaign. Meanwhile, Canada's Prime Minister Mackenzie King, appointed C.D. Howe, a successful eastern industrialist and newly appointed Cabinet Minister, ordering him to prepare the country for war.

After Gladys had left the home, John LaLonde felt he needed to be with Kathleen who would otherwise have been left alone. During the Depression they made frequent runs for survival to the ration train in Moose Jaw, but now the fields were improving, and crops were harvestable bringing in more income than they had in years.

By 1939 his daughter was a determined young woman of seventeen, but somewhat protected from the fear of war by her only child family life. Her mother had come and gone again, and Kathleen had just graduated valedictorian in Marquis' High School and succeeded in being a homemaker for her father in the absence of her mother. The adult responsibilities of housekeeper, bookkeeper and cook for her dad and his farmhands, while being a student, brought a price with it. Kathleen's friends were freer and the lure of accompanying them east in order to help with the military manufacturing effort occupied some of the recent conversations between her and her friends.

LaLonde dreaded the thought of his daughter being away from the farm. They had been separated for a good part of the last school term. During the final school year Kathleen had spent winter weekdays living in town with her high school principal's family, the Silary's. Already she had mastered the domestic operations of the farm enough and pre-prepared food for her dad for weekday periods while she was away. It always flattered Kathleen to think that she had garnered the approval of older people like her principal, enough that he was willing to take her in at his home for the term. She enjoyed being off the farm, because her Marquis friends were more available in the village, but to John LaLonde the weekdays were long and lonely.

The two had developed a team effort in running the farming operation. During autumn 1939 Kathleen drove the grain truck alongside her father's combine for harvest and the two were paid for doing the same for a few other farms. Kathleen's assistance made John LaLonde's farm operation profitable enough for the household to operate without her dad seeking supplemental employment for the year.

She graduated a year ahead of her age group managing to skip a year being promoted early from seventh to eighth grade, but that made it even more difficult for her dad. "She's too young to be heading east with her older grad friends," he thought, so it was time for him to intervene.

"Kiddo, what do you say we head to Vancouver after we're finished harvesting. We could spend the winter there and find work to pay our way. There's nothing holding us here, is there?" He anticipated a positive response.

"Are you serious? Wow! That would be terrific, Dad!" she blurted, as she stopped pumping water into a glass held at the kitchen sink's water pump. Her dad always came through and now the most difficult decision in her life was made easier.

Since the death of Mary's father, Mr. Kennedy, Kathleen's twin was hanging out with a crowd of friends in Moose Jaw where she now lived with her adoptive mother. The Kennedy farm had been sold. Consequently, it was more Kathleen's own feelings about missing her twin sister that made her feel alone in Marquis. As well, she felt a little displaced by the move of her two brothers and her natural father who had left a few years earlier to Ontario and then were absorbed by their careers in the military. Kathleen calculated that her sister would be leaving Moose Jaw soon for training if Mary was accepted in a lab technician course there. It would have made staying at home in Marquis even more difficult until her dad's suggestion provided relief.

The young homemaker guessed that by her father's silence he was beginning to regret her intention to leave home. Mike Griffin had recently passed, and she had hoped to see more of her brothers; however, they enlisted. John Griffin was with the Canadian Air Force contingent in Moose Jaw, destined for England while brother, Patrick, signed up with the Canadian Army's Princess Patricia Regiment in Edmonton and was seldom in Marquis. He would soon leave for Italy and Casino.

Now, after her dad's announcement, Kathleen immediately decided that she would drop her plan to head east where she intended to find work in a military supply manufacturing plant, a recent plan made with girl friends.

John LaLonde recognized that Kathleen was nearly an adult and understood what that meant for his daughter to embark on a new journey and an independent life. Troubled by the prospect of her leaving home, he devised the plan to ease the impact on both himself and his daughter. He had sold all of his livestock during the drought and little work had to be done in the winter but shovel snow and feed the fire, so he concluded that going to the coast would be a good experience for both of them. Moreover, Kathleen would turn eighteen during the winter and benefit by living in the big city of Vancouver before she was out on her own attempting the Ontario venture that he felt she would eventually follow.

The quiet farmhouse suddenly became filled with conversation as father and daughter spent the rest of the harvest season talking about the upcoming trip to British Columbia. One thought pre-occupied Kathleen now and that was the excitement of experiencing her independence at Vancouver! Thankfully, it was all on her father's approval, so her departure from the farm would be easy for both of them. Prior to the new and exciting proposition from her father, Kathleen had given consideration to the idea of seeing her mother in Toronto, but that could wait for now.

At the same time Mary Kennedy's mother, an aging woman, was encouraging Mary's departure for training in a lab tech course. Mrs. Kennedy knew that Mary had to prepare in the event that her daughter lost her mother. That would leave Kathleen's twin sister alone to fend for her own. Mary had always been sensitive and emotional about issues that Kathleen could easily brush off.

"Kathleen you're such a perky girl," Mary would tell her twin. "Why can't I be the same?"

"But you have all the men chasing you. What good is perky for me when you've got the looks?" Kathleen would retort.

Mary was never quite as composed as Kathleen with her emotions, but she was poised, tall and managed to attract the men, so Kathleen was always envious of her twin's stature and height that complimented similar looks to hers. It was Mary who cried when Kathleen left for Vancouver. Both girls were unaware that many future events in the world and their lives would interfere with them seeing one-another or their brothers, John and Patrick for the next five years.

Regretfully, the winter of 1939-40 in Vancouver turned into a lonely one for both. Kathleen's father could not find work in the city, so was forced to look elsewhere, eventually securing employment at a logging camp several hundred miles up the coast near Prince Rupert. Kathleen was left to manage on her own in Vancouver. She stayed for a while in the Vancouver apartment that they had rented together which was located in the False Creek area, then moved to downtown Vancouver nearer St. Paul's hospital where she found work as a dietary aide.

That winter was dreadfully dreary for both. The news of the war and the relentless rainfall made both Kathleen and her dad regret the arrangement which forced them to be apart from Marquis when it would have been best that they were home together. Kathleen spent the lonely hours writing numerous letters to her dad. Meanwhile, he cut wood and ran a horse team hauling fallen timbers out of the bush for a north coast logging enterprise.

Chapter Seven

In 1940 Canada's western seaport city of Vancouver was buzzing with activity, day and night. Both Canadian and American Navies were actively patrolling off the West Coast where shipping activity increased, because the seaport offered less exposure than the east coast to Germany's Navy. For any single man that usually meant that there was competition from the enlisted men for the ladies in town. At twenty-one John Bickert was reserved in his approaches toward the ladies as he had inherited his mother's placid disposition and the task of dating in the larger city was difficult for him. He moved in with his mother's younger brother, Bill Dyck, who had left Vernon to work at the shipyards where incomes were higher than in the interior cities. John was hired at the dockyards too, but the cold damp weather in Vancouver soon discouraged him about his move to the coast.

Social life for John Bickert was mostly related to chats over beers with Bill who was a few years older than his nephew. Bickert declined invitations to join Bill whose social life appeared at its prime in contrast to his own. Other than the occasional outing to area clubs, Bickert preferred to stay at home in the apartment that they shared in False Creek area. There Bickert liked to read because he felt that he put up with enough of the winter rain during the daytime while at work and refused to get soaked at night as well. Within a few months he decided to return to Vernon once he had sufficient earnings to set himself up again at home. Soon Bickert returned to Vernon where he was hired on at NOCA Dairy Products plant.

Meanwhile, Peter Dyck had recently been introduced to Bertha Carey by Frances Bickert and Al Sasges, a man who would marry John Bickert's sister, Gladys. In a few years Peter was destined to be stationed between Calgary and Medicine Hat, Alberta for the course of war. It was love at first sight after the introduction to Bertha. She was attractive having a bit of Shuswap native heritage and possessed a glow about her pleasant face and warm disposition. The couple married on June 27th, 1940 just before Peter enlisted with the Royal Canadian Air Force. Initially, Bertha stayed on in Lumby and Peter went on to serve stationed in Medicine Hat.

Later, the lonely couple arranged for Bertha to travel to Calgary; however, the cost of accommodations was too high for her to stay there on a maid's salary and the couple was forced to be apart again after only a couple of months together in Alberta. Bertha, expecting her first baby, returned to Lumby for the balance of Peter's military duty. He did make it home on furloughs to Lumby during the course of the war.

John Bickert was introduced by his sister, Frances to a Vernon debutant, Ethel Pauline Hiltz. Frances had become the main social convenor for the family. Hiltz, a likeable and attractive young woman frequented swing clubs in the area. The dance clubs had become popular during the war with cadets and military personnel stationed at the Vernon base. In the daytime, Hiltz worked as a hotel chambermaid and then nightly made her trek along with Frances, to the clubs which had also become popular with the locals. Ethel was admired by most of the Bickert family for her beauty, wit and outgoing disposition. Of course, she was successful in garnering John's admiration, as well.

She loved to dance, and John continued to be encouraged to join her at the clubs. Soon the two were dating regularly. Unfortunately, Frances began to warn her brother, about his girlfriend. Apparently, Ethel was sneaking out with other men behind John's back. The warnings became more frequent from Frances, particularly when the couple announced to the family that they were engaged and planned to marry. The final warning came on the eve of the couple's wedding.

Bickert retorted to his sister, Frances, "I don't want to hear of it, Frances!"

So, Frances stopped nattering feeling that the situation was hopeless. Her brother was destined to marry in spite of the warnings, convinced that he had found a wonderful lady. To John, Ethel was good. He enjoyed her affections when he was around her. The couple married in a small ceremony at Vernon's Pentecostal Church on June 29th, 1940. The ceremony was attended by family and friends with a large reception at the National Hotel in Vernon where Ethel worked.

On June 12, 1941, Ethel gave birth to a daughter that the couple named Sherry Anne. The baby was a month premature and weighed only four pounds six ounces at her birth struggling to survive during the first few weeks after the delivery. The infant's dark brown hair, eyebrows and brown eyes matched her dad's. Her round face and squealing laughter warmed the whole family. It wasn't enough to warm the heart of her own mother though as Ethel was feeling tied to the new responsibility of motherhood and silently resented the responsibility that tied her down.

For Bickert the issues in his marriage were troubling; however, the social pressures around him were such that he could not ignore his responsibility to country and the obligation that he felt was calling him to help those who had gone to serve in the military before him. Both his and Ethel's parents were supportive of their marriage and he believed Ethel was adjusting to her role as wife and mother.

Canada's population was less than twelve million people in the middle of World War II; however, the country had the Allied Forces third largest military, with the third largest navy along with the fourth largest air force. Prime Minister William Lyon Mackenzie King had promised to limit Canada's involvement in the war; however, the participation grew. The country's leader began to receive pressure from Cabinet as a result of casualties in the small contingent of forces that he had assigned overseas. When he ordered several soldiers overseas that had been conscripted under the pretences of defending the home front, he had a full mutiny on his hands in French Canada. French Canadians were not interested in fighting overseas defending England. Those French Canadians that had joined or were conscripted only joined with the intent of defending their homeland, not for the purpose of engaging Germany overseas. The rebellion reached its peak in Terrace, British Columbia where French Canadian troops numbering about three thousand were stationed to defend the North Coast. Feeling betrayed by their Prime Minister the men rebelled. The disenchanted Francophone troops took control of a cache of weapons at the camp after witnessing some of their comrades being sent to Europe to fight. The news was silenced; however, enough leaked out to encourage the support of British Columbia men who felt they needed to fill in where the French- Canadian enthusiasm was waning. It took several weeks to defuse the mutiny and bring back order. At the same time King was experiencing a form of rebellion in Cabinet with senior French-Canadian Cabinet Ministers leading a Francophone rebellion garnering French-Canadian voter loyalty to cause a serious schism in the nation.

Eventually, the rebellion in Ottawa and mutiny in Terrace ended, and French Canada joined the rest of the country unified under the direction of senior Cabinet Minister, Louis St. Laurent, whose unifying actions would eventually destine him to become Canada's future Prime Minister. King's deception eventually cost him politically, but for the moment he had unity again and French conscripts joined English speaking Canadians in the fight overseas.

The kaleidoscope of images filling the minds of young men who were venturing off to war must have been terrifying. No moral person could want to leave a family to expose oneself to such an uncertain future, other than for adventure, gain or to search out a deeper purpose in life. For John Bickert the exercise was a moral one, because he was at an age where he felt a sincere pull from the depth of his being calling him to give more of himself. It wasn't the beginning of that form of interior self denial that he had experienced. His upbringing had taught him that people aren't born to live a life only for themselves, but to contribute to building a better society around them. Dropping out of school in order to assist his family when he was thirteen was worthwhile and he grew in the process. It too, was an act of self denial, a part of the Mennonite heritage to assist in building community at the expense of oneself. The decision to put the needs of Europe ahead of his own was a way of fulfilling the need to be selfless, although military service was contrary to the very values of the community he had left at Winkler. He didn't want to kill and being killed was less of a worry to him. Europe was chained to a formidable evil force that called principled men to come and abet the struggle against it.

In May 1943 Bickert joined the Reserve Army committing himself to an effort in preparation for the regular army. The same sense of duty, that prompted the social moral conscience of every young man in the western world to become involved, led John Bickert to the army recruit office in Vernon in mid November 1944.

The pronouncement to Ethel came nearly four years after the couple were married and after the announcement was first made to his parents. He quit his job where he was crew foreman at NOCA Dairy Products in Vernon. That was a few weeks after signing on to the Canadian Army. In mid-November 1944, when Sherry was two and a half years of age, the departure occurred. Ethel offered only a few superficial emotions about John's departure while he stood holding Sherry until ordered along with the other recruits to board the bus.

From Edmonton, Bickert was sent to Niagara Falls. While in Niagara Falls, he was part of a small group of soldiers commissioned to guard the Canadian hydro electric facility at the falls. There he earned the rank Corporal First Class and held the commission for a few short weeks before losing that rank for letting a couple of soldiers take the evening off A.W.O.L. Of course, this was done without the young corporal first receiving the Commanding Officer's approval. The short-lived promotion for the twenty-four-year old Bickert, now bumped down to Private First Class, was not that upsetting. He brushed off the reproach as a humorous and careless event in his life. He knew that he would soon earn the Corporal rank back and giving his friends the liberty of some time off from duty was worth the setback. Bickert told the officer that he would soon replace the stripes that were taken away. Afterwards, he grew a moustache in place of the stripes on his shoulder.

In a couple of months Bickert was sent overseas to England where he remained for the rest of the war. In England he was promoted again to Corporal while simultaneously being assigned to the King's Own Rifle Brigade in England to march as a ceremonial show soldier. It was a posting that was mostly social. He described the position to his family as one that occupied his time polishing his boots and pressing his uniform. As a result of the placement he was never sent to the Continent for combat and fortunately, the war was over less than a year after he was shipped from Niagara Falls to England.

Ethel wrote few letters to John after he left Niagara Falls; however, letters from his parents continued a regular basis. Finally, in a letter he asked for an explanation about Ethel, concerned about both his wife and daughter. A response came from his parents that explained the situation. Ethel had been unfaithful in his absence and had hooked up with another man after dating several more. Annoyed by the restrictions that the child placed on her social life, Sherry was abandoned by her mother and was living now with her grandparents. Everyone including Ethel's parents objected to the situation, but they were unsuccessful in convincing the woman to behave.

It was all so embarrassing to Ethel's staunch Pentecostal parents that the Hiltz's told her not to come around anymore. Almost immediately after John had left for Edmonton, Ethel had moved to Vancouver with Sherry moving in with John's younger sister, Frances, where Ethel enrolled in a hairdressing course that she seldom attended. Frances worked, when she was not babysitting Sherry for Ethel. In Vancouver Ethel frequented swing clubs ignoring both her daughter and her marriage commitment. Ethel was disinterested in the child and was never seen again by her. From that point onward Sherry was cared for by Harry and Helen, Bickert until John would return home from duty overseas.

Peter Dyck had returned home to Lumby in mid 1945, where Bertha was busy with their first two children, Bill and Marie. Son, Bill was four when the family was reunited, and Marie was one. Bertha was then expecting her third baby. The Catholic woman whom Peter married, who wouldn't dance with him during Lent when the pair was first introduced, was providing him with a growing Catholic family. Eventually they would have eleven.

Meanwhile, during the war Peter's brother Jack Dyck had moved to the Okanagan Valley where he purchased a garage in Lumby. He invited his younger brothers, Bill and Peter, to join with him at the garage where Peter immediately would have work to support his family.

Shortly afterwards, Peter was asked to partner in running a commercial airline service between Vernon and Vancouver. He accepted and left Jack's operation; however, it wasn't long before the young entrepreneurs failed in the airline enterprise. Peter rejoined Jack at the garage in Lumby.

It was a monumental task in bringing Canadian overseas troops home. John Bickert would eventually be shipped back to New York on the British luxury carrier, The Queen Mary. He waited six months to travel though as the wounded and troops that fought on The Continent were shipped first. After de-boarding the ship, they travelled by trains and buses back home. It was on March 5, 1946, when Bickert had fulfilled his duty to country and arrived home to rebuild his life.

Chapter Eight

Saskatchewan's landscape began its annual renewal with all of nature's seasonal gifts in the spring of 1941. The chequered mural below the distant horizon again revealed the last harvest's grey stubble, ashen without its golden hue, after a season below the snowy blanket now thawed. Slender willows bloomed, their silver furry buds above streams that trickled in ditches, off the black dirt roads. Pastures were full of cows calving, mares foaling and wary ground squirrels perching where cultivating and harrowing had begun. The province emanated a spirit of harmony toward natural order in each individual creation.

For Kathleen LaLonde the season brought new feelings deep from inside her about womanhood. She was nineteen and had been noticing young men more than before, while radiating mature confidence from spending the past winter alone while her dad worked up the coast in Prince Rupert. Income earned from employment in Vancouver's St. Paul's hospital had given her a new perspective in managing her independence. She was now more attentive to the clothes she wore and the way she presented herself. Her hair was combed differently; she wore make-up and cologne and became forward in her conversation with young men. Kathleen as a social person needed to claim her place. Perhaps something of her adoptive mother had begun to surface in her, even to a fault.

It wasn't long before Roy Gardiner noticed Kathleen. Mary Kennedy had been dating that friend prior to the LaLonde's trip to Vancouver.

Now that Mary had moved into Moose Jaw with her mother after the death of Mr. Kennedy, she was dating others while Roy was left in Marquis, dropping around to see Kathleen since her return. Gardener was a well mannered, handsome fellow that respected the twins and enjoyed both their friendships. Remarkably, Kathleen had changed over the winter and the transformation appealed to Gardiner. For Kathleen, Roy's advances were persuasive enough but somewhat overbearing.

"You're too short for such a long name. I'm calling you Kay," he ordered.

"He even shortens my name to Kay," she complained to her dad while approving of the boyfriend with a smile.

Kay liked that he was polite enough to capitulate when she'd push him away, so she permitted the friendship to continue as long as it had gone on over the summer. Toward autumn all the flirting and warmth of the friendship had become redundant and it was time to end it, not because of Roy, but deeper needs were calling her from within. Those required she find herself again in independence separate from the confines of home and Marquis.

"I have to find another place to live, Roy," she complained, "You're too good looking to fight off much longer," the compliment had a tinge of dishonesty and a deeper motive in it.

Kathleen objected more to the barriers of life on the farm and the smallness of Marquis than she objected to Roy. That same summer John Griffin had gone to England with the RCAF to fly bombing campaigns over Germany; Patrick Griffin was still at war in Italy.

Michael Griffin died in 1932 only a few years after his second marriage which was to Gertie Hanlan a hired housekeeper. At that time the boys, Patrick and John were thirteen and fifteen. Michael, who was in Michigan as a wheat pool operator, lost his job when American immigrations, during The Depression, kicked out working permit foreign workers from the country. Michael Griffin was taken to the border along with his family and beaten by the US Customs officers within eyesight of Canadian Customs officers. He died less than a month after the beating. Michael was buried in 'The Sault.'

Gertie would write the LaLonde's and the Kennedys to report to the twins on their brothers after the natural father's demise. In turn Kathleen would reciprocate with letters to her brothers who seldom returned the mail. Kathleen and Mary's endearing communication did prompt the brothers to contact their twin sisters when as young men they returned to Moose Jaw area.

Kathleen's brothers had returned to Moose Jaw for military service in 1941 and then left leaving Kay feeling abandoned. By then she had assumed the name Kay. It was one of a few names she'd assume throughout life including Johnnie, a name her dad called her. All the friends and family that had left the area that year encouraged a decision about her own future, and it was time to make the announcement to her dad. Her cousin, Phyllis LaLonde and a friend, Doris Hurl, had schemed with Kathleen the night before at a malt shop in Moose Jaw agreeing that they should move to Toronto. In a moment of bravery, Kathleen consented to join her friends on the adventure. She believed that it would be good for her to see her mother again while agonizing over the openness that she had expressed with her friends who teased her about her apprehension.

"Are you going to be able to leave your dad, Kay?"

"Sure, but it's not easy. He'll be pretty lonely," she responded.

With harvest completed, Kathleen finally mustered enough conviction to ask her dad for his approval for her to join her friends whose plan was to find work and live at Ajax, nearby Toronto. Ajax was prompted by newspaper ads that were soliciting Prairie workers to come and join wartime industrial plants there.

For a moment she stood in the dining room entry, her fingers fidgeting with a torn piece of floral wallpaper that curled on the edge of the doorway corner. Distracted from what she set out to say to her father, she studied the paper and remembered that her mother had earlier described it as something that added cheer to the Marquis farmhouse. The thought reminded her that her mother left the home less than two weeks after the re-decorating job was complete. It irritated her that her mom would decorate the home and then leave. "Was the decorating job intended to be a departure gift to the family?" she thought. Then, she re-focused to tell her Dad the news. He was seated at the dining room table. Calming herself, she stopped fidgeting with the wallpaper.

"Dad, I want to go to Toronto with Phyllis and Doris, next week."

She surprised herself that her voice still portrayed a negative tone over her mother's departure and felt it would be a bad opening to the subject. This was something that repeatedly troubled her about her own disposition that she could be sharp with even those she loved.

John LaLonde had grown accustomed to his daughter's intent but understood her defences. Immediately he encouraged her while choking on his words. Although he didn't relish the thought, he realized that he had to consent. The news had come earlier from his niece, Phyllis's mother, Elizabeth LaLonde, the widow of his brother, Frank. Frank had died of a heart attack on the first of February that spring and Elizabeth was concerned that Phyllis was too young to be dating her friend, Amil Sagal. She felt the relationship with Amil was progressing too fast. John had re-assured her that encouraging a trip east might help. The trouble was, he didn't realize at the time that Kay would want to go with Phillis, until he heard that morning from his sister at the town's post office.

"Johnnie you have to be with your friends and you'll see your mother." He always used her nickname when special attention was required, and her voice had indicated it was. Johnnie was a name that had been given to Kathleen since she rode beside him in the farm vehicles as a child.

Kathleen felt her only emotional tie to Marquis was her dad. She understood that her departure would be hard on him, but he'd manage, and she'd write frequently and send along care packages to warm the lonely farmhouse. As for her friend, Roy, she would break the news to him over a beer in the yard Friday evening. He always came to talk to her dad and would bring along a few beers to make his contribution to the social when the three would play Rummy together at home. The Friday evening card game had become a sort of tradition over the years between Kathleen and John LaLonde. It was a time when friends were always welcome to join in but not distract them from the cards as that was when the two would relax together after the week's farm work. Occasionally, her dad's own friends would join in as well. To oblige the tradition, Roy had begun joining in when he began dating Kathleen.

The next week after Sunday Mass, Kathleen, her cousin Phyllis and their mutual friend Doris Hurl (Mitchell), left by train to Toronto. Together, from the coach car they all complained of being homesick before the train had even departed Moose Jaw's station. The gesture was to appease consciences for the guilt felt in leaving home.

Roy Gardener laughed as the threesome boarded the train, "Kay, I'm glad to get rid of you, so I can check out the older ladies in town." Gardener was referring to the fact that the pickings would be slim for a young single man in the small community.

"Look at the goof! Now, he's going to be running around with all the old maids in town." Kay blurted with a chuckle to hide her own tears that surfaced for her father who was standing alongside Gardiner, her Aunt Lizzie and Amil Sagal.

The arrival in Toronto was early on the morning of the third day at the Toronto station where Gladys LaLonde greeted the trio. Afterwards, they all bunked at Kay's mothers for a few nights. It started as an exhilarating meeting for Kathleen and her mom who had not seen each other for a couple of years. By that evening in the apartment, the visit became strained as accusations against her father flowed from Gladys's mouth. Kay reciprocated with blaming her mother for the family break up and the day was ruined by the attacks. Charles Cowperthwaite had become Gladys's new man.

"He is not going to replace my father!" she objected to her friends the next day.

The upset was soon dismissed by Kay when the threesome rented an apartment together with Marguerite Willms, an acquaintance they had met during their first day in Ajax. Marguerite had moved from Lumby, British Columbia for an adventure to assist in the national call for citizen's aid in the war effort. She would eventually play a pivotal role in Kathleen's future.

The girls had all been hired on at Ajax's munitions plant, Defence Industries Ltd., in a job they spent together loading tank and mortar shells for the munitions contractor. The work was temporary employment because the plant was about to shut down and be replaced by the new General Engineering Company (Canada) Plant. It was opening in Scarborough in three months to replace the smaller facility in Ajax. The huge new manufacturing facility with the corporate initials GECO was brainstormed by Defence Minister, C.D. Howe, to assist in financing Canada's military effort overseas and produce much needed munitions. When it did come time to move over to GECO and their jobs at Defence Industries Ltd. ended, neither Phillis, nor Kay were interested in going to Scarborough from Ajax. Doris did make the move, but Kathleen went to work as a salesclerk at Zellers in Toronto and Phyllis decided her love for Amil, was calling her home, so she returned to Marquis.

It wasn't long after the shift to Zellers that Kathleen made a second move over to Eaton's downtown Toronto store where her mother already worked as a seamstress and Kathleen was hired on as a salesclerk. A year later, Kathleen took a third position as filing clerk at General Motors Corporation in Oshawa. GM was also doing some war machinery manufacturing in Oshawa for the Allied Forces. The Corporation apparently produced vast quantities of armaments and military vehicles during the war.

Kay's visits to her mother in Toronto continued to be stormy as Gladys continued to talk negatively about John LaLonde. That and her mother's live-in arrangement added to the discomfort.

Eventually, shortened and less frequent visits substituted for the sleepovers that were always too long and ended in hurtful verbal exchanges. General Motors was a relief to Kathleen, as it provided the necessary separation from her mother where squabbles would continue to erupt.

While living in Oshawa, Kathleen dated Carl Ellis, an appliance salesman who was recently medically discharged from the Air Force. The crafty salesman was suspect by all of Kathleen's friends, but she would not listen to their objections. He was feeding an addiction to heroin that resulted from a two-year morphine pain treatment he was subjected to prior to leaving the military. Unfortunately, his leg fractured in basic training camp and over the course of two years the injury resulted in an early medical discharge. Afterwards, Ellis commenced self medicating the pain with street drugs to replace the morphine that the Canadian Air Force doctors no longer provided.

Nothing could keep her from Ellis. Even though he was hiding the truth about himself and to what extent he would go to feed his illegal habit, the allure of the relationship was enough to move the Prairie girl away from anything that was sensible to her. The marriage ceremony took place on October 25, 1943, in Peterborough closer to Carl's work.

Mike and Gertie Griffin w/ Patrick and John

Chapter Nine

L eaving home can be a lonely experience; however, leaving home having been raised an only child excluded for a period of time from the love and influence of a mother would have left Kathleen exposed to unexpected dangers. Her mother's affection should have offered her much more than words over the phone or in letters imparted and gift parcels provided. To feel the full measure of that love, she needed to experience it in the nurturing gestures of mother-daughter relations: social contact, words, work, smiles, embraces, healing, forgiveness and security. But to have this leave must have been devastating. Once dispossessed of a mother's endowment she lost the most valuable social experience in life that a teenager could expect from a mother. That nurturing couldn't be replaced by a father's love. John LaLonde could only provide a contribution to his daughter, not the fundamental love of a mother that is essential and good in all of nature. Although Gladys attempted to provide that; however, with her mother's life now being shared with a stranger, a discomfort accompanied the strain Kathleen felt from her estranged mother.

Any relationships Kathleen entered after her own departure from Marquis would provide lessons in social development, both good and bad; they would be growth experiences seen from a different perspective than a young woman who had the example and nurturing of both parents. Kathleen would experience complications with people after her mother left the Marquis home and the crust that would develop in her composure would eventually become a defence she'd carry throughout life.

She trusted Ellis, because in the past her father was the stronghold in her life, and she felt her emotions toward Ellis would assure what she required after leaving her Marquis home. Unfortunately, Ellis disregarded that need adding only injury to that which her mother had already inflicted. Any of the attributes Carl had acquired from his upbringing were obscured by the intense cravings he felt for heroin entwining him in a secret life as he attempted to provide for the illicit substance secretly. In due course he began to develop financial schemes to fund the habit. First, he engineered an insurance scam and then robberies. One robbery was a Chinese laundry. He'd drive Kay to see his family in Trent River on Sundays fighting to retain normalcy but after those weekends he succumbed to his cravings again.

Kathleen always felt that the Ellis family respected her. They determined that their new daughter-in-law offered what their son required to fix his shortcomings.

"Who doesn't have blemishes?" They'd ask themselves. "He's always so fidgety, but Kay will fix that." They didn't understand what caused his unsettled behaviour.

Kathleen delivered her first child, John George, on May 7, 1944 and less than a year later informed her father that another baby was due and kept him abreast of her state throughout that pregnancy. What she didn't tell him was about the problems she experienced with Carl who wasn't always coming home at night. He had lost his sales representative's position with General Electric replacing it with a scanty income from work he claimed to have found while his life became disorderly and his temper grew volatile.

Finally, he cried, "I need heroin Kay," melting into the sofa with his head in his hands. The moment of honesty was too late as the addictions forced his life downward. His occasional appearances at home were only to seek refuge from police who wanted to arrest him or from pushers that he owed money to. When Kathleen attempted to hide silver dollars from him by taping them behind a large calendar in the kitchen, he became physical with her. She had hidden the money to have it available for feeding herself and Johnnie. Ellis struck her after finding the money. The incident was so violent that she fell backwards against the apartment wall, temporarily losing consciousness. Then Kathleen understood that she had misjudged the seriousness of her predicament with Carl.

Meanwhile her father was unaware about his daughter's upset, but suspected she was having difficulties, because the phone seldom rang other than at Christmastime when she phoned to announce her second pregnancy. He wondered when regular letters were no longer tucked in gift boxes with her homemade baking goods.

For Kathleen, it was an awakening of what her mother and father experienced in their break-up and how wrong she was to just regard her personal hurt in her parents failed marriage

"Dear Holy Mother of God, Pray for me!" It was as spontaneous as the nuns had taught her to pray in the Marquis school, but more meaningful seeming to appease and bring momentarily peace with each incantation.

Surprised by her sudden re-affirmations of faith, she got out of bed and went to the dresser in the bedroom. She removed from a small box storing trinkets she had brought from her home in Marquis, a rosary given to her by her dad. Since leaving home it was the first time to pray on it the familiar repetitious prayer filled with Hail Mary's that was intended to bring reparation, peace and the Holy Mother's intercession before Jesus, her son. Afterward she retired realizing that the night would be short as early morning baby movement in her womb was waking her and Johnny demanded attention then with his wet diapers.

The next morning, she was more rested and decided to call her father, so she rang the operator from her kitchen wall. Long distance and local calls were all handled through the operators and continued that way until the late 1940's.

"Hello Dad."

"Hey kiddo! I was just eating the goodies from the care package you sent a few weeks ago," he responded.

"What, you're eating stale butter tarts for breakfast?" she chuckled.

"You know me. I do it the easy way. How yah doing?" he asked

"Not so good, I have…a problem," she choked and continued. "I had to ask Carl to leave, because he's been on heroin and beat me up," she strained.

"What!"

"A couple of days ago and he's running around as well" she added.

"What? He…! Are you okay? What about Johnny and your baby?" he pressed.

"Both Johnny and the baby are fine. I was at the doctor's yesterday. He says I and the baby appear physically okay. Although I'm a wreck otherwise," she began to cry.

"I think I'd better come and get you Kathleen. I can leave in the morning. Will you be safe until I arrive?" he asked.

"Carl's gone now. I think he gets his drugs in Toronto," she volunteered after recomposing herself.

"Have you talked to your mother or anyone else about this? You should maybe get to her place in Toronto, where you and your family will be safe," he insisted.

"Dad, I'm okay! I filed a police report and have so much to do to get ready, if I'm going home to Marquis."

"You're coming home Kay. Don't even question it!" he asserted. "I'll wire you some money in the morning."

"That would help. Carl has taken everything!" she advised.

"Figures...! For sure, I'll send the money out to you via Wells Fargo, when I drive through Moose Jaw in the morning. So, we'll talk more when I arrive, Kay."

"Thanks Dad. Drive safely. Bye! Love you!"

"Bye. Love you too!" he affirmed softly, as he hung up the phone.

She was relieved that her dad was okay with the news and that he would soon be with her in Peterborough providing encouragement. They could discuss the details with each other when he arrived. What she had to do now was to begin packing for the car trip. Johnny's baby belongings would take up most of the available space in the car, so she decided that the rest could be shipped by train to Marquis.

"Wow! How am I going to handle this by myself? All my friends are working, and they don't have time. I guess I should call Mom now." she muttered to herself, then picked up the phone and dialled.

Excitement grew in LaLonde that he would soon see his daughter and the grandson. What spoiled his enjoyment for the moment was that Carl Ellis would give up so much for the addiction. Why could he not control himself? He would never understand a son-in-law that had so little respect, that he would steal Kathleen away from her dignity and exchange her for a substance abuse and the life that came with that. LaLonde had always felt that there would be trouble on the horizon for his daughter, when she announced to him that she had married. He composed himself and then picked up the phone on the farm bungalow's hallway wall, ringing his sister with three cranks of the handle located at the side of the phone box.

"Oh! Is that you Gracie?" It was Grace King on the line, from the farm across the road. The phones were on a party line.

"I'll be less than a minute J.J." answered Gracie.

Grace usually called him J.J., short for John Joseph, a nickname he had carried since adolescence. She was the young wife of the farmer across the road, Harry King. LaLonde could hear her one-year old son, Rodney, muttering beside her as she spoke to him from the other end of the line. LaLonde assumed that she was talking to Mildred Hicks, also a neighbouring farmer's wife. Gracie frequently visited Mildred by phone. Harry, Grace's husband, was an obliging friend of LaLonde's. The two farmers would offer each other help on the farms and regularly hunted waterfowl together.

LaLonde would joke to Cy Hicks, Mildred's husband, about Grace's marriage to Mildred. "She spends hours romancing Gracie on the phone, Cy," complained LaLonde.

They'd retort, "What about those hunting trips you fellows always take together?"

The shared rural party line meant John LaLonde would have to wait a couple of minutes before he phoned his sister, Mary Pendleton, who lived in the village of Marquis with her husband, George and their two young daughters, Margaret and Blanche. Mary was always the willing sister to help. She was JJ's kid sister and eight years younger who lavished her affections on the big bachelor brother. She had learned her charity from her mother, Anna LaLonde, who was always a warm homemaker and friend to her sons. While waiting for the phone to be free John recalled how his mother had appreciated his sister's help. John too, had grown to appreciate Mary. She as a youth had given him his nickname J.J.

As he waited for the phone at the dining room table in the quiet farmhouse, he stared at the James LaLonde family portrait that hung from the wall. His father, James had died in 1939 at the age of 81. Anna, his mother, who was failing was living with his sister, Lucy and her husband, Charlie Canon, a couple of miles from John LaLonde's farm. Charles Canon operated the homesteaded quarter of land that his wife's family had come to Marquis from Minnesota to farm in 1902.

A little sadness came over John LaLonde as he glanced at his brother Frank in the family photo. Frank had worked with J.J. in their threshing business, travelling throughout southern Saskatchewan while assisting area farmers annually at harvest time during the early part of the century. Frank died of a heart attack, four years earlier to the day that that call came from Kathleen in the morning. Earlier that day, John attended morning Mass to pray for his deceased brother's intentions and had just come home a half an hour earlier when Kathleen called with her announcement about Carl. Mass was an added annual spiritual exercise for J.J., attended on the anniversary of his deceased brother. Additionally, in the family photo was John's LaLonde's brother, Harry who had died in 1918 of the Spanish flu when Harry was nineteen. All that were left of J.J.'s family in Marquis were Joseph, Lucy, Mary, Lizzie and his mother, Anna, whom J.J. would be sure to call before he left for Peterborough to get Kathleen and Johnny.

He was aroused from his thoughts about his family by the 'Bing' of the phone that signalled the party line was free, so he got up and went to the hall and cranked the telephone box again.

"Can you get me the George Pendleton residence in Marquis, please?" he asked the operator."

"Hello Mary, Kay's got problems with Carl and I'll be driving East today to pick her and Johnny up…."

"Oh John, I'm sorry!" Mary responded, but was careful not to ask what. "I'll let George know as soon as he's home and he'll look after your place while you're gone."

"Tell him that Trixie and Richard are chewing at the posts so they could use a run." He was referring to his horses that were destroying the corral fence. Mary would tell George who in turn would look after John LaLonde's livestock as well as his brother-in-law's chores on the farm. George was familiar with the operation and would take right over in his absence. It always was that way. Family helped one another without questions. Also, he knew that Harry King would take over some of the responsibilities in his absence and assist George.

Before leaving Marquis, for the three-day trip east, he decided that he would drop by St. John's Church rectory in Marquis to see Father McMahon, the Parish Priest, where LaLonde would request some parishioner prayer support for his daughter and advise the priest of her predicament. Father McMahon, a practical Irish Catholic with whom LaLonde had a good friendship, would put all his cohorts to work for his friend's daughter. There had to be arrangements made with the Catholic Women's League, in order to make sure Kay had the friendship of the parish ladies on her return home. Kay was popular with the ladies because of her treatment of her father who was a favourite son of Marquis. With so many of the young men and women now off to war in Europe, or out east working in factories for the war effort, it was nice for everyone in the small town to have Kay returning as the village had lost so many of its young people.

Meanwhile, back in Peterborough, Kay's mind would keep going back to Carl while her father's mind alternated back and forth in his vehicle while it motored between Marquis and Toronto. Mostly he spent time reminiscing over his daughter's years on the farm. Those thoughts were interlaced with concerns over what the community's response would be on her return home. Kathleen's return to Marquis was a gift to the farmer, but it was at the expense of her pain.

"What happened to her life with Carl?" he asked himself out loud.

In the past, her self confidence and maturity challenged young suitors that came around to the farmhouse. LaLonde recalled Kathleen's friend, Roy, who had gone on and married another. She had never taken her Saskatchewan boyfriends seriously like she had Carl. Were the Marquis men too wholesome or too country for her? Maybe she should have been more content with life in Marquis? Perhaps he was wrong? Maybe these were lessons in her life necessary for her own interior growth?

The world had presented a whole new set of paradigms to youth during the war years. The situation in rural life had changed and Canada's quiet, safe communities had been invaded by the war that ravaged Canada too, but in a different way than it had ravaged Europe. Kathleen's generation was influenced by the music and cinema of the day that promoted a carefree attitude toward life, one that would avoid the daily news which carried stories of the serious world events. Musical hits on the radio lightened the emotional load of the War while society struggled with the effects of unsettled times and the young were being exposed to the uncertainty of what the future would offer them. They wanted to explore every freedom that life could provide instead of facing the uncertain future that lay ahead in farm communities. The ambiguous times victimized everyone offering no respect to rural and city residents alike. Those that had gone off to war suffered horrors in their lives and many never returned home; nevertheless, John LaLonde was relieved that his daughter was returning to a safe life in Marquis. Despite her situation, the circumstance was a blessing and he consoled himself that he had not sent a daughter off to war who would never return.

After his arrival in Peterborough, he was busy shipping and assisting Kathleen in the clean-up of her apartment. He had decided that the car was so loaded up that it would be best to put his daughter and grandson on the train at Toronto to travel west to Moose Jaw. Kathleen agreed that it would also be much more comfortable for her, considering her pregnancy and infant son.

The trip home to Marquis appeared full of promise for John LaLonde. While he was East, Marquis people had been listening along with the whole country to radio reports of an improved way of life for Saskatchewan residents who were governed by the newly elected Cooperative Commonwealth Federation, better known as the CCF party, led by Tommy Douglas, a former Baptist minister turned politician. Douglas had taken the party to victory over the ruling Liberal party and his newly elected leadership was offering residents a universal socialized health care system. Socialized healthcare was the Prairie Province's most renowned politician's unique contribution to the North

American continent. Douglas's party was the preference of most farmers in Saskatchewan who made up most of the voting population for the province in those days. He was elected as Premier of Saskatchewan in June 1944, at a time when farmers, had been threatened by the Eastern banks that monopolized the prairie financial community. The contentious political landscape during the election campaign brought threats to farmers from the banks of having their properties seized if they voted the CCF into power. The previous ruling Liberal Party had ignored the plight of the rural residents during both the Depression and war years. Now, it was time for change on the prairies and Saskatchewan would be the first province to oust its right-wing government. With free hospital and medical care, John LaLonde was excited that Kathleen would have her expected baby, without any added financial concern over medical costs and his ailing mother would be cared for free of charge as well.

Federally, Canada's Mackenzie King, had been vacillating on the military's demand for mandatory conscription resulting in a threatened resignation of the country's military commander. Also, a rebellion of King's key cabinet ministers was occurring in Ottawa. They threatened to resign if a draft bill was not presented in the House of Commons by the Cabinet. The Draft Bill was important in order to beef up the troops that were depleted by casualties in Europe. Now King's War Minister, C.D. Howe, had joined the rebels in Parliament causing King to finally acquiesce on the contentious conscription issue. Quebec Cabinet Minister, Louis St. Laurent was attracting voter attention as his leadership of the rebellion won voter favour across the nation. Subsequently, with the Prime Minister's lagging popularity, he decided to rush through new Acts of Parliament, giving Canadian families a monthly family allowance. Senior citizens of the country would get a break as well. They would now receive their first monthly Social Security cheques. Additionally, worker's rights flourished under the formation of the Canadian Labour Congress. LaLonde hoped this all would ease the concerns for his mother and his daughter who he was feeling sandwiched between. These weighed on him both emotionally and financially, prior to his departure from Marquis. His mother's hospital costs and Kathleen's impending delivery when she arrived home could have been expensive.

In Europe, the 156,000 Allied Command troops had successfully stormed the beaches of Normandy and now Germany's forces, had lost 400,000 of its fighting best in the subsequent decimating Battle of Falaise. Meanwhile, fifteen thousand Canadian troops had liberated Holland and were controlling the Northern front while the Allied Command was promising the surrender of Germany any day. All this good news and his daughter's return home were more exhilarating to LaLonde than any concern over her future without Carl Ellis. Kay's life would work out and he could help her with that.

Chapter Ten

With her chubby hand four year old Sherry Bickert reached into a small brown wicker carriage for a doll that her nine year old Aunt Jeanne had passed on to the niece on her fourth birthday. With its rosy cheeks, glowing dark brown eyes and black hair, the shiny porcelain head of the doll looked like a miniature replica of Sherry. Jeanne stood beside Sherry holding a baby blanket to wrap the doll as the two prepared to go out to an evening movie at the Capitol in Vernon with Jeanne's Mom and Dad. Sherry brought her doll everywhere she went. Jeanne had warmed to Sherry after some period of jealousy that erupted when her niece came to the home. Now Jeanne could share what was her doll.

It wasn't often that the family went to movies except during the war years and that Christmas week Bing Crosby was starring and singing in the Academy award nominated film, "The Bells of St. Mary." They all liked Crosby, especially Harry Bickert who thought that the popular actor sang a little out of tune but performed well. It had become a regular occurrence for Harry and Helen to go to movies during the War, without the girls, to see the news clips that in those days were shown prior to the feature film. The Christmas musical was suitable for the youngsters to go along and the hope was that the motion picture screen would bring news of the Bickerts' son's involvement in the Battle of Britain while he was stationed in England. They imagined Sherry's dad to be actively engaged as continuous bombings and the threat of invasion was occurring in the Mother country

Mail to and from England was not getting through that year because shipping was restricted by German submarine interference in commercial and supply lanes between the continents on the Atlantic. Meanwhile, the Japanese presence on the Pacific was doing the same. When letters did arrive, several were tied in a bundle coming on the same day from John who regularly wrote from Britain.

That evening his daughter was seated between her grandparents with the doll on her lap when a newsreel featuring a story of the Princess Patricia Canadian Light Infantry's participation in the King's Royal Rifle Corps lit the screen. Sherry bolted from her seat. "There's my Daddy!" she screeched, pointing at the screen. Then the same group of soldiers kept marching past the camera lens in the news feature. "There's my Daddy, there's my Daddy again!" It was an obvious attempt by the film maker to fool the motion picture audience into believing that the film was recording a large contingent of soldiers marching past the camera. It didn't fool the eyes of the Canadian corporal's daughter who was thousands of miles away. The surprise not only excited the young girl but her grandparents who couldn't believe their eyes that it was their son marching with the group of soldiers Sherry had recognized. Both Helen and Harry had tears of joy throughout the evening and laughed until they arrived home and then continued laughing together in bed that night. They were so relieved that he was alive and healthy believing someday, by the grace of God, he'd be coming home.

Bickert had spent his full service overseas as a show soldier, mostly performing in ceremonial march pasts at official Canadian Government events that were held in England. Politicians, other dignitaries and military brass would visit Britain from Canada and often be greeted by the "Rifles" who would perform precision drill exercises for the guests. For Bickert the commission was a personal victory. His peaceful Mennonite ancestry was always in conflict with the now secularized soldier who hoped not to kill, nor to be killed. The young soldier would be able to live with his conscience as his commitment to King and country were being fulfilled even though he did not have to engage in the hostilities while overseas.

Meanwhile, Sherry grew excited over her father's return to Vernon which was expected as soon as the war ended. Frequently she asked about his absence during the eighteen months he was away. She studied every uniformed soldier she encountered in Vernon. In the end Sherry was always disappointed by a stranger's face instead of her dad's. The disappointment was followed by an affirmation, "My Daddy's coming home someday."

Helen Bickert constantly needed to restrain her granddaughter from bolting outside the home every time the youngster heard a man's voice, or a vehicle passed by the house. Once the girl was advised that the war was over, her anticipation grew more intense.

Springtime 1946 in the Okanagan provided a typical dreary early March with low clouds mixed with rain, fog and frost. Sherry liked to break the ice in the morning puddles frozen over from rain the day before and the cold nights. One day while Helen watched from the kitchen window, Sherry bent over to pick up a piece of ice from the puddle to suck on, but then dropped it and stood gazing toward the end of the driveway. A man in uniform stood with a grin on his face. "Is it my daddy?" She worried that she was wrong, and the man would walk away like other soldiers. Sherry began to cry, and Helen thought there might be something wrong with her granddaughter and went out into the yard to investigate, but by then her son embraced his daughter and was reassuring her that he was her dad.

That day Sherry's loyalties shifted, back and forth, several times between her grandfather and her dad as her loyalty to Harry Bickert had grown and took time to right itself in the young child's mind.

A few days after his return Bickert elected to move in with Peter and Bertha Dyck in Lumby where he was invited to join his uncle's garage enterprise that sold and serviced large trucks to the logging community.

Dyck's Garage retailed White Trucks, the original birth child of Western Star Truck whose large trucks have been seen on the highways throughout North America for years. It started as a small truck manufacturing firm in Ohio and eventually became Western Star Trucking of Kelowna. By 1980, White was insolvent in Ohio and two Calgary based oil companies, Bow Valley Resources and Nova Corporation purchased the Canadian assets of White along with the Western Star nameplate to which the American company had changed the vehicle's name. The remaining American assets took on the Volvo and Autocar names. In Canada the newly financed independent company flourished as Western Star resulting from its newly introduced, popular high cab over models made in Kelowna. Eventually, Western Star was purchased from its Canadian shareholders by Daimler Chrysler Corporation in 2000 and the manufacturing facility left Kelowna and relocated to Portland, Oregon to sister with Chrysler's Freightliner Corporation.

Bickert's work with his uncles at Dyck's Garage separated him, during weekdays from his daughter whom he was incapable of caring for while he worked. She hadn't reached school age yet; so, she continued residing with her grandparents in Vernon while she would see her dad on weekends.

Soon Bickert realized he had unfinished business in Vernon. Now that he had a regular income coming in, he wanted to legally end his marriage to Ethel, so hired a lawyer to proceed with divorce. She had moved in with an Alexander Jackson in Vancouver. The decree, made by a Vernon District Provincial Court judge, was on the grounds of Ethel's adultery with Jackson. She never contested the writ and failed to show in court for the dissolution on April 16, 1946. Ethel was never seen again by either Bickert or his daughter having disappeared from Vernon because of her unpopularity with friends and family.

There were three Dyck children by the time Bickert moved in with the family. Billy was five, Marie three and Tony one. Tony was walking by then and was a handful for Bertha who was still frequently occupied over Marie's childhood demands. Quiet and continuously moving around the house, Tony explored for things to interest him. One day, just before Christmas in 1947, he found a kitchen knife and attempted to pry the Christmas tree plug from its electrical outlet on the wall.

Bickert had been reading a book at the kitchen table adjacent to the living room and hadn't heard Tony for a period. So, he thought that he would check on the boy for Bertha who at the time was doing laundry. The child was blue and unconscious on the floor, beside the tree, with the knife still in his hand. Tony's heart had stopped and Bickert's mouth to mouth resuscitation which he had become familiar with in military First Aid training was now required for his young cousin. After a few minutes had lapsed Tony was revived as Bertha appeared in the living room and stood watching from above while her nephew worked on her son. Tony never was admitted to the hospital as he seemed okay once the event was over.

Sherry eventually moved in with her dad at the Dycks when she started school for her primary grade at Lumby Elementary. It was in September of 1947 that She attended grade one as a classmate with her second cousin, Billy Dyck.

In the late Forties and even continuing today, Lumby is a quiet town having a red sun scorched hillside to the east and peculiar change of the Coldstream Valley from east to west widening to the North toward Mable Lake with flatland scraped level during the Ice Age. The area was first pioneered by Oblate missionary priests, Fathers Pandosy and Richard from France who ministered to Okanagan and Shushwap natives. They were from Portland, Oregon Diocese in the late eighteen fifties assigned to Kelowna area by 1859. At the turn of the twentieth century, Lumby had become an enterprising logging community and in the nineteen thirties enjoyed the milling of logs with the opening of three separate sawmills adjacent to the south end of town where the Coldstream valley widens. The rumbling logging trucks coming in at the end of each day with their loads would park alongside the few village streets.

John Bickert 1945

Sherry Anne Bickert 1945

Chapter Eleven

I t was mid April 1945 when John LaLonde returned to Southern Saskatchewan from Toronto getting Kay and Johnnie on the train. As he drove along Highway One approaching Moose Jaw from Regina's western perimeter, he saw signs of the previous winter remaining where the highway was lined by snow fences that shaded un-melted drifts behind them. Patches of stained snow from muddy livestock hooves dotted the fields providing him with reflections of when he owned cattle, before The Depression Years. The grey plains silhouetted the black outline of Moose Jaw's city core endowing a mural on the Western Horizon reminding him of how the city had grown since his youth when he arrived in a horse drawn wagon at the turn of the century. Thump! He had passed over a frost heave that had cracked and lifted the pavement on the highway. It awoke him to his management of the vehicle as he drove closer to his destination.

When he arrived in Moose Jaw, LaLonde planned to clean up at the Grand Hotel where he would stay in a day room until Kay and Johnny came in that afternoon on the train from Toronto. The tiring conclusion of his trip from Toronto area had consisted of a continuous twenty-four-hour stretch including an all-night drive from Sault Saint Marie where he had visited Mike Griffin's widow Gertie before continuing home.

LaLonde winced as he adjusted the radio dial while rotating his neck and shifting his lumbar spine to relieve the discomfort felt from sitting idle in the car for the last eight hundred miles.

"It's the Happy Gang!" blurted a voice on the car radio tuned to Moose Jaw's CHAB station which had broadcast the program since it first aired in 1938. LaLonde hoped that the cheerful cast of performers would help to keep him from falling asleep at the wheel as he strained sleepily for the final thirty miles of travel into Moose Jaw. Fortunately, Kathleen and Johnny's arrival at the city's Canadian National Station would coincide with LaLonde's plan for the day. He intended to refresh himself with a nap and warm bath at a hotel before their arrival.

After adjusting his window visor in order to reduce the glare of the twelve-noon sun from the southern sky, LaLonde studied a herd of Hereford cattle following a hay wagon as it moved across a pasture adjacent to the highway. It reminded him of how few cattle remained and that now only a few farmers were restocking as water ditches were again refilling since the Drought Years. Recently, it had been easier for LaLonde on the farm; nevertheless, he had chosen not to restock with a herd as he predicted that the work would be too strenuous for him and the monetary reward was not a great incentive to move into livestock. He had always done better with dry land farming in the Marquis area which lies on the plains above the Qu'Appelle Valley providing fertile conditions for growing grain crops. He was now fifty-two and a nagging pain across his lumbar spine was becoming more prevalent occasionally preventing him from lifting the bales of hay required for feeding.

Late in the afternoon that same day, LaLonde stood on a crowded station platform watching the locomotive slow to a stop ahead towing the train's passenger cars from Toronto. Kathleen and Johnny were two of the last passengers to disembark. She moved slowly off the railway car stepping down while holding Johnny. It was an effort for her to manoeuvre while her son leaned outward forcing her to support him. LaLonde noticed his daughter's struggle with the tot and rushed through the crowd to grab his grandson. Kathleen let out a short breath and panted, "I'm glad that's over!" It was the train ride across the country that she was referring to. Fortunately, earlier LaLonde had a chance to unload the car at the Sagals' house where his niece Phyllis and her husband, Amil now resided. It meant that he could take his daughter and grandson strait to Marquis from the station.

LaLonde laughed at his grandson's exuberance in the car offering the toddler a toy windmill that the boy could play with in front of the automobile's dash vent. Johnny put everything in his mouth though. The toy was intended to entertain the child as he balanced on his mother's lap as they drove the twenty miles to Marquis.

After a few minutes, a line of baby chatter erupted while the child attempted to stand on Kay's lap pointing at his Grandpa whom he recognized from the short stay they had together in Peterborough earlier that week. The train's ride had obviously not tired the boy.

One thing about LaLonde's daughter was that she never knew when to slow down and rest. She liked working past midnight on projects in the home and seemed still to manage to arise in the morning to continue. He wondered if that would change with a baby to care for. He looked forward to some of her homemaking though.

"I'm out of baked goods and the house could use some fresh rolls." He volunteered.

"Oh, it could, could it?" She responded adding, "What about some Hot Cross Buns?" Did Aunt Mary make any for you yet?" Kay couldn't decline her dad although she worried that she'd have the energy to do that for him.

"Just wondering, how you'd roll out that pastry with a toddler in your arms. Maybe it can wait?"

"I'll manage it." She ended with a smile.

Spring seeding could not be done until the thaw was complete as the fields were too soggy. LaLonde's only chores on the farm, were to milk and feed Nelly, his only cow, and look after a few chickens and the two horses. He intended to run grocery errands for Kathleen and that would be an opportunity for him to show off his grandson and socialize with friends in town. Eventually, those outings became a sore point for Kathleen who envied the time her father had with Johnny while she was restricted from the outings, because she was not that ambulatory during the remaining weeks of her pregnancy.

On the evening of May 28th, 1945 Gracie and Harry King, were just settling down in their home after dinner dishes and having put their one-year old son, Rodney, down for the night. The telephone rang. It was LaLonde on the other end of the line.

"Kay's ready, so we're dropping Johnny off in ten minutes," LaLonde announced.

Providence Hospital's old brick facility was a prominent structure in Old Town, Moose Jaw. It had stood for a good portion of the first half of the twentieth century and serviced the area for years, run by the Roman Catholic religious order, The Sisters of Providence.

The next morning at 5:30 in the exact same delivery room as my mother and her twin, Mary had been born to Mary Anne Griffin, twenty-three years and three months earlier, she gave birth to me, Paul Francis, her second son.

Great Grandmother, Anna (Zoller) LaLonde arrived for care at Providence's geriatric ward. Great Grandma had been weakening fast with a failing heart accompanied by dementias and subsequently needed the nursing care. During the time, Grandpa John LaLonde, along his brother Joseph and sisters Mary and Lucille, regularly attended at their mother's bedside where she continued to stay until her death.

James LaLonde had passed away six years earlier at age eighty. He was survived by his seventy-four-year old widow, Anna.

"J.J., where did they take my baby?" Anna pleaded with her son from the hospital bed.

That May, her dementias were further aggravated by the medications offered for her failing heart. She had heard about my birth and her confused mind interpreted the arrival, as a baby that was hers. Anna regularly asked my grandfather and others attending her to bring me to her. Her death was on June 9th, 1945. Later, I was told that she did get to hold me before her passing. Anna was buried in the Marquis cemetery beside my deceased Great Grandfather James. At the same cemetery, was buried Mary Anne (Forrester) Griffin.

Historical documents record that James LaLonde was born on July 5th, 1858 in Perth, Ontario. Perth was first a military camp in Lanark County, a bushy area west of the Quebec border on the boundaries of Upper Canada. The British in 1791 had divided the colony of New France (Quebec) into two: Upper Canada and Lower Canada. Upper Canada was predominantly inhabited by united English-speaking folk from the British Isles, military, natives and Francophone loggers who didn't care politically over who managed the area. Perth had become the political centre for Scottish immigrants who were most of the British Empire Loyalists of the region. Then, Perth had become the Ottawa Valley's first Capital City. It grew from the organization of government, courts and commerce that caused the area to develop.

During that period the residents of Upper Canada had to come to Perth for the law courts and other commerce. Early attempts to separate Upper and Lower Canada occurred in Perth when in 1820 wealthy Loyalist families held general elections for the region, electing William Morris as the first Prime Minister. The system of government continued, and he was re-elected again in 1823 while during the governing William Lyon Mackenzie was recorded as having been evicted from Perth's Parliament for being a "radical agitator." Apparently, efforts of British rule in the Colony were being managed haphazardly by the Loyalists since 1812 when the Brits needed the Loyalists as well as native assistance to push back the Americans who were attempting to annex the Colony. The British were inciting the Americans by interfering with their European trade, by searching American ships where they found British naval deserters who joined the Americans. Additionally, the British were accused of inciting the native population. Eventually, with the building of the Rideau Canal for exporting lumber and other products, the area south and east of Perth, known as "Bytown" eclipsed Perth with its influence and became the Capital city for the new Dominion, known today as Ottawa.

During the development of the Dominion, Francophone loggers settled north of Perth at the "French Line" near Davidson. They had moved east out of Montreal and were recorded as having entered the area to harvest the timber while having no allegiance to French or English governing bodies keeping to themselves offering no interference to the Loyalists. More of an issue to the Loyalists were the Irish Protestants who brought their Orange affiliation with them and agitated the Catholic and Anglican population in the area. It seems that for a time the French and English in the immediate area were somewhat united.

James LaLonde was the son of Xavier, who himself was born in Perth in 1815, around the time of the Colony's military camp being assembled there. Xavier and Margaret Noonan married in 1842 and afterwards moved with their family and James from the French Line to North Dakota in 1879. They then travelled on to Minnesota a couple of years afterwards. At the time when the LaLonde's left, Canada was experiencing a depression. The dire circumstances in the newly formed Dominion led many Canadians to immigrate to the USA. Evidently, after Confederation in 1867 a huge migration of labour into Canada resulted in a temporary deflationary period for the Dominion's economy resulting from the temporary excessive labour force arriving. Although prices were lowered and goods were cheaper in Canada, work was not so plentiful. The low wages created labour unrest and a temporary drying up of capital from Europe and England which was needed to expand the small nation's economy; consequently, industrial development diminished in the young country. Ultimately, Canada's economic growth rate stagnated during a twenty-year period from the mid seventies until the West's gold discovery and wheat boom in the 1890's which eventually reversed the trend to economic boom for the

Dominion. Then the LaLonde's accompanied many of their Canadian countrymen back to Canada.

Prior to their return to Canada when James LaLonde settled in with his parents Xavier and Margaret in North Dakota, he married Anna Zoller in 1887. At that time the Dakotas had not yet joined the Union and James was twenty-nine years old. Anna had given birth to her first two children Frank and Harry in 1888 and 1889, respectively. Third son John Joseph LaLonde was born in Otter Tail County, Minnesota on May 18, 1892 and subsequently, daughter Lucy was born in 1893, followed by Mary in 1900. Minnesota territory had joined the Union in 1858, so census information provided our family tree historian, Ken Cannon of Ottawa, who is the youngest son of Lucy LaLonde, to provide me with ages and dates related to the Xavier and the James LaLonde family. Cannon's research also provides any reader with the necessary historical data on the LaLonde family history in Canada and the USA since Jean Luc LaLonde came to New France as a soldier for the King of France in 1636.

When James and Anna LaLonde moved back to Canada in 1902, they brought with them all of their family and livestock in a harrowing trip across the prairies. Many ex-patriots from Canada were enticed along with the LaLonde's back to their native Country by the Wilfred Laurier Government. Canada's wheat boom was in full swing and those willing to farm were being given land by Ottawa. Parcels offered in the Prairie Provinces were to be homesteaded at a cost of ten dollars per quarter section and James chose a quarter a couple of miles northwest of Marquis. The only requirement of the gift was that the man from Minnesota would have to build a dwelling on the property. In 1904, Anna LaLonde gave birth to her youngest child, Joseph, at the Marquis homestead home. Joseph was the sixth child that Anna had delivered in the family homes over the years.

While living in Minnesota and prior to returning to Canada, records indicate that James and Anna had adopted a child, Catherine Thompson, who was born in New York in 1897. The adoption took place in Otter

Tail County, Minnesota, but soon the child passed away of unknown causes and never moved to Canada with her adoptive family.

My birth in Moose Jaw was at a time when society was harsh on marriage failure. Often divorcees were punished by social attitudes that were uncharitable and generally oppressive toward single adult women in general. Kathleen found that the close-knit Marquis community disregarded the stigma and was hospitable toward her.

I was baptised Paul Francis Ellis on July 23rd, 1945, by Father Charles McMahon, at Marquis' St. John's Catholic Church. Mom still retained the name of Ellis, so my brother and I continued to carry the Ellis surname legally until I turned twenty-one. Appointed as my godparents were Phyllis (LaLonde) Sagal and her husband Amil.

Great Grandma Marie Anna Frances LaLonde had been promised that I would be named after her, if I was a girl. As a compromise, I was given one of the middle names, Francis, a name I disliked until becoming a teenager when I heard more about the life of St Francis of Assisi.

Chapter Twelve

At just over two years, I stood on my Grandma LaLonde's sofa in the middle of a hot, muggy summer's day in east Toronto looking out of her third-floor Victorian tenement apartment window observing the busy street below. My grandmother had given me a soda cracker to chew on, intended to pacify while I sobbed over my mother's departure minutes earlier. She had left that day to have her marriage to Carl Ellis dissolved in the Ontario Court.

I kept teetering, balanced between the back edge of the musty smelling green velvet sofa and the window's ledge where my attention shifted between the street view and the unfamiliar-setting I had been left in. Voices from neighbours across the hall in the building derided each of my emotional outbursts.

"Be careful of the window, Paul, or you will be out on your head, down on the street! See that man below with the ice wagon. He'll pick you up and take you away with his ice if you fall onto it," Grandma warned as she peeked over my shoulder toward what had distracted me. The man stepped up on his wagon to remove a large block of ice. The suffocating July air was the reason for the opened window, to move air through her apartment.

An interesting feature of my grandmother's refrigerator was an ice tray and fan positioned on top of the fridge to cool the room, but that day it had run out of ice. Scarcely a minute after my grandmother's warning came was a knock at the door of the apartment. A man's voice on the other side of the door announced, "Mrs. LaLonde, it's your iceman!" I let out a scream panicking that the stranger on the other side was there to take me away. Grandma opened the door as the vendor rushed to put a large cub of ice on the top of the fridge into the empty tray. The stranger left as abruptly as he had arrived, so that I could be calmed.

Those childhood images still linger when I think of my first memory of Grandma LaLonde. The short stay with her was in the late summer of 1947.

It wasn't until twenty years later that I saw Grandma again. At twenty-two I made the trip to Toronto while enroute to a convention held in Montreal at the 1967 World's Fair Expo site. That was the year we Canadians celebrated one hundred years of Confederation. Expo 67 was held in Montreal to coincide with Canada's centennial. At the time, I was working for Capitol Records of Canada and had just been married in February of the same year. On a flight from Edmonton to Montreal I arranged a layover at Toronto for a few nights to travel by rented car to Pefferlaw, Ontario, in order to meet my Grandmother LaLonde who was living there with her eighteen-year old son, Charlie, half brother to my mother. Charlie's father had died several years earlier, and Grandma had taken up residence in the Lake Simcoe shoreline village.

Much like my mother, Gladys LaLonde liked to talk. She possessed the same exuberant attitude as my mother while joking and showing off her dance steps in front of me, spending hours philosophising on life. It was remarkable that my mother's adoptive mother was so much like her; however, when John LaLonde was mentioned her mood darkened to anxious and startling. For every defence my mother could give for her father, Grandma offered an offense. It troubled me that a woman could be so cheerful yet vexed about someone my mother and I had admired so much. She attacked my grandfather for about ten minutes before she quit, realizing that I was not participating in the conversation. Her attack consisted of a litany of ramblings related to his time spent with others and a disdain for his cold regard toward her. "He built curling rinks, churches, schools and harvested farms rather than staying home while every lady in town curtsied to him," she complained

The little Pefferlaw home that my grandmother inhabited with her teenage son had a bedroom divided by a curtain from the living area. It was sorely in need of some repairs. Obvious to me was that she had suffered at least materially while being apart from my grandfather and mother. I couldn't help but feel affection for her as she entertained me.

Seeing Gladys LaLonde on that visit prompted a consideration that I should initiate some interrogation into my natural father's whereabouts. I asked her if she knew anything about his current life. At first, she winced at my question and then brought out a newspaper article. The article was headlined "Man and Wife Sentenced for Illicit Drug Enterprise." It was a story about Carl and his present wife, Ruby Ellis, being arrested and having their five children taken away by Social Services after the pair were sentenced to eight years for drug pushing. Apparently, Carl had not yet changed and although twenty years had passed was involving even a larger family circle in his illicit habit. The article stated that he had already spent over fifteen years behind bars for past activities and was again, back in jail for another eight-year stay. For the moment the news article succeeded in tempering any interest I had in finding my birth father.

To this day I have only one memory of Carl Ellis. It was lunch hour sometime in 1948 on a summer's day on the Marquis farm and I was between three and four years when we returned from Lumby. A strange man came to the door and my mother and Grandfather told him abruptly to stay outside while John and I remained in at the kitchen table. I could see from my vantage point at the table that the stranger was accompanied by another man who stayed in the parked vehicle a distance from the house. Then the two left almost as fast as they had come in. It was an upset that was enough to create a permanent impression on me that remains today. Recalling the event to my mother years later, she advised that Carl Ellis was the visitor and that he was still on heroin at the time. He had come to Saskatchewan and was stopped by Regina RCMP for vehicle inspection. The police in turn advised my mother that he was around, and they were attempting to keep him under surveillance.

Mom had been granted her divorce from Ellis during the time we stayed at Grandma's in Toronto. The grounds for the divorce were his adultery and abandonment, witnessed by a private investigator that my grandfather hired.

I have a few memories of Marquis. One of those memories is falling out of my grandfather's car from the back seat where I was sitting with my brother John. We had each been given a bag of Jellybeans to occupy us while on a Sunday drive. The mishap was explained to me as being my fault resulting from my fiddling with the car door that I leaned against.

Another episode that I recall was my brother, John deciding to copy his grandfather by attempting to siphon gasoline. He had seen Grandpa do this believing he could do the same in a near disaster that almost killed him. The result was that John fell to the ground in the farmyard unconscious as I watched. Eventually, I realized the situation was serious and went to the farmhouse to tell my mother and Grandfather, "Johnny drank the gin!" The situation was quickly rectified as the statement aroused curiosity about what John was into.

Driving farm equipment was yet another temptation for four-year-old John. He talked me into being his leg extensions to engage the starter which was on the floorboards beside the brakes, clutch and gas pedal. What John had figured out was that if I were to crouch between his legs on the floor below and press the starter, the truck would lunge forward a few feet. So, with each kick from John I obeyed hitting the starter while he steered the 42 Ford farm truck across the extent of the farmyard until our grandfather caught us.

The farm in Marquis provided a sketchy, but memorable place to grow as young children where we were free to roam an endless landscape with the little legs that carried us. We played in towering wheat fields each summer where I'd search for my brother in trampled mazes he left behind as he'd run from me. Always I'd find my way back to him.

Chapter Thirteen

Lumby's Sacred Heart Catholic Church's pastor, Father Harrison, regularly met to play Rummy in the Willms' home located across Park Avenue from where his church faced, and the small rectory house stood behind. Parishioners, Peter and Bertha Dyck, who resided below Mr. And Mrs. Willms and their twin daughters on Lumby's Shuswap Avenue, usually attended the gathering. In late summer of 1947 John Bickert and his friend Tommy Shields joined a Rummy evening on invitation from the Willms twin sisters, Marguerite and Margaret. Over the fence, outside the Dyck's backyard garage, where Bickert resided, is where he had become acquainted with Marguerite Willms. He offered to repair Marguerite's automobile. She and her twin were already dating other young men from the area but had other plans for Bickert.

Marguerite, who was better known by her nickname, 'Snip' was Mom's friend from Ajax, Ontario, who had returned to Lumby after the war. She was awaiting a decision from my mother about the possibility of our family coming to Lumby, for Mom to work as housekeeper and parish secretary for Harrison.

People joked about Harrison who irreverently referred to himself as bedlam's best friend. "Rome tells me to remain celibate; however, that's as far as my manhood is concerned. The rectory needs a woman's help, but Lumby hasn't any nuns," the priest would apologize while people commented about the chaotic rectory.

In the end, my mother's concerns about her experience with dreary British Columbia winters were alleviated as more of Snip's letters reassured her that the Okanagan's climate was drier than that of the Coast. She phoned Snip in October 1947 advising that she could come to Lumby the next month and take the position the priest had offered her through Snip.

Permitting a twenty-five-year old single mother and her two youngsters to invade the small Church rectory and impose on the priest's ministerial life was a brave undertaking for Harrison. Soon gossip began; however, it dwindled as everyone adjusted to the little rectory being transformed into the noisy family home with a celibate priest and his platonic family. Mom tidied and did parish secretarial work while John and I became intent on re-decorating the rectory residence with toys and leftover food items.

My recollection of the time spent with Father Harrison is limited; however, fond memories of the cheerful cleric remain. His bellicose laughter, magician pranks and entertaining wit always put both adults and youngsters alike at ease. It was a warm experience to have had the priest around us to aid in our departure from Grandpa LaLonde and the Marquis farm.

That autumn my brother disappeared, and a search party was quickly arranged to look for him. A good six inches of fresh snow had fallen, and John apparently became distracted wandering away from the rectory while oblivious to the alarm that he would cause. Mom searched for him in one direction while Harrison went in another with me straddling his shoulders during the hunt. The priest found a trail of partially covered footprints left and followed them finding that John had wandered into the bush above Lumby and was asleep under a snow laden spruce tree. It was a fortunate find as there was little light left in the day. The man carried my sleepy brother back to the rectory while I stumbled through the snow behind.

Often the good priest would forget to close and latch the rectory door before leaving for daily Mass each morning and John and I would escape the residence to track him down. It would become necessary for the priest to explain to the curious congregation regarding the mysterious commotion that would erupt in the church's sacristy while he was celebrating Mass. "Sounds like my two little house guests have gotten loose from the rectory," Harrison whispered to the altar server. Everyone soon understood what the interruption was.

On one occasion my brother and I explored the rectory's basement which served as a cold space where the Knights of Columbus kept food supplies for Sunday Church breakfasts. Finding a couple of large crates of eggs, we bowled every one of them across the basement floor breaking several in the process. The mess only made the jovial Harrison laugh more at the predicament he had gotten himself into with live-in youngsters. The church and rectory both bring back fond memories as it was a good home for us to be introduced to in Lumby. The small rectory has since been re-built, but the church and new rectory continue to be located a few paces from each other.

The experience etched permanently some priestly attributes in my brother, John's character. He was old enough to be impressed by the Catholic Mass and our priest friend had earned my brother's endearment. For years afterwards, John would play the priest role and I would altar serve beside him in his pretend ceremony which became common play.

Soon after our arrival at Lumby the introduction was made. When first introduced, my mother and John Bickert studied each other, convinced they had met before.

"Did Snip say you're from Saskatchewan, Kathleen?" Bickert interrogated while his eyes moved back and forth between Willms and my mother, curiously.

"Yes, from Marquis, just outside of Moose Jaw," Mom responded.

It continued to trouble the pair until a few days after the meeting when they discussed one another's pasts and both calculated that they had met briefly, years earlier. Their memories were of the chance encounter at the bus stop in the False Creek area of Vancouver. Mom would take the bus from there to her work at St. Paul's Hospital and Bickert would catch the bus to work at Coal Harbour. On that one meeting they had studied one another with fondness hoping they would eventually get to meet again.

The set-up had been arranged much earlier prior to my family's arrival from the Prairies. The Dyck's were made aware of the planned relocation to Lumby of Mom and her two boys through a conversation with Snip Willms. The first formal date was at the Church's Christmas party and dance, an event that had been arranged by Father Harrison and the Dyck's, successfully touching off a romance for my future stepfather and mother. During the next spring, Bickert proposed to my mother. Unfortunately, a problem existed preventing her from accepting his proposal. Before either party could consider any re-marriage in the Catholic Church, my mother's first marriage and divorce needed the Vatican's examination.

All this had to be done by a petition being sent off to Rome through a process involving the Roman Catholic Bishop of Nelson. Nelson's Bishop Johnson regularly visited his priests' parishes and was often in Lumby. He asked the priest to prepare the case in writing advising that he would work on presenting the application to Rome. The expectation was that the process would take three years to complete before a decision from Rome would come. It was a tedious situation for any anxious couple; however, Catholics accepted that the Church is never too quick to re-marry members. Today this process and examination for annulment has quickened, in the case of prior Catholic marriages, as local tribunals in each diocese will do the scrutiny work in conformity with Canon Lawyers. My mother's marriage to Carl Ellis was not a Catholic one, so the process was different.

In the autumn of 1949 Rome ruled that the marriage could go ahead. Apparently, Bishop Johnson had made a trip to the Vatican himself on other matters and his visit assisted in speeding up the paperwork that decreed in favour of the couple's future together.

In the course of all these events Mom felt it was best for her to return to Marquis in 1948, while she awaited a response from the Church. Her courtship of John, whom Mom referred to as "Bick" remained in Limbo. He drove the whole family, including our prospective stepsister, Sherry, back to Saskatchewan where we would reside separate from them until the union of both families could re-occur, when that was permitted.

The letter came in the early autumn of 1949, but not from Father Harrison; he had moved over to Cranbrook from Lumby, transferred to a new parish. It arrived in the hands of a new priest, Father Les Trainor who was assigned as Pastor for the Lumby parish. The marriage could proceed. So, in early October we were loaded into the car by our mother and grandfather and we all rode to Lumby for a wedding that was held on October 17th, 1949.

I recall being introduced to my new grandparents, Harry and Helen Bickert, when we arrived. I was older and likely had met them before; however, I don't recall any prior meeting. We stayed overnight with the Bickerts at their small home in Vernon where conditions were a little crowded; so, we moved over to the Al Sasges house for the second night.

During the interval that we were away in Marquis, John Bickert had been taking instructions in the Catholic faith from Father Trainor and was baptized a Catholic before Easter 1949 at Sacred Heart Church. Earlier Bickert's younger sister Gladys had married Al Sasges, another Roman Catholic and she converted, so encouraged her brother to do the same. Gladys had apparently followed a girlfriend into the Catholic rite. In the end, my mother asked Gladys to be her Maid of Honour and my new dad asked Al Sasges to be the Best Man for the nuptial

For the wedding Mom was dressed in a full-length sky-blue satin dress and John Bickert was in a dark brown pin-striped suit. The Lumby and Vernon families from the Dyck and Bickert sides were both well represented at the ceremony. Sherry, John and I all stood in the front row of the church with Grandma and Grandpa Bickert on one side of the church pew and our Grandpa LaLonde standing on the other side as we saw our parents married.

Afterwards, Mom and Dad honeymooned for a couple of nights at the Oyama Inn, a small hotel that was located on the south end of Kalamalka where the colourful lake meets Woods Lake. Unfortunately, the hotel was demolished in the early 1980's when Highway 97 was converted to four lanes. The quaint inn had consisted of only a few rooms overlooking the aqua marine waters of the south end of Lake Kalamalka.

After the honeymooners returned, we all moved into a basement apartment at Lavallette's Ranch House, a building still standing one mile south of the Lumby cemetery on the west side of Creighton Valley Road that runs south below the cemetery toward Echo Lake. After the war, the large house had been divided into small apartments to provide income in order to support the struggling ranch operation. We first lived in an apartment on the lower level on the southwest side of the building's basement, where one of my few memories was that of my Grandpa LaLonde assembling a new set of maple bunk beds, given as a housewarming gift to John and me, that continue to remain in the family today.

A few weeks after our family had settled into the small rural apartment an unexpected knock was heard at the entry door. It was late in the afternoon on a mid November day and Peter Dyck greeted my mother at the door with some very upsetting news. He asked Mom if he could speak to her outside of the apartment away from the children. Apparently, a logging truck had fallen on the pelvis of our new Dad while he had worked under the large truck while lying on his back. The jack that was holding up the front axle of the truck had failed. Seriously injured, with his pelvis and internal organs crushed, Dad was rushed earlier that afternoon to Vernon's Jubilee hospital.

All three children were taken to Bertha Dyck's to be watched while Mom and Peter went on to the Vernon hospital where dad was undergoing surgery. The injuries resulted in Dad having an extended recovery period in the hospital followed by several months convalescing at home. In due course he made a full recovery and resumed work as a mechanic at Dyck's Garage. It was a tough first year for the family. Fortunately, Workers' Compensation had been available in the province of British Columbia and Dad did receive benefits to provide for the family.

As I recall, Lavallette's building services were a little rustic. There was no bathroom in the apartment which would result in all of us taking our turn bathing in a large galvanized steel tub in the middle of the open kitchen floor. Baths were usually a rare event and not so glamorous, but a very necessary weekly occurrence in those days. All the kids got to bathe in the same tub of water, one after the other, with hot water added to warm the water. Guess who got to bath last? I was the youngest, so my sister Sherry went in first, then John and finally me. In the beginning, the soapy water was enough to leave our big sister Sherry complaining about her younger brother's dirty feet and she succeeded in convincing our parents that she should be the first in. I recall how I used to lick my finger after the bath and clean out my naval that was still soiled. I wasn't the dirtiest kid in town either. Everyone must have been a little dirty in those days considering the lack of bathing. I recall how amused I'd be over rummaging through the Lavallette garbage pile. I became quite fond of a hat that I found.

After a year at the Lavallette's, we relocated to a house my parents purchased on the corner of Shuswap Avenue at Maple Street in Lumby, when news came that Mom was expecting the first new addition to our blended families. The home was set in a friendly neighbourhood within steps of the three Dyck families.

The merged Kay and John Bickert family

Chapter Fourteen

I recall once being corrected by my dad as I approached the chiropractor's office. I asked Dad when I would get to see the quack? "Shush, he's a chiropractor!" he cautioned. Later Dad explained that he jokingly had referred to medical doctors as sawbones and chiropractors as quacks, which was his way of maligning both practitioners' professional efforts. His effort to explain away a poor choice of words to describe the doctors made little difference to me. It was easier at five to pronounce quack than chiropractor. I got used to Dad holding his hand over my mouth each time we approached the chiropractor's office.

The visit occurred in the spring of 1950, after I sustained an injury while sitting on a high kitchen stool that had no back for me to lean against. It was offered to replace the regular chair I normally sat on for dinner. We had company that night and there was a shortage of seating. Inexperience with the new chair resulted in my falling backwards sustaining a compression fracture to my fourth thoracic vertebra. Subsequently, the injury left me with recurring pain in my upper back throughout most of my childhood along with other health issues that would immediately commence and weren't explained until much later in life. The mishap was the beginning of my lifetime relationship with chiropractors. From then on Dad and I began the ritual of visiting the Vernon practitioner together.

Prior to starting school in 1951, I have memories of my head on my mother's lap feeling the baby's feet move against the wall of her abdomen while anticipating what our new arrival would look like. I would stay at home alone with Mom during the daytime while John and Sherry attended school. News of the birth of baby brother, Irven Joseph, came on July 7th. Two hours after that announcement more news came that the baby had died succumbing to a heart defect, known as Tetralogy of Fallot. The walls of Irven's heart chambers were not completely formed. It was the continuance of my mother's affliction in bearing children after first suffering heart failure in giving birth to me.

That August, prior to commencing first grade, I fractured my left arm at the anatomical head of the humerus which sent me to the Vernon hospital for two weeks. The stay resulted from the difficulty doctors experienced in resetting the bone. After putting me under general anaesthetic on three separate occasions the fracture was finally reduced. For each re-set the bone was re-broken and set again and I was quite irritable over the ordeal.

I had earned the nickname 'Southpaw' prior to the fracture to slight that I favoured my left hand. The injury required that I switch to my right hand when I arrived at school for first grade as the arm was casted all the way to my shoulder.

Mrs. Moore, the elderly grade one teacher had some sort of religious hang-up about left-handed people. She kept threatening that I would be taken out and burned at a stake for not quickly improving the dexterity in my right hand while I struggled to cope with the cast. Moore's demonic reference tormented my dreams as she coerced me with a wooden pointer to switch hands and tearfully convert for her.

During that first couple of weeks, while back in school, I recall being warned by the teacher, not to play on the street where the power company was putting in new power poles. Now no teacher could honestly expect young boys to pay attention to such a warning? "You'll fall in those holes and you'll never get out!" she admonished.

As soon as we emptied out of the school my cousins, Tony and Ray along with Brian Pattie, a Lumby neighbour and classmate all headed over to investigate the power pole operation. After spending our lunch hour where we weren't supposed to be, we arrived back for class and we were all taken to the principal's office where the principal proceeded to give my cousins and friend, Brian the strap. When he got to me, he stated that, if he strapped my only good hand then I would fall even further behind in my schoolwork, so I was sent back to the class unpunished. Fifty years later, Brian Pattie complained to me, "Why didn't you get the strap?" I reminded him that my arm was broken. He still feels cheated.

Not long after the arm had healed. I came down with conjunctivitis. I could hardly open my eyes resulting in more lectures from the teacher who suggested that I should not be such a sickly child, or I'd fail first grade. The relic had been hired when teachers received less than six months training.

While I went through the trauma of the cranky prods of Mrs. Moore and her pointer, on weekends I was suffering a sort of rebellion toward preparation for my First Communion at church catechism classes. Roman Catholic children prepare for First Holy Communion at a time when they supposedly reach the 'age of reason' and are consciously aware of what The Sacrament offers them. I resented school all week, conducted in a less than hospitable environment, along with the added responsibility of learning, by memory, the Baltimore Catechism, a course of responses about the Catholic faith. The thought of receiving Jesus in a wafer did mean something beautiful to me as the thought of consuming His pure and holy presence offered something very special. It was a time when the test of being young and Catholic attending lengthy Sunday High Masses seemed overbearing. First Holy Communion preparation during that period of Church history required children, along with adults, being required to abstain from eating from midnight the night before until communion was given near the end of each Mass, which would be around noon on Sunday in Lumby's Catholic church. The fast, intended as an act of separating one's temporal food from the spiritual, was always difficult, particularly when no temporal food was offered until noon.

As play, John continued to enjoy playing priest. Later, at about age twelve, he would mix in the role of mimicking hypnotist with that of a Catholic priest. He'd hypnotize victims by instructing them to unknowingly balance a piece of furniture on an index finger or to hold items on the end of their noses while in the trance. It was quite a remarkable show, the hypnotic act he performed at a very young age. It was always easier for John to get Protestant friends to consent to hypnosis than to have them yield to Catholic confessions in his mock-up confessional set behind a living room chair, positioned to offer penitents some degree of privacy during the play rituals. John would drift from his priest role to that of being the Judge Himself sitting in his confessional absolving sinners direct from our home. I was often the sole willing penitent and John recited sins on my behalf in the makeshift confessional. It served as a convenient spiritual exercise to have him debase me with his own examination of my conscience.

When we moved from Lavallette's Ranch to our Lumby house on Shuswap Avenue at the corner of Maple Street, the previous owners left behind a big gentle Red Irish Setter dog. Shortly afterwards, Lucky had a stray kitten park itself on his doghouse doorstep and the dog adopted it as his own. The two became inseparable sharing rations and sleeping under the porch in the doghouse. Unfortunately, a wretched neighbourhood paperboy would kick the dog when he came by to deliver papers. Initially, Lucky would go out from under the porch to greet the boy in a friendly manner; however, the greeting was never amicably reciprocated. Eventually, the dog developed a hatred for the contemptible visitor who threw rocks. Lucky came out of hiding and took a bite out of the paperboy's shoulder. Subsequently, the town constable ordered the dog destroyed.

I volunteered to bring Lucky with me to the boy's home, a farm located a couple of blocks from our house. This was in exchange for my pleading to my father for a few extra moments with the pet before he took the dog to have it destroyed. When we approached the farmyard, the farmer whistled at the dog from a distance and as the dog ran to him, he fired a rifle striking the dog in the left rear leg. Lucky yelped dragging his torso before receiving a fatal wound to the head. I fell to my knees in horror at the sight blaming my Dad for being part of the malicious event.

Soon afterwards we were given a new puppy from our dad and my feelings ameliorated. Ricky was a golden Cocker Spaniel. Both cat and the puppy slept together in the house afterwards.

For three summers John and I travelled with our cousins, the Dyck boys to Camp, Lourdes, located outside of Nelson on Kootenay Lake. It was run by Bishop Johnson, a kind man who would drop by to visit Father Harrison while we lived at Lumby's Catholic Church rectory. The camp was situated on the remote shoreline of Kootenay Lake, thirteen miles east of Nelson, where the Canadian Pacific Railway tracks passed on the south shore behind the perimeter of the camp that was inaccessible by automobile. If we didn't arrive by train, we would be ferried across the lake on the bishop's launch a large leaky dilapidated wooden hulled boat. No mother would ever trust her child in it, if she cared to go and inspect the camp's transportation link that regularly ferried children. Mothers and fathers seldom looked out for children in those years. They had special faith that the Supernatural did that. They were too occupied with other younger siblings in their homes to watch the growing ones who were permitted to venture away.

John and I always looked forward to the camp experience. The launch was part of the lure Lourdes offered. Just as Christopher Columbus had on the Santa Maria, a picture of The Virgin Mary "The Star of the Sea" was displayed above where our bishop sat steering his boat that would often incur mechanical failure while crossing the lake. The entrustment worked for the Spaniards and seemed to work for Bishop Johnson and the children of Nelson Diocese.

Each rustic outdoor cabin was nestled in a wooded area of the camp behind the beach. Apertures were framed in the cabin walls for windows without panes providing the youths with mosquito filled nights in the partially exposed annual outdoor camping adventure. Camp was divided into separated two-week sessions for girls and boys each attended by a hundred or so campers of varying ages from six to eighteen. After campers arose at six-thirty to bath in the frigid Kokanee Glacier fed waters of Kootenay Lake and attend daily morning Mass, they would eat breakfast catered to by seminarians from throughout the diocese who'd assist the bishop. He would occasionally vacation nearby in his own cabin with Pal, his one-eyed dog. The bishop and Pal fished in his wooden rowboat for Kokanee lured by the renown, Willow Leaf, the cleric's favourite tackle.

The seminarians arranged the fun for the campers. At least once during each camp adventure, an afternoon ordeal after a half hour nap or quiet time, was boxing blind folded where the competing boxers punched it out until the weaker one was down. You had no choice as everyone participated after being sized up by the seminarians!

Some boys were sore losers and still complain as elderly adult men of the hammering they took at Catholic summer camp.

Mornings were spent with outdoor games and swimming that would take the campers through until lunch hour. Those were followed by afternoon hikes and more swimming before dinner and then nightly campfires consisting of roasted marshmallows, hot dogs and concocted seminarian "ghost" stories. The days were always full of enjoyment. Sherry attended the girls' camp just on one occasion.

The balance of the summer days, were usually spent with Lumby area cousins and other neighbourhood playmates on the village streets with weekend trips to Kalamalka or Okanagan lakes with both parents and the Bickert side Grandparents who would picnic and swim with us.

The village was an easy town to raise a family in. Children played in yards bordered by wooden plank sidewalks. The only two or three roads that had pavement were the highway through town, Shuswap and Park Avenues covered with mud mixed in with fallen timber bark that had dropped off the loaded logging trucks. Small cottage shaped housing, peculiar to that day, were what families resided in and continue to today.

The three active sawmills often left the village full of smoke, particularly on the days when air inversions lowered the haze in autumn and winter months. By six years of age, I was suffering immensely from bronchitis and asthma. There was no treatment offered me and by then we had stopped seeing the chiropractor after the pain had subsided in my back. I would cough, snort and wheeze day and night.

"Paul coughs a lot," my parents would remark brushing off my suffering while they chain smoked contributing to the environmental effects.

Frequent injurious encounters with logging truck booms were a peril for me at that age. The booms connected the two sections of the extended logging trucks only when they were used for hauling. When parked the rear extension of each truck was drawn up onto the front section. With the boom protruding out the back of the equipment, I'd often collide with them while manoeuvring around the neighbourhood forgetting the area hazards that I should have become accustomed to. Once I was knocked out cold after running home from play at the full speed my legs would carry me colliding with the eight-inch thick solid steel extended booms. Eventually, I came to when a neighbour picked me up off the street and helped me home. Brother, John nicknamed me 'Egghead' for a few years, until he found another name that was more appropriate designed for whatever humoured him. 'Buckled Kneed Chicken Breast' or 'Pickle Puss' were handles I wore from age seven until I was about fifteen. Those chicken and buckled knee references came as a result of my slightly malformed chest and knees from a mild case of Rickets when I was a child. The metabolic bone disease still was common in children when I was young, but in spite of the name it earned me, it provided something to have in common with my Grandpa Harry Bickert.

John and I would spend any rainy day listening to Superman, The Lone Ranger, Roy Rogers or Gene Autrey radio shows or reading similar character comic books. They were the popular heroes for the day and the extent of indoor entertainment for children during the period. Fights would seldom erupt between us as we were faithful playmates since Marquis. Most of our outdoor activity was spent around a creek or a stream, riding our bikes or hiking the hills often transporting along with us stolen cigarettes from our parents' stash of 'Roll Your Owns.' We had several cousins living within a block of home and they provided extra entertainment to us as we'd watch them choke on our pocketed smokes. I don't recall any of the other kids providing cigarettes to John and me. Perhaps their folks didn't smoke. We seemed to be the sole source of it as if we were the neighbourhood 'pushers' of the day. I had my first cigarette when I was not yet six needing only a little encouragement from my big brother. Of course, no consideration was given to my bronchitis.

On Halloween nights we roamed the streets of the small town until late in the evening, without any parental supervision, as the town was safe except for ourselves and friends that mimicked the role of young vandals soaping up windows and overturning garbage cans all usually ignored by adults who let the kids have their fun for the special evening.

Canada had not developed a widespread immunization program against polio until 1954 and in 1952 our whole household came down with the polio virus. It was a mild sickness and we were generally unaffected other than my sister Sherry was left without hearing in her left ear from an earache that she developed during the illness. For a while afterwards John had stomach problems which eventually disappeared.

The epidemic occurred a year before the Salk vaccine was developed, the first vaccine that was widely used before Sabin oral vaccines. Unfortunately, many people contracted the disease even after the general mass immunization programs were widely promoted. Per capita the effects were not noticeable as few were disfigured by the illness.

Geoffrey Michael was born on August 15, 1952. He was one of four babies born in the immediate neighbourhood during that summer. Aunt Jean Dyck, Uncle Bill's wife had a son, Alan and two other ladies had daughters. It was the beginning of my mother becoming socially involved with other women in the small town. They formed a club called the Lend-a-Hand to help one another with baby needs.

Kathy Mary was born less than thirteen months later on September 18th, 1953. She died two weeks later from a stroke that resulted from a high fever during a battle with infant jaundice. She never left the neonatal ward at Vernon's hospital.

I feel that adjusting to tragedy in a family is always much easier when a family has faith comforting death; you believe and pray that your deceased sibling is watching over you in heaven. Today, I still invoke Irvin and Kathy's intercessory assistance before the Lord, trusting that they are acting out their role as loving family members in heaven interceding for us. Sorrows in our family always appeared short lived as our busy household was full of faith and activity spurned on by my mother who seemed to lead in matters of faith.

When bad news arrived at our home, we could usually look forward to a visit from my grandfather, John LaLonde who'd come and visit for a month or two in autumns after Prairie harvests on the Marquis farm. That year was no exception.

My Dad had two sisters and a brother living in Vernon then. Edward, the younger of the two brothers, was an announcer at CJIV Radio and spent most of his free time with a guitar in his hands when he wasn't broadcasting. Jeanne Bickert, a teen CJIV Radio talk show host was a local celebrity at the same time as her older brother, Edward. Older sister, Gladys Bickert (Sasges) was a mother to a couple of children by then while Uncle Al operated Sasges Cement Plant and trucks. Dad's sister, Francis Knapper resided in New Brunswick with her husband Wes until divorcing him in the early Sixties and returning to Vernon.

Edward Bickert became a very progressed jazz guitar musician and left Vernon in the autumn of 1953 to move to Toronto where he became a well-known Jazz recording artist. His career was marked by appearances in Carnegie Hall, the London Palladium and other world theatres. He recorded several albums on the Commodore label. Eventually, before retirement he was awarded the Governor General's, 'The Order of Canada.'

Chapter Fifteen

After completing the 1953 spring seeding, John LaLonde climbed off his Massey Ferguson tractor and stood wiping the dirt from his face onto his shirt sleeve. Making his way slowly across the farmyard, he supported his right loin then moved in front of the water pump where he pumped a dipper of water. He had been suffering all week and that day the backache was accompanied by weakness and traces of blood in his urine. Unfortunately, seeding had fallen behind because his work had been held up with a late spring thaw and what he described to neighbours as a lumbago attack forcing him to stay inside to convalesce for a week. He used the remaining contents that he poured from the dipper to wash his hands and face and then stood in thought musing over his condition. "Perhaps stones?" he thought out loud. "Hell, with it," he continued as he gradually moved to the inside of the small farmhouse to telephone his doctor.

By the end of May he had the medical results. It was an inoperable and non treatable cancer of the right kidney that had affected him. The doctor advised that there was nothing medicine could do and that he had less than six months to live.

LaLonde was not one to feel sorry or talk to others about his concerns over impending death. Over the years he had grown to accept that Providence was of a higher order than he would care to question. Historically, LaLonde men didn't live long, and he wasn't going to be the exception. His brothers were all deceased and only he and his sisters were still alive. The simple, austere and solitary life that he had lived didn't provide him with the luxury to self indulge, nor did it give him any reason to expect that his neighbours or his family who had struggled over the years would want to listen to his own self pity. LaLonde upbringing taught that life had its graces and an early death with advance notice would likely be one of them, so he would make the best of it and prepare himself to meet The Lord. He wanted to make his death easier for those endeared to him and would spend the balance of his life with my mother and her family.

George Pendleton could assist Mom after my grandfather's death with an orderly sale of the farm assets and Lucy and Mary would console one another. Later Mary who was freer to travel could follow him to Lumby when it was near the end and Mom would need more family to be with her to offer support.

As a final indulgence my Grandpa bought a new 1953 88 model Oldsmobile. It was a gem for that day and the finest vehicle he had ever owned. He knew that he would not have it for long but wanted my parents to benefit from the vehicle that would accommodate travel for their growing family in Lumby.

Surprising everyone he arrived in mid-summer that year after deciding to leave harvesting to his brother-in-law, George Pendleton. He drove into our yard in the new green vehicle and used the excuse for the purchase that it contained a seat which he could sit in for twenty-one hours while he was on the road between Marquis and Lumby, a trip he always made in one long day's drive.

Mom had gone out grocery shopping and John and I were in the cellar examining the remains of a summer flood that had filled our basement with water. There was one light which lit the cellar and it went out while we stood perplexed in the muddy cellar over how we could possibly find our way to the stairs.

"Hey, turn on the light," John bellowed.

Then the light went on and we quickly made our way upstairs before the light could go out again discovering our Grandfather, who had a grin on his face. His prank was rewarded with our usual cheers and enthusiastic welcome.

Grandpa's illness was not announced to us until much later that summer, so at first the visit appeared to be a normal one. It wasn't long before my dad was busy changing our living room and porch area with a renovation to accommodate an addition for our grandfather's bedroom. In the beginning it all seemed so perfect to have him living with us.

It wasn't until later in the autumn that I recall his health was on a visible decline. Loss of weight, colour and general deterioration were rapid by then and he would slip in and out of consciousness by late autumn. I don't believe there was ever a formal announcement made in front of the family that Grandpa was dying; it just became obvious that he was gravely ill. Occasionally, I would lie down with him on the edge of the bed and straining he'd offer a few words, placing his arm around me. His rosary was always in his hand during those months. I recollect that there was a parade of well wishers, including Sacred Heart Parish's new Irish Catholic priest, Father O'Reilly who arrived regularly to minister the sacraments to Grandpa and offer some Irish humour.

Grandpa died on Dec 16th, 1953, closing a memorable chapter in all our lives. It was a bitter loss for my mother who had lost her babies Irvin and Kathy in the first four years of her marriage. Now, losing her Dad was an added anguish.

The period we spent with Grandpa before he died was a gift I will always cherish. I recall that summer taking a few walks with him before he was bedridden. He frequently wore a blue woollen cardigan sweater that he boasted my mother had given him years earlier. I recollect how he would pull me toward him with his hand over my shoulder offering his grandfatherly affection and I would sniff his body and the sweater that always smelled of his shaving cream. It provided me with a comfort and feeling that I was at home and safe with the man whom I had known and loved very early in my life. Those walks and the private times seemed to mean as much to him as they did to me. Today, when I see my own grandsons, I like to wrap an arm over their shoulders and do the same. To let them know that their presence is special to their grandfather, even if few words are offered. I know that the affection is a warm gesture that they will remember.

That sweater that Grandpa LaLonde wore was eventually given to me by my mother. As a child I was always impressed with how big a man he appeared to be. Years later, when I received the sweater from Mom, I discovered that he wasn't big at all. I was twenty at the time when the sweater was handed over to me. Then, I was one hundred and sixty pounds, five foot ten inches tall and the cardigan was snug. It is still in my possession today and is probably eighty- years old by now.

Grandpa's sense of humour remained during those months. I recall how he would chuckle when Mom or the Irish priest would come to his bedside to humour him with their Irish yarns during the last few days of his life. He broke out laughing at my brother Geoffrey who was a one-year old toddler at the time, actively engaged in clearing all the knickknacks off end tables in the living room. That afternoon I was spread across the couch half asleep and Geoffrey whacked my head with an empty beer bottle. The bottle had been used that day by my mother as a dampening bottle while she ironed. Mom would poke holes in the bottle cap sprinkling its contents to dampen her ironing. She had a series of hot ironing plates warming up on the wood stove that would hook onto a handle that she'd exchange the cold plates with hot ones from the stove. It was a primitive form of ironing, commonplace in those days.

Grandpa must have been observing my little brother from his bed, when Geoffrey thumped me over the head. At that moment I wasn't as humoured as my grandfather was; however, I eventually joined in with his laughter realizing little Geoff had successfully belted his big brother.

Before dying, he decided to return to Saskatchewan to make some changes to his Last Will and Testament. He wasn't satisfied with the way that he had prepared the document before and wanted to change the executor of the estate to my mother.

In mid-December that year the family climbed into Grandpa's car and drove from Lumby to Sicamous's railway station. Our grandfather was transported ahead of us in a hired ambulance to deliver him to the train. Accompanying Grandpa in the ambulance was Aunt Mary Pendleton who had come from Marquis to be with us. I recollect it as a sombre trip. Our teary-eyed mother asked us to join in a short prayer for our grandfather while we followed in the Olds behind the ambulance headed to Sicamous to board Grandpa and Aunt Mary on the train headed east.

The next day, after returning home from school during lunch hour, the phone rang. I had just left the kitchen and gone into the adjacent bathroom and I could hear my mother crying while on the phone, followed by my brother John who began crying along with her. When I came out, I understood my grandfather had died. Then, I cried too. He had died in Medicine Hat's train station on December 16, 1953 before ever arriving at Moose Jaw.

That winter was particularly difficult. The loss, the empty room and death were now revisited. My childhood mind had a strange perspective about Grandpa's death. I recalled how it always troubled me seeing Lucky's doghouse while it sat unoccupied under the back porch after the Irish Setter's death. Now my grandfather's room seemed too close a reminder in our home. Afterwards, I refused to sit in the living room for some time because Grandpa's room was too visible from there. Dad eventually demolished the room as it was too much of a solemn reminder to the family of our grandfather's illness and our home needed the living space.

My parents went to Saskatchewan to arrange the funeral in Marquis and stayed for a couple of weeks while we were babysat. Grandpa was buried next to his mother and father at the Marquis cemetery. Nearby Mom's maternal mother, Maryanne Griffin, is also buried. It was Christmastime and the whole family felt the loss as our parents travelled to Marquis for the funeral.

John Joseph. LaLonde (May 18, 1892 – Dec. 16, 1953)

Chapter Sixteen

It appeared the loss of my grandfather resulted in the kindling of a deeper relationship between my mother and her estranged mother. Perhaps as a result of Gladys LaLonde being more sensitive over remarks made about my grandfather during that period. Letters from the East were arriving more frequently after Grandpa's passing along with packages with gifts of handicrafts and the occasional telephone call. The barrier to my grandmother's attachment to Mom had for years been strained by the antagonism her mother exhibited toward John LaLonde. Perhaps being second in line was difficult for her.

After the funeral my parents began to busy themselves with redecorating our family home. The house was old and tired and needed a change. Grandpa's illness and passing was a factor in my mother's feelings about the house and for her decorating always provided an emotional lift. The main floor of the house consisted of a small kitchen, bathroom, living room and my parents' bedroom from where stairs to the second level were only accessible. It was an odd configuration to have stairs in their bedroom. I believe that the room may have once been a dining room that was converted in order to accommodate our larger family. On the second level there were two other bedrooms. One was Sherry and Geoffrey's room and the other was where John and I slept.

The makeover consisted of a full repainting as the small budget permitted. I do recall the odours from the oil-based paint gave me horrible headaches for days. Of special interest was Mom's kitchen floor mural that consisted of a large red apple painted in the middle of the floor with two big green leaves attached to the stem. The floor mural was in the middle of a grey background with a black trimmed circle bordering. It's all quite amusing to think of the decorating choice intended to cover old linoleum. Mom's sewing flair provided the kitchen and main floor living areas with homemade draperies. When real estate clients came to view the house, my parents made certain that the kids weren't around for fear that we'd point out to potential purchasers whatever the dwellings deficiencies were.

That Easter Mom planned a family excursion to Prince George where we visited her twin sister, Mary, who had recently relocated after marrying Jack Norman, a Kraft Foods salesman. "Mr. Cheese," Dad used to call him. Mom and her sister had not seen each other since the War on a visit occurring prior to my mother's departure to Toronto and her marriage to Carl Ellis. She often complained of her lost Marquis family that had become so fragmented over the years and with the passing of her father the distant relationship with siblings Mary, John and Patrick troubled her. Some of them would send the occasional Christmas card, but otherwise there was little contact. Distance, budgets and road conditions throughout Western Canada made travel less common in those days so attempts were seldom made to see one another. Having forgotten my childhood experiences in Marquis's Prairie cold, I was quite impressed with Prince George's chilly temperatures.

Oddly, throughout life, Mom claimed that both Mary and she possessed inner premonitions that alerted each to the needs of the other. This strange talent would surface from time to time and my mother would concern herself over the forewarnings and then make a telephone call to her sister. Usually, the intuition was correct and further convinced Mom that they possessed a special gift. Knowing the events that affected the other's life was reciprocated by each when both of their fathers died and, of course, the death of Mom's babies, were occasions for Mary to exhibit her own clairvoyance. They also claimed that they felt each other's childbirth pains. For my mother the bizarre sixth sense continued up until the last episode in 1984 when Mary happened to be in New York City with Uncle Jack and Mary had taken ill. Her sister apparently doubled over a parked car's hood in Manhattan while experiencing severe abdominal cramps that hospitalized her. It was then that doctors advised that she had terminal cancer. Meanwhile my mother was served notice in the form of stomach pains that persisted until Uncle Jack phoned with the news about Aunt Mary's illness.

I turned nine in the spring of 1954 and at that age 'Cowboys and Indians' was a preferred form of play. As politically incorrect as the play could possibly be today, Western heroes that were depicted in comic books in those days were Gene Autry, Roy Rogers and the Lone Ranger, all idols that assisted in cultivating our behaviour. These models would portray law abiding gun slingers, living as purveyors of freedom and advocates of the West's good small-town folk in the Nineteenth Century where their towns had sissy sheriffs protecting them. The feeble lawmakers couldn't muster up the courage to strike down rebellion in their midst. From the oppression of villainous outlaws and renegade Indians the hero gunslingers would free the West over radio airwaves. After listening to weekly radio shows which would reinforce the comic book imagery, in order to partake in the heroics, we'd rehearse our own gunslinger acts in the neighbourhood by mimicking the deities while playing those roles with toy pistols, rifles and bow and arrow sets. The radio broadcasts were equally as impressive to our minds as television programs that came along later in our childhood. The terribly insensitive games to any First Nations people of the day were played and encouraged as entertainment.

In one such game during May of 1954, I decided that I would climb a neighbour's fence to escape the "Indian" who was in pursuit of me. Usually, the villainous Indian and outlaw roles were assigned to the younger boys. They always lost in gunfights, so those roles were never taken up by the older boys. The fence that I was climbing was positioned parallel to a neighbour's garage and my plan was to attempt an escape to the other side of the garage from its rooftop. Up the fence I went and then onto the garage roof where I managed my best Gene Autry stunt rolling and then up onto my feet again, while blasting my cap gun at the renegade in response to rounds from his toy Winchester rifle. As I sprang back to my feet from a stunt roll on the garage roof, I tripped on a loose shingle while approaching the ladder that I planned to mount and descend. Unfortunately, I fell over the ladder and knocked off it another friend who was climbing up. Off the ladder he fell to the ground behind me. When I hit the ground, I fell backward into a two sectioned wooden apple crate. My friend landed directly on top of me with a crunch so forceful that the crate's midsection cracked in two from the impact of my compressed lower ribcage. Besides fracturing several ribs, I ruptured my left kidney. Dazed and in pain I lay there unable to move and fell unconscious. Minutes later, I awoke with my dog Ricky licking my face.

Before I awoke, John, along with my two outlaw friends, had all run home in order to tell my mother about the mishap and my condition. She came along and loaded me into a wagon and together they pulled me home.

Within a short time, I had passed a large volume of blood that was assumed to have come from internal haemorrhaging, enough to alert my mother that I was in serious enough condition from the fall. She phoned Dad and I was driven to the hospital emergency room in Vernon. That resulted in another three-week stay at hospital and numerous procedures to investigate the extent of the injury that I had sustained.

My brother John always seemed to land upright like a cat. Instead, I landed on my head or some bone would break resulting in my being left alone in the hospital and bedridden for weeks afterwards. Today, family still finds humour in reminding me of my life full of mishaps.

I recall being told from the side of the hospital bed that our dog Ricky had gone missing after my injury. Apparently, he chose to stay in the friend's yard where the mishap occurred remaining quietly out of sight guarding my bike. Eventually, they notified my family of the dog's whereabouts. The weeks spent at home after the hospital stay and hearing how the dog had missed me, endeared me to the new pet whom I had somewhat ignored after his becoming a replacement for Lucky.

Unfortunately, those hospital stays caused a lot of emotional pain in my childhood. I was held back in third grade that year as I missed considerable school time and was unprepared for promotion. It was the first personal painful setback in my life, but one of four upsetting events for me during the third-grade school term, my dog being destroyed, my illness from the kidney injury, my grandfather's death and then the failure of third grade. Childhood was full of lessons for me and death was just one of them. Those provided a definite influence on my formation.

———◆———

In the summer of 1954, the family moved to Nelson, BC. Dad and Mom had been planning the move for a few months but did not make the announcement until near the end of the school term. The principal reason for relocating was that Dad had heard from Peter and Bill Dyck that the brothers were considering leaving the garage partnership in Lumby and were going into the logging business. Their older brother, Jack, who was nearing retirement age, would soon sell the garage. Rather than face an uncertain future, the move to Nelson would result in an immediate economic improvement for the family as my father was able to secure good employment there.

Two pet rabbits that John and I had been given earlier that year and had raised since they were about six weeks were about to be orphaned since moving them from Lumby was not practical. We gave the rabbits to a young Lumby butcher who misunderstood the intentions of our gift. The man was already on our front lawn by the time we made it home from play that day. The two skinned and gutted rabbits were lying on a newspaper beside him with their white fur coats draped across the clothesline above. The butcher did the work that his profession required without thinking that what we really wanted was for him to provide the rabbits a safe home. We both laughed and cried at the same time. Afterwards we became very definite in expressing ourselves clearly.

Chapter Seventeen

The West Kootenay region always unveiled a pristine and majestic beauty in the summer and continues to do so today. Located in a refreshing deep, narrow and green valley on Kootenay Lake, it provides a quality area for British Columbians to reside. Annual moisture in the form of spring rains and winter's heavy snowfall maintains lush healthy foliage peculiar to the area which possesses numerous thundering creeks and countless deep freshwater lakes. Thirty kilometres west of Nelson the Kootenay River joins the Columbia, but first a series of hydro-electric dams with their impressive waterfalls add charm as the Kootenay gorge narrows and then turns south before the Cascade Mountains when the river empties into the Columbia at Castlegar.

Nelson commenced its development during Victorian times and the buildings of that era are abundant in the small city located on a steep hillside on the south shore before the West Arm of Kootenay Lake constricts to form a river just past Nelson. Kootenay Indians established early camps in the region and fished on the shoreline eating wild fruit and nuts from the healthy forests that provided their sustenance over several thousands of years after the glaciers receded. Some evidence of their temporary primitive earthen dwellings still exists today on Elephant Mountain which faces south toward Nelson from the North Shore.

Prospectors came in the latter part of the nineteenth century for gold, silver and copper followed by American railway builders who arrived on the invitation and generous hospitality of the British Columbia government in Victoria encouraging them to build the first railway segment to the region. The gold and copper claims were disappointing; however, generous supplies of silver were present to export. After the railway, more prospecting occurred with claim disputes, murders, legal judgements and hangings portraying the lawlessness of some of the inhabitants in the small community which made few rich during that period.

A forest fire wiped out the shanty and tent hamlet in 1885 before streets bearing the names of early pioneers Hall, Ward, Stanley, Latimer and Josephine, wife of Ward, were titled and in 1897, coinciding with the hamlet receiving the Letters Patent designating the City of Nelson. As mining continued to develop hydro-electric dams were built on the river to service more growth. Then another railway line was added to carry the metal and lumber that were exported from the area.

Over the early Twentieth Century the area experienced an increase in population with the advent of the railway servicing the mines and then commercial activity developed to service that expansion. Government offices opened and area policing headquarters were established adding to the stability of the centre.

The Roman Catholic Diocese of Nelson constructed Notre Dame College in 1950 which received its university status by 1963, about the same time its enrolment began to decline following the short period of prosperity for the area. By then, Nelson had become the hub of the Interior of British Columbia before quickly losing its status to the rapidly developing communities of Kamloops, Prince George, Kelowna and Cranbrook.

Nelson as the jewel and 'Queen City' of the Kootenays was the most prosperous town of the Interior during 1950's. The city benefited from the the Canadian Pacific Railway which had a large repair depot for locomotives. Kootenay Forest Products, which was a thriving sawmill operation, along with commerce that was coming from logging and mining helped. It offered a much more versatile economy for the period than what was offered in the Okanagan. Higher wages and a private Catholic school were additional features.

The Nelson Maple Leaf's hockey team was renowned as the main rival to the Trail Smoke Eaters of the Western International Hockey League encouraging a terrific community pride. Nelson also hosted an annual Midsummer Curling Bonspiel. The town was alive, and residents loved the small city's activity.

My parents purchased a charming Victorian home for seventy-five hundred dollars. The dwelling at 716 Mill Street still stands as a heritage building designated protected by the provincial government.

Just down Mill Street was St. Joseph's Academy, run by the Roman Catholic Diocese of Nelson. The students were taught by the Sisters of St. Joseph of Peace, a religious order from Bellevue, Washington. The school functioned as both a convent for the nuns and school to provide income for the religious consisting of grades one through twelve until 1960. There were approximately three hundred and fifty students attending the facility in 1954 when the Bickert children arrived.

On the same block as the school, was the Roman Catholic Cathedral of Mary Immaculate, a magnificent turn of the century structure that today is a heritage monument adding allure to the hillside. The fully restored Cathedral stands as it did in its early years, but the old school has since been torn down and replaced by a newer facility on the same property that the old building I attended.

Bickert family after Janice's birth

In my second year of third grade I was taller and thicker skinned discovering how to finesse my way with assurance and diplomacy. I wanted to demonstrate that I was a winner not a failure. I read the news in the papers I delivered and became worldly always engaging in current event conversation and challenging others to attempt to do the same. It was how I liked to manoeuvre around the year I lost. I enjoyed that I could convince friends on my own viewpoint.

Although my self worth had been reduced by the event, what followed was a new period of self discovery giving rise to strengths. My failure had become a stepping stone to my own moral growth and subsequent failures in whatever situation would make me more resourceful. As a boy of nine, I had yet to discover that I would be humiliated more than once in life.

That year, I enrolled in piano lessons with Sister Jean. John opted for freedom and I would join him by deciding not to continue after the first year of Royal Conservatory lessons. I wanted play time with my friends and brother. Sherry continued and completed Royal Conservatory sixth grade then never played the piano again. When I was thirty, I began to play again.

John and I took an interest in Cubs and brought along other neighbourhood boys that we encouraged to participate in the Wolf Pack nights. We'd be awarded a bright brass star for our green Cub hats for each recruit. One of the boys that I recruited was Richard Joyce, who remains a friend to this day. Richard would take pleasure in challenging my youthful worldly deliberations. As a retired High School teacher living in Kamloops, Richard still enjoys sharing his perspective as we email one another our thoughts on current social issues. I, a conservative and Richard a liberal, usually provoke one another's need to set the other straight.

During the early morning of September 8th, 1954, the week after we moved into the Mill Street house, Janice Mary was born. She had both my sister Sherry's dark brown eyes and hair and was delivered by Caesarean section. To the relief of our parents and the whole family she appeared healthy. Unfortunately, a couple of days after the birth Mom noticed Janice was bruised and had sustained a blow to the side of her cranium that possibly had occurred since her last feeding while she was attended to in the hospital nursery apart from my mother.

When the baby was delivered back to Mom's hospital room for the next feeding my mother immediately inquired of the nurse, "What have you done to my baby?"

The nurse denied that anything had occurred. Mom's concern was that the right parietal and temporal bones of Janice's skull were bruised and indented, as if a blow had occurred, a change from earlier observations made of her newborn. Also apparent was Janice's unsettled disposition unlike before when the baby rested at ease in her arms.

A week later, when both were finally released from the Kootenay Lake Hospital facility, Mom's concern continued as doctors brushed aside her distressing over Janice. The family's physician did agree to investigate the complaint, but advised he felt Janice would be okay; hence, my mother capitulated leaving the matter alone to make the best of her new baby and not spoil the arrival with her protests.

Six weeks after Janice's birth, the family awoke during the night to a disturbance in our parents' bedroom. Janice had gone into convulsions and Mom and Dad were hurrying about in preparation to take the baby to the hospital emergency. Janice suffered a massive cerebral haemorrhage along with seizures that night. Subsequently, brain damage occurred in both her cerebellum and the cerebral hemisphere adjacent to the cranial bone injuries that were an earlier concern leading to a serious disability that my little sister would have to endure for the rest of her life. Janice returned home a few weeks after the ordeal visibly changed to the whole family.

Unfortunately, my little sister would grow up in a community that had little more than a church basement to offer as baby sitting service for the mentally and physically challenged of her day. Nelson received no public funding from the provincial government to assist the disabled then, but did its best under the circumstance to provide what today would be viewed as a grossly inadequate service for the needs of the disabled.

Afterwards, a neighbouring nurse from the hospital told my mother that she understood the injury to Janice's cranium to be the result of an accidental dropping of Janice in the hospital nursery. There was never an effort made by my parents to confirm the nurse's accusation.

It was a time in our Canadian legal system when people accepted personal injury being not so inclined to attempt revenge or to seek compensation through the courts. Janice was only one infant of many in those days that was injured by careless or unfortunate medical procedures. At the same time as Janice's infirmity many thousands of North Americans were maimed by the drug Thalidomide that left the victims disabled with complete limbs missing or malformed. Without trial testing, during the first trimester of women's pregnancies, the drug was prescribed to ease the symptoms of morning sickness. The horrific size of the event made our concerns for Janice miniscule in comparison.

Although, her birth forever changed the structure of our home with the special attention she required in order to support her life, she was always accepted as a blessing not a cross. My mother penned a special citation to Janice in her poem 'Little Girl Blest.' The verse explains the special meaning that our mother found in Janice's infirmity.

> "She causes apprehension, for we fear
> She will not reach the goals for which she strives.
> She seems to be so near yet so apart
> From those she loves and, in whose lives
> She fails to find a pattern for her own.
>
> Though in our loving hearts she holds a place
> Far wider than the care less ones
> Who keep the pace and grasp whatever comes?
> Of learning, without struggle as is hers.
>
> How little does she know that we have fault
> (Not disco ordinate such as she)
> But hers have brought her nearer to perfection
> Then those of us who seem to perfect be.
>
> True love within her heart will grow
> For Love is what she feels clear through
> And gives abundantly, so we will know
> That this she has in common with the others.
>
> We say "She is not normal, is retarded,
> With portions of her baby brain erased
> And is not gifted as a child might be."
> But who can say what hidden gifts encased,
> In her by God makes her advanced

In blessed Heavenly security?"

Mom found a deeper meaning in the disappointments and crosses she bore in life. It was her belief that those were making a better person out of her and that the hurts provided a deeper and a more enriched life, augmented by a wisdom that came from her soul with each new lesson.

Janice today continues to grace those she encounters in life. Most who have faith conclude that she and all the others that share disabilities with my sister have a special purpose in our world making those various handicaps tools to teach society that God has a place for each in one another's lives.

Janice grew slowly and strained to survive in her little spastic frame left rigid. Her mouth and tongue flesh constantly had thrush, a result of repeated infections caused by wounds that were inflicted by a spastic jaw and teeth rendering the inside her of her oral cavity. She didn't sleep well because intracranial pressure caused headaches nightly. She would cry and her discomfort was felt by everyone. While we'd lie in bed each night, we'd erupt in spontaneous prayer for Janice. Each of us needed interior comfort that could only be appeased by a hope that a loving God would hear our whispered words from pillows dampened by tears of hope that our household would be delivered from its predicament and that Janice would be healed. For the moment answers came in the form of graces that offered interior consolation.

We were a family of five children, all having special needs while four of us were left to sort out our own problems as our parents had more important business to attend to for the sake of Janice. We all became ruggedly independent and understood that, that was what was required of us, to be responsible for our own selves.

The quality of parenting in the home was ample and even though the amount of attention scarce, we were loved. It was all a new growth phase for us as family. Sort of a test to the measure of strength we possessed for enduring trials together as a unit.

I got my first paper route that autumn after Janice's birth. The circuit involved delivering the Vancouver Sun to sixteen homes that were located on the opposite edge of Cottonwood Creek from the roadway that connected Nelson and Salmo. The chore was quite remarkable, when I consider it today. I recollect that The Sun newspaper was weighty, full of advertising that would accompany several sections of the news, much more so than today's papers. Many days the paper would be an inch thick. In those years it was the principal publication of Western Canada, published long before television and the Internet devastated the printed news enterprise. My paper bag would bulge over a foot out most days.

The delivery involved walking up a long hilly stretch of highway for two miles with the heavy paper bag equal to half my body weight dangling over my shoulder. I was quite lopsided on trips back and forth over Cottonwood creek, a swift moving body of water that winds its way down a steep grade of hillside under narrow makeshift bridges that were often wet and slippery from the mist off the creek. The moss that was growing on the wooden logs was an added hazard to the crossings. With the delivery of each customer's paper, I would often be forced to straddle the logs with the paper bag dangling from my side as I attempted to shimmy my way across. Each customer's overpass was enough to scare the wet corduroy pants off me. Though terrified, I was making social advancement in my age group as I delivered the paper to residents at the base of Toad Mountain.

It was almost certain that I would have to make one or two extra tours each week, to get the dues from each customer. Along with the barrage of encounters that I met from malicious dogs that roamed the circuit, I eventually became a pretty thick-skinned paperboy. At nine years of age the responsibility prepared me for greater and more challenging dealings in life.

During the month of February, my Dad gave me a ride to the route and was upset as he watched me deliver a paper to my first customer's house. That evening he asked if I would be willing to quit the delivery because of his concern over my safety. I was perfectly willing to oblige him for the easy exit from the risky and unrewarding enterprise.

Most children in those days enjoyed responsibility and were more independent because neighbourhoods were safe and freedom to roam was permitted. Although families were larger and normally households had only one wage earner working, there was balance and less stress imposed unlike today's households' dual income demands and busy schedules conflicting. The doors to homes were always open if help was needed.

Mom was always at home when we came in the door. Dad's income managed to provide for the family and Mom's homemaking was commendable. She kept an orderly and clean home, cooking, baking, sewing, darning and knitting. Whatever it took to keep our growing family fed and clothed she delivered. She was never depressed, seldom temperamental or distracted from her homemaker role. Dad was steady and reliable with his work always admiring our mother and demonstrating openly his affection toward her.

I seldom recall seeing a parent at a school play or children's sports event when I was young. Before I left home, I played hockey, little league baseball, was in Cubs, Air Cadets, and later Sea Cadets, but never did my parents come to observe me once. They had responsibilities and their life was to provide a warm home with love, food on the table and a bed to sleep in, otherwise my responsibility was to grow and be responsible for my own actions.

We lived for just over a year in our Mill Street house until a business opportunity ten miles away from Nelson attracted my parents. They purchased a confectionary, called the 'Welcome Inn.' It had a home attached and they renamed the enterprise 'Bick's Inn' intended to be an opportunity for my mother to assist in bringing extra income into the home while Dad continued at his new job at the International Harvester Truck service outlet in Nelson, called Central Trucking.

The original proprietor of the Welcome Inn was Mrs. Walton, a cranky widow who was moving with her teenage daughter, Twyla to a small house behind the property. She had purchased the business several years prior and after retirement had become bored and a nuisance pestering us with her complaints that we didn't keep quiet enough for her predilection. She wanted peace and quiet and the noise of children at play on the adjacent property to her retirement cabin was a constant annoyance. Her daughter Twyla's fondness of our family further incensed Walton. Twyla left home and moved to Alberta with a boyfriend, abandoning her mother's harrying behaviour toward her and others. Unfortunately, she was killed that same year leaving her mother devastated. Walton became a recluse whom we seldom heard from afterwards.

The store was eleven miles outside of Nelson requiring that John, Sherry and I be bussed to school every day. First, I attended Willow Point School six miles toward Nelson while John and Sherry continued to attend St. Joseph's Academy. Willow Point was a two roomed building adjacent to the lakeshore. It housed six grades, both divided equally. I attended grade four in a class mix with grades five and six. My teacher was Mr. Searle, a stout and mean-spirited man, who had a penchant for corporal punishment.

Each day we'd leave ten-mile for our day at school joining the group of country passengers that rode the bus with us who found purpose in bullying. We were the new arrivals and they didn't feel we deserved to fit in. Twyla Walton, who had just graduated from high school, was seasoned at riding the bus along with the feisty group of students that controlled even the bus driver's behaviour.

I didn't get to share the ride home with Sherry and John as I took a different bus from Willow Point and that experience was a double challenge for me. The bus driver would drop me off about half a mile from our home by a small orchard ripe with apples attracting both deer and black bears. Although the wildlife had earlier been disinterested in me when the fruit was plentiful as the pickings thinned, the black bears would approach to see if I was offering food from my empty lunch kit that contained a leftover odor. The family consisted of a mother and her three cubs of less than a year making for a touchy situation. I was sensible enough to understand how unstable the circumstance was. As my late afternoon departure from the bus would often be accompanied by whistles and jeers from the hardy group of country students seeming to want to excite the bears, their insensitive attitude never did cause a situation. During the same time in history there was tremendous turmoil being broadcast on the airwaves about the bussing issue in the South of the USA. In comparison I experienced my own kind of school bus bullying that was faced by African Americans in Mississippi.

The country school at Willow Point became known for its sinister Halloween Parties. On October 31st, 1955, I attended my one and only Halloween Party at Willow Point. The strange ordeal was run by teacher, Searle and the other teacher at the school. That evening Dad dropped me off at the school on his way into Nelson with Sherry and John going to their planned evening to Trick or Treat in the city. When I arrived at the Willow Point Hall, I was immediately blind folded and shuffled into a corner with a bunch of other classmates who were as mystified as I was over the event. Then, I was led with a couple of the children to a plank that we were told to walk across which was explained to us as being positioned above a bed of hot coals. Our hands were guided over the apparent bed of hot coals and then we were hoisted up on to the plank. Petrified we proceeded left foot in front of right and then right in front of left. We all successfully crossed the plank. Although there likely were no hot coals under what was likely not a plank above ground at all. It was an unusually traumatic exercise for a fourth grader. The evening was not a fun event as we were tormented by 'Sinister Searle' most of the evening.

During the next couple of weeks in school I was issued corporal punishment at least a dozen times. Usually, for not giving the right answer to a question in class. I had been absent from school with bronchitis and the cruel teacher felt he should make an example out of me for getting behind in my work. Instead of using a strap, he would select a willow tree branch and have the toughest sixth graders administer the punishment while he stood by and mocked his victims. Of course, those that administered the willow branch were never to receive the punishment themselves.

I was moving in a lot of pain as I recall and had some pretty severe welts, all up and down my backside from three of the corporal punishment sessions that day. We were warned by the teacher not to discuss what went on in the class with our parents or we would receive more of the same when we returned to class. I intended to be silent about the ordeal in front of my parents. That night when I took my clothes off to put on my pyjamas my brother was horrified to see the lash marks on my backside spread from shoulders to rear. John called in my parents who then extracted an explanation refusing to let me return to the school the next day. I transferred back St. Joseph's in Nelson and afterwards the Willow Point teacher was placed under investigation by the school district and subsequently removed from his teaching position.

Sister Ida Mary McCauley was like an apparition compared to Mr. Searle. Her happy round face and quiet character were such that every boy in fourth grade was fond of her. The nun was particularly kind to me, understanding what I had just been through at Willow Point School. The rest of fourth grade was better than any other previous year and substantially improved my outlook on school.

Chapter Eighteen

From the front of the classroom the nun shouted, "Red light in the sky!" We all bailed from our seats to take cover under our desks while placing hands over our heads remaining in a crouched position. Eventually the teacher advised that all was clear, and we could come out from under our desks. The peculiar exercise was first introduced in Lumby by Mrs. Miller in third grade and came again at least once a week during fifth grade in Nelson. The teacher would close all the window blinds, so that we could not see whatever horrors we were supposed to be protected from. The exercise began during the Korean War which ended in 1953 and some teachers carried it on through the Russian Communist threat. Both exerted their influence on our childhood lives particularly the Cold War as a result of the new nuclear threat. I suppose the drill was a way of protecting our eyes from the explosion of a bomb. I don't imagine there would be any survivors if a person could see the explosion, so the point in the exercise was senseless. Some of the nuns who taught at St. Joseph's were Americans and were more inclined to have the 'Red light in the sky' drills as frequent as fire drills. It was in my sixth grade the routine ended. A degree of uncertainty about my safety and the safety of where we lived was beginning to develop as I'd read news headlines of the day or be told by nuns that war was part of a chastisement that would come if people didn't behave and act as children of God. I presume my feelings were aggravated by my developing insolence making me feel guilty at age eleven over almost everything. The year was 1956.

On February eleventh that year my thirty-four-year old mother gave birth to her last baby, Patrick Gerard, born at Nelson's Kootenay Lake General Hospital. She had been married to Dad for a little more than six years and by then had gone through five full term pregnancies with three of her babies surviving, leaving her and my father with six children. One would think parents were never that busy in that period to find time to mix and have family?

Patrick was named after Mom's brother, but my new baby brother's middle name had a significant meaning. It was attached to our mother's prayer devotions to Saint Gerard, the Patron Saint of distressed mothers. Father Feehan, a Redemptorist Parish Priest for Blessed Sacrament Parish in Nelson, alerted her to the saint's powerful intercessory work before the Lord, particularly for mothers in her circumstance. Apparently, she had expressed some concern to the priest about yet another pregnancy in her troublesome history. The regular intercessory prayer requests that she would make to the saint were pronounced to the family requesting each member unite with her petitions to the saint. She trusted that Saint Gerard would ask the Lord for his heavenly assistance in the health of this baby and her delivery. The prayers seemed to have effect as our mother had the easiest pregnancy and birth and the baby was healthy. Mom was about to turn thirty-three.

After Patrick's birth, Mom was busy operating the store and coffee shop, which required a lot of extra time from her day. Caring for Janice, the new baby, Patrick and four-year old Geoffrey was too much for her. Patrick and Janice were both in diapers. Geoffrey was a complete nuisance to watch over by then and Mom's homemaking was hurried by the Bick's Inn that had a lunch counter. The meal preparation for the odd customer that would come into the struggling business was quite eventful and always occurred when the household and Mom were quite unprepared. The fledgling operation had peak times, namely in July and August when the Kokanee Provincial Campground had visitors. That also coincided with the business season of the Starlight Drive-In across the road from Bick's Inn. On summer evenings the outdoor theatre would bring business right during supper hour up until bedtime. I recall how embarrassed I felt over the uneasiness created in the home when a customer would arrive. I never liked the intrusion on our privacy; however, enjoyed the sweets that Mom would reward us with from her store shelves.

My parents attempted everything to get motorists to stop in to shop or eat. They began to hang or erect signs in front of the business. The billboards had cartoon images with humorous slogans attached to them intended to attract customers and depict the wit of the operators. Nothing worked though, not even Mom's great homemade huckleberry pies and desserts. It was only pocket change that the business earned to supplement our father's income at Central Truck.

The arrival of supplies for restocking the shelves was an interesting event to witness. There was one small supplier that operated in Nelson who offered my parents credit for supplies. I recall the scepticism that surfaced in the family and how distrusting we were over our dad's ability to judge consumer likes and dislikes. With each wholesale order arriving we would hurry to examine the contents of the order disappointed to find most were packaged in quantities of not less than two dozen in the same box with everything from toilet paper to chocolate bars of unpopular brands. The very business Mom was attempting to build, Dad sabotaged with his selection of unpopular cheaper items that were poorly received by the public.

The problem was that Dad's work at Central, located on Front Street in Nelson, was one block away from Malkin's warehouse and that resulted in his doing most of the shopping for the business. He shopped bargain products that no one else, customer or family members included, were interested in consuming. Selections were based solely on price and not consumer preference. The toilet paper was too rough! The jam was always marmalade and the cereal Kellogg's All Bran or Post Grape Nuts. The only consumer that would finish off the last twelve boxes of whatever was left over on the store shelves was dad. He was learning a lot about how the head of the household cannot force undesirable consumer products down the throats of a family that is pre-conditioned to the latest consumables that are advertised to the public through the media. If it didn't have Good Housekeeping's seal of approval it likely wouldn't be easily imposed on the family.

For my part, I discovered a way of swindling my parents out of chocolate bars for a short period of time by agreeing to help Dad finish off a box of Post Grape Nuts, if I would agree to marmalade on my toast for a week, provided I would be allowed to choose a favourite from the confectionary's shelves. It worked for a short time then it ended when they insisted that if I was willing to eat those items with chocolate, I should be willing to eat them without chocolate.

During the summer of 1957, I volunteered during summer vacation to care for the younger set of siblings while Mom looked after the store. By then, Sherry had found work as a sitter in Nelson and she'd leave early in the day with Dad. The work care giving for my three young siblings was a tedious commitment at that age, but I managed to stick with the work for the six-week interval that I agreed to. John was freer spirited and didn't want the extra income the job offered to distract him from his summer break. He liked to taunt me for my choice. The pay was a dollar fifty per day and at the end I had enough money to purchase a bus ticket for travel to the Okanagan.

I decided to visit my grandparents and see Okanagan cousins. It was my first trip away alone. At twelve, the sense of self satisfaction and personal achievement I earned was enjoyed most when I ordered and paid for my first restaurant meal in Penticton. The restaurant was adjacent to the Bus Depot. I had a two-hour layover before the transfer to the Vernon bus. It was an impressive buffet meal, and nobody was there to tell me what I had to eat. For dessert I had cantaloupe with a scoop of ice cream and have enjoyed the dessert ever since. After that trip, during the following summer, John and I collected pop bottles along the highway in order to finance that summer's vacation together. He had shared the experience from his previous summers' successes in bottle collecting that was not so confining for us as my babysitting work. It didn't pay as much but riding my bike and collecting bottles with John was much more enjoyable.

While living at ten mile we were quite accustomed to trekking out on our own where we'd climb the mountainside or go off to other area points of interest. The country home and store were a popular venue for our friends from Nelson to overnight with us and enjoy the liberal assortment of sweets that came from the store shelves. One activity was trekking to Kokanee Park and beach. The beach was quiet with a long sand bar that stretched out into the water allowing us to walk a good distance into the lake. It was a special intrigue when we'd swim, as the glacial waters from Kokanee Creek were warmed on the sandy prominence making the lake's water more bearable.

Joining us on one swim at the park in early August after my return from the Okanagan visit were Phillip and Michael Lindsay, sons of a couple who were close friends of my parents. That swim almost ended in a catastrophe, except for the grace of what I believe was Divine intervention taking place in our lives.

We misjudged the force of the water spilling from Kokanee Creek and three of us were washed off the sandbar into deeper water in the lake. I realized that it was serious after I saw that Phillip and Michael were no longer around me. I ducked under the water to see if they were swimming submerged, when suddenly, I was swept deep below the surface by a powerful undertow current as well. I passed under Michael and viewed upward to see his lifeless body and vacant eyes wide open as he and his brother floated near me. I figured they had drowned already. As I struggled to get to Phillip who was closest to me, the situation was hopeless as I could not swim against the current. Soon, I no longer could see Mike and I feared the worst. I then realized that I could not get to the surface myself, as I was out of breath. Taking in the water, quickly weighed down my body. I was several feet below the surface in dark water struggling with all my effort. In seconds, I stopped struggling, as I was no longer able to fight the current. I was exhausted and had swallowed too much water and felt that I was drowning too.

I lost consciousness. Then, I recall feeling like my head was going to explode, with a horrible headache; I coughed out water from my lungs and stomach and in seconds I was sitting up on the beach and looking at John. Moments afterwards, Phillip and Michael came around spewing-out water beside me.

What had happened? Where was the person(s) that rescued us? John could not answer and stated that he never spoke to them. He just knew that there were two men that had assisted us and brought us to shore. John also stated that he helped rescue Michael but couldn't explain anything else. The three of us were all on the beach, lined up side-by-side, coughing out water, except for John who was flabbergasted along with the rest of us. The predicament he witnessed was incredible! Not a person was anywhere on the beach to attend to us and ensure that we were alright. It was midday in the middle of the week, in a British Columbia Provincial park that seldom had more than a half dozen people present on any weekend, let alone weekday. After assessing the situation and the depth of the water that we were in and distance from shore, none of us could imagine that two men could have had time to rescue three boys and come so far out into the water and do it in the time necessary to succeed. It's hard to explain and continues to amaze us to this day.

The Lindsay's and my parents together ran an ad in the Nelson Daily News for a week, asking those who assisted in saving their sons to come forward so they could be thanked. No one ever came forward.

Sometimes you know when something special has happened in your life. We all knew that that was a very special event and has forever convinced me that the Supernatural does exist and is good.

Late that same summer, my brother and I decided to take a bike ride together with our dog, Ricky. It was our intention to spend the night out camping somewhere as far away from home as we could journey before darkness arrived. After packing some food for meals, blankets for bedding, along with mosquito repellent, toilet paper and a few other essentials, we started out on our ride. The highway from ten mile continued over a hilly landscape as it left our house and wound its way to Balfour. Our Spaniel, Little Ricky followed running behind us the ten miles to the Balfour where we took the Kootenay Lake ferry to Gray Creek. It was getting dark by then, so we only managed a one-mile jaunt up the hill after Crawford Bay where we chose a flat piece of land to set up camp. The trouble was that in our planning we failed to find a camp area near water. We did manage to get a fire built in the night and prepared some grub before rolling ourselves in the blankets from head to toe to be protected from the mosquitoes that were attempting to devour us. Ricky became occupied with some noise in the bush after we retired and disappeared for some time before returning to the campsite. He eventually settled down before the embers in the fire lit between us totally disappeared.

The next morning, we were so frustrated with the mosquitoes and required water, so chose to head home. While making our way back to the ferry we noticed that our dog was beginning to appear lame and falling behind. On investigating the cause, we discovered that he had worn the padding raw on the bottom of his feet. The dog couldn't continue, so we engaged a trucker to assist us by taking our pet back home which the trucker would be passing on his route into Nelson. Later that day when we arrived home, Mom advised that the dog had been taken down the road to the veterinarian to be treated for his paw wounds and was now safe sleeping in the living room with the wounds treated.

A couple of weeks later, I spent time hiking on the hillside with the dog who, seemed to have recovered. We passed time for a couple of hours in the bush across the road from our house, investigating a trail which led to a spot above Kokanee Creek and a favourite bush of wild hazelnuts. Strangely, on our return as I was about to cross the highway, Ricky didn't want to follow me. I thought that it may be his feet that were troubling him again, so lifted and carried him across the road. He was fine as soon as I put him down and didn't seem to have a problem at all with his feet.

The next day I was in Nelson visiting friends and at the end of the day went to my Dad's work to catch a ride home. He informed me that he would be returning to the shop later but wanted to talk to me on the way home about something. It was unusual for Dad to give me a ride and then return to the shop as he usually let me stay at the garage and eat a snack with him while I waited for his extended day to end. He seemed to be having a difficult time saying what he wanted.

"Paul, I have some bad news that I really don't want to have to tell you. Are you ready for me to share it with you?"

"Ah…. Sure, Dad what is it?" I asked.

"Ricky was hit by a truck in front of our house and died a couple of hours ago." The shock left me in tears.

1957-58 was a cold and snowy winter at ten-mile, so cold the West arm of Kootenay Lake froze over making for perfect skating conditions. John and I had the bright idea of loading onto a sleigh an old pot-bellied stove that sat in our yard and then to take it with us to Kokanee Park to warm us while we skated on the frozen lake. The sand bar from where we swam in the summers sheltered the water from the turbulence of the lake's wave action in winter providing a thick cover of ice. We were determined to have the convenience of heat; so, before going off for a skate, pulled the stove on the sleigh a good distance to the park and out onto the ice in order to prepare a fire. It was quite a feat to transport that old stove about three quarters of a mile in winter! We skated off, but on our arrival back at the original location, there was no stove just a hole in the ice. The stove had sunk to the bottom of the lake. It was a pretty entertaining moment for both of us as we stood and laughed at each other over our mistake.

That same winter we encouraged our parents to embark on a new enterprise in the store speculating that if they put a Juke Box and converted a portion of the living quarters into a 'Rock and Roll Room' it would be a terrific venue for teenagers to come, spend money on cokes, etc. and help the struggling business. They reluctantly agreed and talked a Juke Box vendor into the idea, to our delight! It provided free entertainment for the family and any friend that came to visit. I never recall a paying customer coming to compete with us on the dance floor for the hits offered. Unfortunately, it was another worthless enterprise for the confectionary and our parents.

Chapter Nineteen

We all prayed our grace before eating, but seldom did it orally in unison as a family, other than for special occasions. It was customary to bless ourselves with the 'Sign of the Cross' and mouth our own benediction silently before and after meals. Since Lumby there was a plastic napkin holder on the table to remind us to do that. It had become the table's centrepiece having inscribed on it, "Bless us O Lord and these Thy gifts." In addition, the reverse side reminded us to say a thanksgiving after each meal with the inscription, "We give Thee thanks for all Thy food and benefits..." It's a treasure I continue to have in my possession today.

I recall starting my grace before breakfast one morning while distracted by Janice. It was an upsetting moment for me to view my sister's frustration while her mouth reached to contact a piece of toast as she fumbled it in clenched hands that spastically waved the food in front of her contorted face. Janice's body was typical of a severe Cerebral Palsy case. At four she had a tea towel tied around her waist anchoring her in the highchair as her torso flopped around and her arms waved food in front of her mouth. Her clothing was always soaked from drool and food stains and the floor around her was covered with portions of the meal. For the moment all I could think was, "Can't there be some more that I can ask of God than just a blessing for myself and my meal?" By then, Janice's plight was greatly affecting the whole family.

In spring 1958, six months before Janice had turned four, Mom met Mary Murphy, the wife of Doctor William C. Murphy, a Nelson

Chiropractor. Mary had sat in on some of my mother's discussions with other women at Catholic Women's League socials in Nelson and the subject of Janice's condition was brought up, particularly her inability to walk or sit up other than if someone supported her spastic frame. Janice's Cerebral Palsy condition, diagnosed by the family physician, had left her an invalid since her stroke at six weeks. Meanwhile Janice was getting no assistance from area allopathic doctors who recommended that she be institutionalized at the coast for her future care, suggesting that such a facility would alleviate some strain on the family. The suggestion repulsed my parents, so when Mary Murphy, the chiropractor's wife suggested to my parents a chiropractor, Bill Murphy, attend and examine Janice, my parents accepted the invitation.

Murphy described Janice's condition as one that required intensive Chiropractic care and he recommended it be undertaken at a Chiropractic hospital suggesting the Spears Clinic in Denver, Colorado. He advised that that facility had extensive experience with Janice's type of case. Fortunately, after a few adjustments done by Murphy himself, Janice began to respond with less rigidity in her body. It was enough encouragement to give my parents hope that the trip to Denver could be beneficial. Meanwhile Murphy's work allowed Janice to sleep better at nights which was a benefit.

The six hundred bed Spears health facility was founded in 1943 and operated for forty years until the deaths of the brothers who had opened it. The two chiropractors had made the facility known for their successes with medicine's failures utilizing chiropractic programs of care particularly successful with spastic paralysis patients. Spears Hospital's chiropractors gave Janice from fifteen to twenty-four chiropractic adjustments to her spine and cranium daily alleviating her nerve pressure enough that Janice was independently sitting up within days. The hospital released Janice to Murphy's care in Nelson within two weeks.

The cranial moulding techniques that had been pioneered by the Spears brothers were applied around the area of Janice's brain that was flattened from the impact of her apparent fall in Kootenay Lake General Hospital's nursery. She had waited four years before her recovery commenced. Remarkably the hospital waved all the fees for Janice's care as it was customary for the hospital to do a means test for the patients that they admitted. Historically, the generous chiropractic brothers were known to have provided a soup kitchen to hundreds of thousands of visitors to the facility during WWII years and they were continuing their philanthropic ways years later when Janice was helped.

My sister was attempting to pull herself to an upright and standing position within weeks of her return to Nelson. In less than four months of her release from the remarkable facility she was taking her first steps, an obvious contradiction to the medical prognosis.

I had been billeted to Dr. Murphy's home while my parents accompanied Janice to Denver. The rest of the family went to other friends' homes while we all started back to school that September without Mom, Dad and Janice. While staying at the Murphy's, I became so impressed with the young doctor that I decided that someday I, too, wanted to become a Chiropractor. It was a dream that lingered for years afterwards.

Chiropractic is not a treatment. In fact, the profession does not care to use the word treatment in its application, as treatment infers that there is a modification or alteration of what is normal to the patient's body. Treatment is usually given for the purpose of alleviating symptoms, a form of chemical or structural manipulation. Chiropractic utilizes an adjustment or re-alignment of the spine or cranial bones for the purpose of restoring function which allows the inherent recuperative ability within the body to heal. Any reference to spinal manipulation or a forced alteration from the normal is more of a medical term. It's the nerves that transmit the vital, intelligent life force electrical impulses that traverse along the final common pathway of the nerves to tissue cells and the organs to restore health. Growth, respiration, assimilation, circulation, digestion, motor function and temperature along with thought, reason and repair and others need the intelligent life force to make for a healthy and vital life.

The misunderstood profession provided Janice the opportunity to function more normally with what was left of her nervous system after the infant stroke had destroyed thirty percent of her baby brain. After the adjustments she reached her maximum human potential, with the seventy percent of nerve tissue still intact without interference from the effects of damaged cranial bones or misaligned spinal vertebrae occluding the nerve pathways.

There is no doubt, that it was a Chiropractic miracle for Janice. When she returned to Nelson after two weeks, I recall her eating by herself and then beginning to talk on her own while sitting independently and socializing with me for the first time and her own laughter after she began to say her name. "Yah-yah-iss," she'd say. "That's right Janice," we'd encourage while she experimented with her new babyish jabber at four years.

Murphy's chiropractic practice in the community of Nelson was generally respected for its results and professionalism. He was a member of the first graduation class in 1949 at the Canadian Memorial Chiropractic College in Toronto.

He left a Legacy of a daughter and a son-in-law, who are both chiropractors, as well as the Bickert brothers Paul, Patrick and John who all became chiropractors, as a result of chiropractic intervention in our sister, Janice's life.

It seems that the mentally challenged offer so much to the world without any awareness themselves of how much of a gift they are to those around them. They just do well at benefiting others, unaware of their value. I think it's their special circumstance in life that enhances the state of their souls and the closeness that their lives place them to the Divine, by being little ones in our society they do great works. They are not full of themselves or distracted by material conquests and shallow endeavours. They emulate holiness in life. Most are inherently good and grace the world around them. It seems the disabled person's life fosters humility and purity of heart and mind.

Over forty-seven years later, we sat and watched as my sister, Janice at fifty-one years crossed Bernard Avenue as it intersects Richter Street in Kelowna. She moved her spastic frame across the intersection and the light had turned amber before she was halfway through the crosswalk. Her facial muscles were slightly distorted as she watched her caregiver who had already arrived at the other side of the street ahead of her standing on the sidewalk while waiting for Janice to complete her crossing on her own.

My disabled sister finally arrived on the sidewalk from the crossing several seconds after the light had changed to red while cars with impatient operators were passing her, barely giving her room to manoeuvre around them. I was too far away from her or I would have left my vehicle to assist. As Janice followed her caregiver across the next intersection, I realized her right arm with its little hand was extended ahead of her to balance herself as she pushed forward toward her destination. It made me more aware of the effort she made to survive with her disability that remained. "Lord thank you for Janice," I whispered to myself as I contemplated the humble and determined person Janice was in her little frame. Janice as an aging adult woman standing less than five feet tall would find it more difficult to negotiate such tasks than in her past with a left side becoming more rigid with age.

My heart was always full of love for Janice, but more so that day as it overflowed for my sister. At that moment I was compelled to offer the thanksgiving prayer while I sat in my car with my wife, Marlene beside me viewing her. In the seat behind were eighty-four-year old Dr. Bill Murphy and his wife Mary. The two were anxiously awaiting a hastily arranged reunion with Janice that had taken years to occur. The chance encounter of the retired Chiropractor coming to Kelowna for care for his own failing health provided an opportunity for Janice and the Murphy's to meet for the first time in more than forty years. It was a short visit before they travelled back to Nelson from an overnight stay in Kelowna. The moment seemed to cheat Janice who deserved so much more time than she was given that day with the Murphy's. But Janice had her schedule of day programs for the mentally and physically challenged and Murphy's had little time before their bus departed to Nelson.

I had been in Nelson a couple of weeks earlier and dropped by to visit Dr. Bill Murphy and his wife Mary at their home where they announced that they would be taking a bus to Kelowna. It seemed inappropriate for this Chiropractor, who had been my mentor, to be suffering in his own health. At eighty-four he was experiencing intention tremors, characteristic of Parkinson's. Murphy was always an active athletic person from youth well into his old age. Long after I left Nelson, I would hear stories of him climbing up mountainsides with skins on his skis and leading the way ahead of men less than half his age while attempting to get the best out of the rugged hillsides that towered above the narrow valley around Nelson. Murphy was an outdoor and skiing enthusiast. He particularly liked alpine treks with unbroken snow far away from the ski resorts that were overcrowded.

I wanted him to see my sister before he left, fearing that this opportunity would never happen again as the man was now old and frail. I hopped out of my car and moved quickly ahead as Janice was sitting herself down at the bus stop shelter located in front of Kelowna's First United Church on Bernard Avenue.

"Hello Janice, I've got somebody in my car that would like to see you." Janice was startled for a couple of seconds, not expecting to see her big brother during that outing where she had been folding church bulletins as part of her weekly routine.

"Oh, hi Paul." she smiled as she got up and hugged me and then followed me a few steps to the car that I directed her toward.

"Do you remember Dr. Bill Murphy, Janice?" I asked.

"Yes!" She shrilled and pushed me out of the way while simultaneously Mary Murphy peeked out and greeted Janice.

"Hello Janice!" Mary injected.

Janice looked past Mary, wanting to see Dr. Murphy first. I was a little embarrassed for Mary; however, she understood that Dr. Murphy was Janice's hero.

"I remember you Dr. Murphy! You're my Chiropractor," she affirmed."

So, then I understood. Despite the countless number of adjustments that Janice had received from her brothers, John, Patrick and Paul, it didn't matter. Janice's number one Chiropractor was still Dr. Bill Murphy. He was responsible for making the biggest difference in her life and she remembered it and loved him. Janice was four years old then; however, her awareness was enough to recall the change in her physical body that Murphy had made possible and nobody was as important to her at the time. Dr. Murphy was immediately embraced by my little sister. "I love you Dr. Murphy," she said as she kissed him on his right cheek.

The emotional reunion brought tears to everyone's eyes and moved Bill and Mary immensely. I'm certain that they understood how deeply indebted Janice felt toward them. No other patient could express that gratitude more than a person that was as humble and loving as my sister. Bill had saved her life from a much greater disability and the few moments that the Murphy's and Janice had to visit with each other on the city's street corner were well worth the effort. No doubt the encounter emphasized to the aging man what an impact his life's work was and rewarded him enough to satisfy him for the rest of his days. He passed in February 2010, four years later.

That evening after the Murphy's left Kelowna, I recalled the sequence of events around the birth of Janice. The birth announcement was made to the family on the morning she was born, September 8, 1954. It was The Feast Day of the Nativity of the Blessed Virgin Mary; hence, the name given Janice Mary. I had come downstairs in our Mill Street home in Nelson and sat staring at the piano that had been brought to Nelson from Lumby after being shipped from Mom's Marquis home, subsequent to the death of Grandpa LaLonde. I had not practiced my piano lessons the day before and knew that my music teacher would be disappointed. I was supposed to bring my piano book to school that morning and was resenting the responsibility amidst the excitement of the birth of a baby sister.

A babysitter looked after us while mom was in the hospital. It was always customary for my mother to prepare breakfast for the family in the morning and I silently objected to the strange woman in the kitchen. John and Sherry announced the birth to me that morning after I had come downstairs. I suspect they had either heard the news from Dad before he left the house, or it came from the sitter. I voluntarily excluded myself from the excitement, because I was pre-occupied with my impending piano lesson.

It was a frightening moment. I recalled the death of Kathleen Mary, who had died before she came home and the loss of Irvine Joseph before her. Both infants had preceded the birth of Janice and I presume now that then I wanted to protect something inside of me although I should have felt excited about the good news. Although the events of the deaths of my other two siblings seemed distant, I was reminded of feelings that were left behind in Lumby. Janice's birth announcement for a moment brought back sadness from Lumby. Was our new happy home in Nelson going to be a place of sadness again over yet another loss? The feeling lasted only for a few moments, but it is still vivid in my mind today. Then artificially, for the sake of John and Sherry, I began to convert the emotions to excitement while moving over to the dining room table where we all chatted over our morning breakfast. "What is her name going to be? When is she coming home? Can we go and see her? Is Mom going to let us hold her?" I asked as I finally joined in. The rest of the day went better as I began to get caught up in the event.

That morning at school, I made the announcement in a class show and tell session and Sister Mary James, who was a happy and warm nun, pulled me up to her and held my face. "And you're going to be the best big brother, aren't you, Paul?" She gave me a big grin then moved me toward my seat after my announcement. I looked at my friends in the classroom and they were all as excited as I was. What a day! I had good news, and everyone was happy for me. The excitement of a new birth overcame my fears.

After school, when I walked home with John, we hurried a little faster than normal, both expecting something of a surprise when we got home. Although, it was doubtful to us that our mother would be home with our baby sister we did anticipate more news on the event. When we arrived at the side door of the house the sitter was there to greet us with more news. "Her name is Janice Mary," she announced. The name sounded agreeable. It aroused more excitement for the two of us of what this new sister would look like.

"She'll be good looking if she doesn't have a pickle puss like you Paul," John chided. I could hardly wait to see her and laughed at his suggestion.

It was obvious to us that Dad had made the announcement by telephone to the sitter from the shop at the GM dealership where he worked at the time. This was likely done while he checked in on how our little brother Geoff's day was going. Geoff, who was two years, was required to spend the day alone with the sitter. The young Russian lady was a friendly person that seemed to enjoy the responsibility of caring for the family in our mother's absence.

Six weeks later Janice's life was changed forever by a cerebral haemorrhage. I went off to school with John and Sherry and on the walk down the hill we scarcely said a word to one another. Sherry had tears in her eyes and silently sobbed. John and I were hurting as well. We were fully aware how Sherry had mothered her new baby sister during the short interval that Janice was at home. We were mostly the observers as we allowed our big sister to lavish her attention on Janice, as it was special to watch Sherry do that. Now we had doubts that we would ever have Janice home again.

By mid October Nelson was dreary and wet. The narrow valley became quiet when the autumn clouds moved in. The scent of the fallen leaves and the colours remaining on the branches gave one a sense of finality. That autumn did bring a special solemnity to it. Janice did not return home until the snow had fallen. Although she was still a baby to love, we all knew she had changed and so had we.

I often wonder how many others suffered as much as my sister did to change lives around them. For me Janice was the main reason I had become what I was. She always was a model of sainthood in our family and her life graced our lives in ways we probably didn't understand. She was the reason I had become a chiropractor and not just my patients benefited from that work. More important, Janice had added a broader perspective to my faith over the years.

I believe that I've grown to understand the merit in trials and suffering and have been more inclined to place value on these in my life, rather than abhor them. Having shared life in a family with a disabled sister brought perspective to my whole family. It matured all of us.

Janice Mary Bickert (at 62 years)

Dr. W. C. Murphy, Chiropractor

Chapter Twenty

Sometime in autumn 1958, we moved back into Nelson from ten mile. Our household was still a little behind from the struggle of the Bick's Cafe business and the cost of the trip to Denver. Mom and Dad were unable to purchase a house at the time, so we lived in a rental. The first rental house was a relic in such dire need of demolition that we remained in it for just the winter. It was one of Nelson's earliest dwellings situated on the upper side of the four hundred block of Victoria Street, one block above Baker Street, the city's main commercial street.

One hardship for the family was to see our mother find work outside of the home. Just prior to Christmas that year, she was employed at Pierre's Café located in the Greyhound Bus Depot. Although, Dad's income had improved, the sale transaction of the store and home up the lake had not completed. That required a wait for the sale proceeds financially strapping my parents with meeting the mortgage at the ten-mile property while paying rent in Nelson.

The Greyhound Bus Terminal was located just below our rental home separated from the Victoria Street dwelling by a steep Nelson hillside. The restaurant operation had a juke box and soda fountain and served up burgers and light lunches, common for the Fifties, but it did possess a fine dining establishment on the lower level not expected to be domiciled in a bus depot. The top of the Neon sign that sat on the corner of the café below Victoria Street was visible from the living room window. We all felt very short changed and our home life suffered while Mom worked over the Christmas break. She did not arrive until late Christmas Day because of her work catering to restaurant patrons where she worked. Her employer and his wife were well respected by the community and my mother felt the same for them.

Mom usually put those special details on Christmases but had left Dad and Sherry in charge to place their best efforts on the event before she finally made it in the door around seven Christmas night. All day long, I recall looking from behind the Christmas tree out the window to see if Mom was coming up the stairs from Pierre's. We seldom saw her throughout the season while she worked numerous hours to bring in the necessary income to pay for gifts while dad struggled to meet the payments for the two properties. From that moment the decision was made that my own children would never be without their mother in the home convinced that there would always be ample income to prevent that. My father always wanted the same, but his work and circumstance placed that consideration out of his control that year.

In April 1959, my parents found a much better rental for the family at 907 Third Street. It was a large post Victorian home that had several large rooms and a suite attached to the house. While I attended seventh grade that fall at St. Joseph's Academy, my brother John went off to attend St. Louis College in Moose Jaw, Saskatchewan, a private school run by the Redemptorist Fathers, a Roman Catholic religious order of priests and brothers. Sherry was attending LV Roger's High School by then as St. Joseph's had reduced its classes and downscaled to accommodate only grades one to nine.

In those days it was customary for Catholic religious orders to foster vocations to the priesthood in young boys. Families were encouraged to send their sons to these private Junior Seminaries. Daughters were often sent to convent schools to consider becoming nuns. Those schools would give the developing youth a sense of community life in a cloistered type of atmosphere sharing life that religious orders are known for. The schools, no doubt, were also intended to provide a source of income for the congregations of religious.

After the departure of John there was more room, so my parents decided to rent out the extra space. It was first rented to an alcoholic man that frequently relieved himself urinating on the floor when he was too drunk to find the bathroom that was provided for him. The bottles that he emptied would fill his garbage along with beer cans that Mom would empty for him. The substance abuse could have poisoned the reprobate, but he survived long enough to be evicted by my parents. He died from liver cancer shortly after leaving. Later we took in a couple of young spirited bachelors who assimilated well into our family home and remained for almost a year.

In 1958 I had Sr. Fidelus in seventh grade, a tall skinny lady who never smiled. I mistakenly judged the nun as indifferent and cold when I compared her to, Sisters Ida Mary and Callistus, who cared for their students. It was many years later that I was informed that she had left the order to marry. I recall the redness in her face when she would talk to me. It was as if she was ready to explode or needed to let out air.

Shortly after that school term commenced, Uncle Peter Dyck, my grandmother's younger brother, phoned from Lumby about my cousin, Tony. Apparently, Tony was having issues regarding his attendance at the Lumby's Junior High School. My cousin was an intelligent eighth grader, who had a reputation as being disruptive in the school district. In fact, his school days remain a legend in the small community of Lumby. Had his parents not intervened Tony would have succeeded in declaring a coup d'état over the Vernon School District's Lumby Junior High. He was incredibly intelligent, convincing and conniving to the point of his peers joining him to spend weekdays to play hooky in area resorts. His Machiavellian standards of instructive independence were all to the chagrin of the district authorities.

Uncle Peter's call was to ask a favour of my parents, if they would mind taking Tony into our home for the rest of the school term. It wasn't long after Tony's arrival that the pranks started in Nelson. They were nothing other than minor misdemeanours that I willingly joined in. Tony had the wits to get away with almost anything. My parents realized early that Dad's younger cousin was a handful; however, their belief was that most of his escapades were good clean mischief related to skipping classes.

On one school day outing after Tony and I left the house with prepared lunches in hand, while making as if we were going off to class, we instead hitched a ride to Ainsworth, a small town less than thirty miles from Nelson. We were destined for its hot springs and pool that was open year around and was usually patronized in winter months by middle aged Doukhobor couples that frequently came from their farms in the Slocan Valley to bathe. There was leisure time in winter months for them to enjoy the hot springs joining in with area students that skipped class. The Russian sect's contra cultural behaviour approved of student truancy never reporting teens that bathed with them on school days.

After a good day's entertainment at the hot springs we returned that same afternoon expecting to appear as though we had attended class after thumbing a ride back to Nelson with a gentleman who wore a business suit. The man did inquire why we weren't in school that day.

"Well sir, the school boiler burnt out, so the school was closed for the day," replied Tony.

"That's interesting?" He left the conversation with that.

The next morning, Tony and I were summoned by Sister Fidelus to the school principal's office. The Principal announced that she had just received a visit from some authority inquiring about the status of the school's heating system. The nun informed the official that there was nothing wrong with the heating. It took little time before the two school authorities put their heads together to decide who was missing from St. Joe's the day before.

Sister Fidelus reassured the principal that we were good students and followed us back to the classroom with a smirk on her face. 'Good job boys!" She quipped after we were out of hearing range of the principal.

She really did have a sense of humour buried under the stoic look and habit she wore! It was the one and only time I saw her smile all year. I expect that she enjoyed our rebellion, envisioning a little of us in her own insubordination toward the religious life. For me, it was the one redeeming quality I recognized in her, to undo what had transpired earlier between us.

I commenced playing hockey that winter along with Tony who had played the sport before in Lumby. In the beginning teammates mockingly called me "Star." I didn't mind shrugging off their frustration with me. I played the sport until I was seventeen, gradually catching up with the other boys in performance.

It was the end of seventh grade in the summer of 1959, that I was given a paper route by the Nelson Daily News and commenced my deliveries at six each morning, six days a week. After each delivery I served Mass for Father Lange, the Redemptorist priest at Blessed Sacrament Church in Fairview at 7:30 a.m. The popular Redemptorist was particularly impressed with my effort and awarded me the head Knight of the Altar citation for my daily attendance.

Dad was forty that year and in his prime. I recall how good he looked as he'd move around Central Trucks, strong and confident in his position as Service Manager. He was given a substantial increase in income by his employers that year. The partnership was prospering as the fifties ended and Nelson grew in commerce permitting the International Harvester truck dealership to reward its employees accordingly.

John returned to Nelson from St. Louis College at the end of the school term advancing to his tenth grade at L.V. Rogers while Sherry graduated that June and moved to the coast for her nurse's training.

My brother kicked the tar out of me a couple of times to re-establish the pecking order, enough to make me realize it was best for me to find my own friends for awhile.

Chapter Twenty-one

I thank my parents for the sense of pride and confidence instilled in me, but immaturity distorted any ability I had to manage the gift.

It was something they possessed in supervising their home and family that allowed all their children to grow without fear of individual shortcomings. We were quite confident of where we stood.

Some credit must be given to the period and the communities that we were raised that reinforced that development. Freedom from superfluous parental observation allowed us to discover what was best for ourselves through trial and error as corrections mostly came from our peers rather than parents. Being rebuked by friends was much more effective at straightening out one's perspective as it was less complex to understand. Today, it appears as though regimentation and structure stifle youth, while the youth of my day were permitted to roam and interact more; hence, revelation was an automatic part of formation leaving us to experience life independently where we found what gifts we could unearth, consequently fulfilling ourselves.

As I'd wander up and down Nelson's steep hillsides, to and from Baker Street reinforcing my independence from home, I could become self absorbed by my adolescent musings that never amounted to much more than momentary lapses where I'd attempt to figure how to walk without my corduroy pants making a ripping noise between my legs. Experimenting by holding my shanks an extra foot apart, I'd assume a ridiculous stride. Whack! Someone would throw a green unshelled chestnut awakening me, that there were more important things in life than to become self absorbed!

Much of life in those days made people pragmatic. If I departed from my pace toward maturity in the town's small but ever real circumstance, I didn't pause long before a friend, sibling, parent or event prodded me. Then, daydreams were seldom part of adolescence as society expected more from you after childhood. Everyone contributed from youth on.

Psychologists have written volumes about the complexes that develop in individuals who have experienced failure as I had when I was eight. That failure in third grade compelled me toward success in those areas that I knew I had the advantage. I converted the negative and lead physically and socially, first with my peers and then in odd jobs.

By fifteen I became more aware of my father's contribution to my development. He influenced my appreciation of the value of effort when I observed him both at work and home. Before then, Mom was more my role model, I seldom noticed Dad contribute until I worked at more manly tasks.

I always admired his deference toward my mother and the rest of the family. Regardless of what she or his kids dealt him he was never harsh and seldom disagreeable. His only complaint, "That's nonsense," if he was troubled by others. Child, friend, neighbour, co-worker, employer and his children would rarely challenge him, because they did like him.

Mom was more inclined to give lengthy dialogue on matters that concerned her including times she disagreed with him. It was her nature. Unfortunately, I inherited my mother's wordiness and have never acquired the talent, to in a word or two, express myself as my father did. Mom was the only person who'd ever oppose Dad. She expected lengthy deliberation from him as one or two words were seldom enough for her, even though she loved and admired him, his simple, quiet and direct form of communication exasperated her.

What I really found most appealing in my father's life was his ability to work and live so silently, communicating non-verbally through facial expression with little dialogue while he earned respect from everyone.

My attempts at being a better person through the example of my father were beginning to take form as I took notice of where I fell short in life through his model. My behaviour always challenged what I required in myself from my father's example.

Peers had their way of provoking a response in me too, mostly about my conceit. "You're full of shit, Paul!" That's all it took in corrections that were terrifically effective.

Church involvement was part of the contribution that youth of my day made. Catholic boys became altar servers. Girls sang in choirs and assisted with changing altar linens and attire. By fifteen, I began a cleaning enterprise securing a job as the janitor at Blessed Sacrament Church and rectory working for the Redemptorist priests. That work, along with serving Mass, newspaper delivery, hockey and Sea Cadets kept me well occupied aside from school.

I had a wonderful teacher that year, Sister Mary Lourdes, an older woman from whom I received a commendation for perfect attendance. I worked extremely hard to catch up, because her warmth earned my attention and aided in my discovery of some academic prowess.

I joined sea cadets after switching over from Air Cadets which I had first attempted for three months the prior year. The Air Cadet corps handed me drumsticks and required that I rap on a wooden block each Monday night for the duration of the weekly two-hour meeting. At the beginning they promised me a set of drums, but the waiting exasperated me, so I quit. In retrospect, I believe that I was so uncoordinated they saved themselves the agony of listening to my discombobulated clatter. No one attempted to encourage me to stay in Air Cadets.

In Sea Cadets I was happier. It was an all boys' league in those days. Air cadets had a much older group of teens with few young recruits.

The smart looking naval uniform and the reward of attending summer camp at the end of the year were both enticing.

In summer 1960, I went to Vancouver Island's Goose Spit Navy Camp with several other Nelson cadets where I enjoyed one good week out of two at the camp. John worked that summer with Harry King our neighbour from Marquis who had moved by then with his family to Kelowna where Harry and Grace bought a motel. Rodney was John's childhood friend from Marquis, so the summer with a friend was a cheap holiday for John.

Sea Cadet Camp involved daily drills on the parade square, followed by afternoons sailing in two-man dinghies in Georgia Strait. We had one outing on a Navy destroyer. Norm Boulet, who's been a good friend over the years, attended the camp with me. He eventually became a well-known artist with much of his artwork displayed throughout North America in public buildings, including hospitals where the artwork would raise charitable funds for both public or private institutions.

The perfect getaway ended on the afternoon of the eighth day when I fell backward while wrestling with another cadet. Ironically, I slipped on a banana peel, whacking my head on one of the barrack's bunk beds and was knocked out cold. I sustained such a serious concussion sending me to Sick Bay for a week and was apparently comatose. During the unconscious episode Canadian Navy doctors discussed air evacuating me to a Victoria hospital; however, they felt it too risky, so they transported in doctors from Victoria to examine me. Eventually, I regained consciousness by the end of cadet camp and was bussed home to Nelson with the rest of the cadets. For weeks afterwards, I remained quite forgetful while suffering headaches. Eventually the headaches were helped by a couple of adjustments from chiropractor, Dr. Bill Murphy.

After my recovery I resumed my handyman work and the church cleaning work while delivering newspapers. John had returned to Nelson from Saint Louis College in Moose Jaw by then and worked the rest of the summer at a service station but had handled my paper delivery while I was absent.

Entering the Sixties brought change as society transformed with biases being discarded and tradition becoming reformed. It was all on account of a revolution in communications. Canada moved from a closed to open society, all discovered through the medium of television. It entered our homes with images stirring public senses altering lifestyles, thinking, politics and religion. Racism with its televised live news stories of the oppression of the African Americans to the south were telecast simultaneously with other stories of French Canada wanting to be culturally liberated from English Canada. Universally politicians, who in the past hid their impetuous handling of issues, began to carefully deliberate them in front of the visual press. Peace rallies grew as wars became distasteful and the consumerism of the 1960's consumed us.

We were being influenced daily with new products invented and televised in commercials faster than any Industrial Revolution entrepreneurs could dream of. New gadgets and appliances entered our home as convenience and expediency became a matter of necessity. We rushed home to view television after work or school preparing and eating meals instantly served from containers that were taken from freezers and popped into ovens.

How we ate, slept and thought was transforming. Mom and Pop would dress formally for photos in front of each new automatic appliance which replaced the household's manual ones. The kids traded in their single speed bikes for multiple geared models and automobile seating went from bench to bucket eliminating at least one family member from travel. Birth control pills, scorned by the Christian faithful, would eventually be consumed by women to reduce family size and accommodate the Hollywood model of the modern household fitting it into more compact automobiles. Hairdos shagged while clothing was psychedelic, language slanged and even lengthy High Masses sung in Latin on Sundays became low Masses recited in English before the Sixties decade was half over.

I recall Mom selling the family on TV dinners, which appeared at the table one evening as a reheated anaemic display of meat and rubbery vegetable leftovers covered in tinfoil. It was every modern mother's aspiration to disguise leftovers for kids that hated the re-served food. Along with that trend came instant porridge in bags, noodles in boxes, orange juice and milk in cartons replacing bottles. Instant puddings, cocoa, and cake mixes substituted for home baked goods and fried food was now touted as healthier fried in hydrogenated oils. Later we discovered to the contrary that that product hardened arteries at double the pace of animal fats. The TV Dinners were likely my mother's most inglorious moment. Dad's most shameful moment in front of the family came when he appeared out of the bathroom with his eyebrows shaved off. He was so sick and tired of them being full or dirt and grease from work. He overdid it and was carful not to do it again, on account family objections.

During the period, one neighbourhood kid found a reject appliance in someone's garbage bin that provided his household with a form of colour TV, way ahead of the real colour sets ever appearing on the scene in Western Canada. The plastic translucent screen was a lens that sat on the floor in front of the TV and cast a rainbow of colors over the black and white picture tube. It only worked ideally when the black and white television transmitted scenes that otherwise could have been seen in colour as green grass at the bottom of the screen or blue skies at the top of the picture. The colours were always superimposed green on the bottom, pink in the middle and pale blue on top. So, skies appeared blue along with clouds, birds, treetops, ceilings and chandeliers. Floors were always green with shoes, cats, dogs, hamsters and dirt. Faces, shirts, dresses and neckties were fleshy pink. To any serious critic the device was hilarious!

"See you guys, we've got real colour!" The kids pitched to their parents and enthusiastic friends they invited over to view the acquisition. The useless thing was tossed out a couple of weeks later when the mother stumbled vacuuming and knocked it over rupturing the lens.

Jack Parr was on TV hosting a late-night talk show on NBC. He'd demonstrate gadgets like vegetable slicers, transistor radios, household cleaning tools and so on. Most won the approval of his viewers and were added to homes making the device's designers instant millionaires. The viewers were no better off for having purchased the items though.

I never recall my folks ever buying from television. I would wait until I was sixty, to one day attempt that, being conned twice by infomercial hucksters who came to television, on a regular basis, long after Jack Parr did. Never again! When those infomercial guys have your credit card number, they're always sending you stuff and billing it on your card forever after. The only escape is to cancel the card or to be the author of your own funeral.

Dad seldom ever bought anything from stores other than tools for his work. He once splurged and bought a fancy German made Loeve Opta stereo. It was the finest Jack Parr recommended. The machine lasted in the Nelson appliance store less than a week after my father spotted it and he couldn't resist! He made the family so proud of his purchase. And then, out of Mechanics Illustrated Magazine he purchased a membership in the Columbia Records Club, an organization that pestered its membership to pay for at least one new stereo vinyl recording, of course for double regular retail price, each month. My dad purchased the six that came with the initial order and then pleaded 'temporary insanity' or something of the sort, to get out of ordering any more. He seemed to have a knack for getting rid of nuisance mail. I discovered years afterwards that the Columbia Record Club was not a division of Columbia at all. It only purchased discontinued catalogue recordings from the manufacturer at a discount and sold off the product at full retail to its club members. Occasionally, the record club would offer a current album as an enticement to joining the organization. Anyway, thereafter my dad only ever played the half dozen or so albums he purchased from the mail order company. The rest of the time the kids of the household monopolized the stereo.

The fifties provided Kootenay community residents some of the best senior league hockey in the world. The Western International Hockey League (WIHL) could even impress NHL players who would visit Nelson's Summer Hockey School annually where they'd train promising hockey youth in the community. In those days, the six WIHL Kootenay franchises were extremely competitive as an over abundance of amply qualified candidates for an annual National Hockey League draft would end up in farm teams or with the WIHL. When the NHL expansion finally occurred, it swallowed up the profusion of hockey's best talent including players from the Nelson Maple Leafs and the Trail Smoke Eaters, two of the best in the world's amateur leagues.

I would lie on my bed listening to road games of the Leafs as my idolized home team would battle it out with the arch rival, Smoke Eaters in Trail. Otherwise, I'd faithfully attend all the home games with the majority of the town's youth.

In the daytime my favourite television show was Dick Clark's American Bandstand. It featured anything teens ever needed to know about Rock and Roll's popular scene along with its artists' live appearances. Any new record I acquired was worn out within weeks on Dad's Loeve Opta. He'd never object to the use of it. Rock and Roll was like a religion to youth in my day. The music would capture every emotion. Like art was always capable of doing, it transformed our society in the Fifties and Sixties with its trends and attitudes.

My mother would spend each Saturday from three until five with Dad grocery shopping. Ours was always the fullest fridge in the neighbourhood. Each grocery shopping ritual would provide at least a dozen large paper bags loaded with food and sundry items purchased for the grand total of thirty-nine Canadian dollars. That was enough to provide a family of eight ample supplies for a week in those days.

Mom was a great cook, until she would ritualistically deviate in her food preparation. Saint Patrick's Day was one of those occasions when we'd be surprised. If you didn't get green dyed tuna fish sandwiches, you got clover leaf shaped iced sugar cookies and a bottle of green lime Kool Aid. The drink would leak all over our lunch bags along with the rest of the lunches that sat on a shelf at the back of the classroom providing the whole class with green soggy lunches. At Christmas you could be certain to have rum balls, plum pudding, fruit cakes or shortbread in your school lunch. We were always well fed and sweetened up.

Dad's contribution to the evening meal was doing the dishes. On Sundays, after church, he'd cook breakfast. The routine was never broken. On weekday mornings he'd rise early, and I'd have a bowl of cereal or toast with him and then go out to do my papers. Oh yes, that's when I was introduced to grapefruit. I ate the half slice he'd hand me, obligingly. I eventually began to like it. He would always read the same Popular Mechanic magazine each morning awaiting the next edition. Occasionally, I'd bring home an extra Nelson Daily News and he'd exchange for that.

By autumn 1960, I commenced selling newspapers at the toll station entrance to the Nelson Bridge. That replaced my North Shore delivery route after I succeeded in convincing the newspaper circulation manager on the idea that the paper route was superfluous and a sales location at the bridge entrance would make more sense. This continued with my handyman work that resulted from placing ads in the newspaper, "Handyman Will Perform Odd Jobs." The phone rang frequently with requests for my help. I even put in a concrete sidewalk that year and was hired on part time by a commercial cleaner, operated by a cantankerous Dutchman. By then I was a healthy one hundred and sixty-three pounds, standing five foot nine inches.

The commercial cleaner's erratic behaviour and poor command of the English language were enough to eventually discourage me from continuing my work with him. I went back out on my own again, but not before performing some incredible cleaning work for the European immigrant who seemed to always be a little annoyed at me for taking business away from him through the newspaper ads that advertised my own enterprise. I recall one cleaning job that he assigned me to, cleaning windows on Nelson's Hume Hotel, which today still stands on the corner of Ward and Vernon. Friends suggested that hiring his competitor may have been his intention to see me killed on the job. The Ward Street side of the building was hilly, so placing a thirty-foot extension ladder to clean windows on the Third-floor suites was a perilous endeavour. I would get distracted during the cleaning by some passers-by and the ladder would begin to slip along the building and leave me dangling with my hands grappling at adjacent window ledges to prevent myself from falling to the ground. More than a couple of times during the job I had an audience of friends below, placing wagers that I wouldn't make it through the week before I would be hospitalized again. "Bickert, you're a goner," remarked a friend and then he proceeded to place bets with friends on my future.

One day I was asked to clean out a couple of motel units at the Bluebird Motel. The unit had been rented by people that left it in disarray and filthy. I engaged my brother John to assist with the cleaning responsibility which was contracted by the commercial immigrant. John had the bright idea that we should use ammonia for oven cleaner insisting on placing the ammonia in a pot and turning the oven on to boil the cleaner in the pot, surmising that the steam would loosen the oven grit. It seemed plausible to me. Surprisingly, when he turned the oven on it was necessary to evacuate the building for the rest of the day because of the fumes. Paradoxically, our employer was more annoyed at me for using up all of the ammonia than he was for the salary we collected for the additional hours we spent sitting on the lawn outside the motel, while airing the fumes out of the room.

Eventually, the Dutchman and I had a major disagreement. The week before the upset he drove me to a house where he wanted me to spend the week weeding and cleaning overgrown shrubs out of beds that were left unattended by the property's owners. When my boss went to collect from the homeowners, he discovered that he had sent me to the wrong house. Since he was never paid for the job, he told me that he wouldn't pay me for the weeks work. I quit and that was the end of my relationship with the cleaner.

In retrospect, the man's most redeeming quality was that he provided a good service at a fair price to all his customers. I could only reason at the time that his disagreeable disposition was because my own enterprise was taking what little business away from him the small city could provide to support his household and not because I fell short in my work effort. Much later, I realized that I likely overvalued my work as do most young people.

In spring of 1961, I was in ninth grade and during my second year in cadets I faced another embarrassing ordeal. I had been sick and hospitalized for three weeks with double pneumonia at a critical time during the cadet training. The league was studying sonar and mapping techniques which were necessary requisites for promotion to Seaman First Class. I was not prepared for the exam as I had missed the required preparation during my illness and was mostly occupied with catching up in my schoolwork. Unfortunately, I failed the sonar and mapping exam. The failure was not announced until the stripes and awards were handed out to every other cadet except me. Again, I felt the hurt of the failure. I had succeeded in everything else that year but had failed in what was most important for me.

I used to experience a reoccurring dream of running as hard as I could. I was either chasing or being chased by someone or something. First, I recall chasing my brother John through wheat fields to the dugout pond that was located a few hundred feet from our Marquis farmhouse. No matter how hard I ran, I couldn't catch him. I dreamed at night where I'd be out of breath attempting to catch up and was behind no matter how hard I tried to keep pace behind him. I expect there was something more to the dream than just that frustration. I'd always awake breathing hard feeling my heart racing. Much later in life in other dreams John was replaced by another figure. When I was eight it was my teacher who wanted me to keep up in class and then later another teacher would have me read without taking breaths. At fourteen, I was rushing to the confessional and there I'd find Monsignor Monaghan had left before I had confessed. At twenty-one, I dreamt I missed my wedding ceremony and at twenty-nine, just as had happened at eighteen, I had missed chiropractic exams. Always in the day, I'd run as hard as I could, but failed to keep step while dreaming at night. What was it about my makeup that while I slept, I ran rather than rested and while awake running as fast I could, never produced satisfaction for my sleep?

I don't recall when the dreams finally left; however, I expect that it was when I stopped attempting to be who I wasn't or then it could have been, when I stopped attempting to impress who I couldn't. I always went as fast as my will and legs would carry me in life but never satisfied my dreams. I expect that I had subconsciously run life's course as a series of races from youth until old age attempting to satisfy mentors, employers, teachers, confessors and vanity, because I could not satisfy myself until I won. Failures were too painful.

That was the last year that I attended Sea Cadets and St. Joseph's School. I was about to go off to Edmonton for tenth grade in September. The bitterness of the Sea Cadet ordeal was enough to drive home to me that failure could only be measured in degrees of pain. Experiencing it in my Latin class and then socially in the cadet corps was numbing. Whatever character that was built by it was not understood until years later.

The Franciscans Friars of Western Canada accepted me for tenth grade at Saint Anthony's College, their all boys' boarding school in Edmonton. Attending that school would be a pivotal point in my life. After leaving home I would discover what I really was called to be. Saint Francis of Assisi, the young saint who changed the Church in twelfth century would have a degree of influence on me while his friars taught more of the real manhood I required.

Chapter Twenty-two

By the mid Nineteen Fifties, cartoonist, Walt Disney had a couple regular shows on television. One was Wonderful World of Disney and the other, The Mickey Mouse Club. Simultaneously, on swamplands in the countryside outside of sprawling Los Angeles, images of an incredible fantasy were physically taking shape, Disneyland, his dream, was under construction. The metropolitan area had grown to have more automobiles within its city limits than all of Canada's vehicles combined.

Interstate highways were constructed to accommodate the modernized American family which toured more than the rest of the world travelling in large automobiles possessing broad bench seats suitably accommodating families of the day. The renowned cartoonist had judged the American hunger for theme park holidays long before anyone else conceived of them. He had found the perfect medium to advertise his newest investment, on his own television shows. At Disneyland a family of six could spend the whole day for less the five dollars including eating, refreshments and admission. I wouldn't get to visit the theme park until it cost a hundred and fifty dollars a day to take the five of us. Today a family will spend close to a thousand dollars a day.

At home in Nelson we were isolated by poor roads, mountain ranges and few television sets that delivered a selection of just three Spokane network stations. America was already boasting of more television sets in each household than bathtubs while Canada still hadn't finished installing bathtubs in most houses.

There's a special sentiment that surfaces in my mind going back to our family of eight travelling off for short vacations to visit Okanagan relatives. It's a combination of feelings from my earlier childhood living in Lumby mixed with the warmth I sense for my grandparents, cousins and other relatives or friends who lived in and around Vernon. The large Oldsmobile had been sold to facilitate the budget. Despite the crowded replacement vehicle's ride, there was generally a relaxed form of cramped family closeness enjoyed in the small foreign vehicle as we ventured out contorting, complaining or outright fighting on route over British Columbia's substandard Interior roads and passes.

Travel was limited for us in the Fifties. Our household, like most of the day, was on a tight budget and it was even more difficult to fit our family into a vehicle. Ours had six children compared to that day's four child average. Dad's British made Austin would ideally transport four occupants, not the eight of us, but we did manage some short excursions on long weekends to see Okanagan relatives. My father's annual two weeks' paid vacation, as reward for his five-and-a-half-day workweek, was frequently not taken but surrendered in lieu of collecting an extra paycheque for the year's work. In 1957 he traded Grandpa LaLonde's 1953 88 Olds on a 1949 A40 model Austin, England's contribution to the Post War family. The extra cash left from the trade provided my parents with a much-needed financial boost.

For a few years we enjoyed the large American automobile dream of the Fifties in the inherited 1953 88 Oldsmobile. It was nearly the industry's best and had all the attributes of the period's fast cars featuring a General Motors 'Four Power Package,' consisting of power steering, brakes and styling. Whatever that fourth referred to, I suspect it was the Rocket 88 V8 engine.

Everything needed to be fast to impress while rockets were being blasted out from every continent by the world's military powers compelling the automobile manufacturers to advertise and name their products so for improved sales. Cadillac had a Hydra-mastic transmission, Chrysler the push button transmission and Ford the Comet. But at one hundred and ten miles an hour our dad would demonstrate to John and me that he could take his Rocket from nine mile to eight-mile on Nelson's North Shore in forty seconds a feat no other dad could achieve. It was the one bit of insanity our dad possessed, his 'lead foot,' on the accelerator. Never mind the widow and four other siblings he'd leave without a dollar's insurance should a fatal accident occur. He required this of his sons, to enjoy the experience with him and he did it on a few occasions to prove the point. I'm certain that if my father's own Catholic confessions to the town's pastors consisted of a sole expiation, that would regard his speeding habit, his only evident weakness outside of tobacco which was a social fault and as I expect, not a sin.

The automobile manufacturers didn't install seat belts, so, the cars and people were likely thought to be indestructible. Fewer vehicles were on Canada's highways; hence, menacing vehicle accidents were rare enough to go unnoticed. If the Russians didn't nuke us with a surprise attack and 2-4 D didn't wipe us out by polluting our rivers and streams then Dad could have, with his roll your own cigarettes or the penchant he had for speed. The joy of speed for Dad finally rested as the frugal budget measures brought our father to his senses. The Olds was traded for the A49 Austin and John and I were humiliated along with our father who, until that day in 1957, had only two ounces of pride remaining, his 88 Oldsmobile and his attractive wife.

Subsequently, treks to the Okanagan were made in three different series Austins from 1949 and 1957 until 1965, as he continued to trade to larger and newer model Austins accommodating for the growth of the family's expanding rear ends. There seemed to be an abundance of those cheap foreign vehicles on used car lots and afterwards dad could afford the small amount required to upgrade from the cheapest that he first acquired, the A40 Austin, then an A50, finally culminating in a near new A90 Austin. By then we were nearly fully developed and the extra room made little difference. Travel was always confined to Easter weekends when my parents preferred to enjoy a spring break-out ritual more common when the family was younger, and we could all squeeze into the vehicles.

Most frequently we used a route that went south of Nelson to the Washington State towns of Metaline Falls and Colville. It entered back into Canada outside of Grand Forks near Christina Lake.

The trip was shortened when in 1962 the Blueberry-Paulson Highway opened between Castlegar and Christina Lake knocking another two hours off the drive. That eliminated the need to drive the Cascade route, a horrific gravel road that wound over treacherous canyons and steep passes which was usually avoided. The few times that we did use the Cascade highway, I hated it. In those years, the alternate Monashee route was equally dangerous. Mom's prairie roots left her cowering in the vehicle on any mountain passes bringing strong objection to my father's suggestion that we take either of those highways.

Although I looked forward to the periodic family visit to our grandparents' home in Vernon, I never really relished the nine-or-ten- hour drive over the infrequently serviced gravelled highways that connected the Interior cities of Nelson and Vernon. I recall when delivering newspapers reading reports of whole families being wiped out in motor vehicle mishaps that would usually involve a logging truck or some large tractor trailer unit running into a carload of vacationing family members sending them plunging over the edge of a cliff to their deaths.

Those memories of five of the six siblings piled two-deep, across the back seat, squirming and elbowing our way through the length of the round-trip journey are very vivid. The windows were shut tight to prevent one of the younger ones from falling out or developing earaches from the wind. Each roundtrip tour to Vernon consumed the better part of each long weekend leaving little time to visit at our destination.

The travel was more difficult for Mom who would spend most of the night before departures preparing and packing. Exhausted the day of travel she was usually a little cantankerous and Dad would endure the brunt of it. This seemed to be the time that the worst of my mother's disposition would show. Poor Dad, driving his family through treacherous passes and having to cope with my mother's litany of complaints over blunders made during the course of his married life, all as a result of his failing to load a box of sandwiches she had made during her trip preparation. I can't imagine a worse time to pick on the man, but that was Mom's moment to unload her cannons for his shortcomings; notwithstanding, the fact she risked sending the family over a cliff for a moment of domestic victory that resulted from Dad's inability to communicate. Somewhere between Lumby and when I turned a teen Blessed Mary's Rosary, the weapon against Satin's furor, had been forgotten and traded for Mom's need to put my father down and feel triumphant for doing so.

What was amazing was the patience of our big sister, Sherry, who would be the only other victim in the family, sustaining more a form of physical injury during the trips she made in back seat. The load of younger siblings that she carried on her knees was laughed off with her jovial attitude.

Travelling the roads with the vehicle's dense smoke provided by both Mom and Dad chain smoking their roll-your-own cigarettes would be considered abusive today. The haze would billow through the stuffy vehicle mixed with road dust pouring in through vents left open as a gesture of sympathy for the non-smokers.

Sherry, who graced every trip, had the ability to calm her younger siblings with choruses of "Row, Row, Row Your Boat Gently Down the Stream," alternating with her screechy soprano rendition of "Early One, Morning Just as the Sun was Rising." We'd all join our sister's concert; however, eventually to be silenced when Dad had had enough of the performance suffering sore ears from Mom's earlier protest. He'd whistle a melodic tune of his own quieting the family and likely to defy Mom's scolding.

My big sister would balance Geoff on one knee and after the singing and dad's whistling ceased would have a Hardy Boys or Nancy Drew novel on the other knee to read orally, chapter upon chapter entertaining her restless companions from the back seat. That's when John and I would shuffle Janice or Patrick between us to keep Sherry reading. The vehicle would stop, only when one of the passengers detected a sickening sweet odour that emitted from either young Janice or Patrick's soiled diapers, made of cloth and not disposable in those days. On that signal Dad would stop driving and vacate the car, then load the corner of his mouth with some chewing tobacco, posture a grin and lean against the back fender of the Austin while watching the rest of the kids head a good distance down the road to answer their individual calls to nature. After a twenty-minute break, which would occur at various points along the route, we would eventually be encouraged back into the car as Dad threatened us, by slowly rolling the vehicle ahead toward Vernon, alerting stragglers that he meant business and was on his way. Mom had no reprieve on the road which could have added to her cranky disposition at the time. She changed the diaper silently and stayed in the car. Perhaps it was a demonstration that she was still annoyed with him or she was merely upholding some other feminine call to modesty with the absence of facilities in the mountains. Half a day's drive and she had vented all her hostility renewing herself with normalized conversation before we'd enter the Okanagan.

I have always felt a mixed home allegiance between the Okanagan and the Kootenays. The openness of the desert valley, bordered by the green irrigated landscapes closer to the lakeshores, offered familiar orchard and lake aromas in sharp contrast to the refreshing cedar and spruce aromatic Kootenays which display lush foliage and dark forests.

The trip along the lakeside, just before approaching Peachland from the south, was always exciting as we'd work our way toward the ferry that crossed the lake to Kelowna. I recall that the road at Peachland was lower in those years, just a foot or two above Okanagan Lake. On one occasion, there was a storm over the lake, stirring up waves that washed across the highway when we travelled south of Peachland. There was a line of cars slowly passing through the water from waves that submerged the road. Eventually, the road was built high enough above the lake and waves never washed over it again.

Prior to the building of Okanagan Lake Bridge in 1959, Kelowna was the smallest of the three Okanagan cities, having a population of eight thousand residents. Penticton was the largest with about eleven thousand and Vernon had about nine thousand inhabitants. The most popular tourist town in the fifties was Penticton, with its beaches on both sides of that city, making both Skaha and Okanagan lakes popular beach areas for tourists.

In those days none of today's Kelowna existed between what is known as Gordon Road to the upper part of Highway 33, where there existed a convenience store and post office outlet. Otherwise, the area from Highway 33 to Gordon Road was strictly inhabited by farms and orchards during the fifties. Some were tobacco farms.

I recall, as we approached the Kelowna airfield then, that there were a number of B-12 bombers, relics from World War II, mothballed on a field that subsequently Kelowna's Flightcraft Industries occupied. It was entertaining to see those huge aircraft left as a reminder to passers by that a war had recently ended. The airfield had no commercial flights operating at that time but was utilized for private aircraft. Vernon's airfield also stored a few larger military aircraft in those days.

The trip to the Okanagan in the summer of 1961 was the last trip with Sherry. She went on to Vancouver that autumn for her nurse's training. John enlisted with the Royal Canadian Navy and the next summer I was off to Edmonton to school.

Chapter Twenty-three

I would seldom enjoy early morning rising for my newspaper sales; however, I always got caught up in a mood, being mesmerized by the early dawn's metamorphosis that occurred each day in the small community of Nelson while it came to life. Then, at 5:30 in the morning, five days a week, Dad would wake me and often go back to bed for an hour before his own day needed to begin. I couldn't seem to rise on my own, but having Dad get out of bed made me responsive to the call, respecting that I was the cause of his losing sleep on my account. I would leave the house fifteen minutes later after giving some affection to Sambo, a black Cocker Spaniel Lab mix, given to me by a newspaper customer when the dog was a puppy. Sambo would gesture a token lift of the head and tail, then flop back down to sleep.

A bundle of thirty newspapers was always waiting for me over the fence on the bridge approach in a service shed which stood a hundred and fifty feet from our home's back yard on Third Street. We were living there when I first commenced my paper route that involved the delivery along two miles of the North Shore, across the bridge. In winter months it was always cold and damp near the lakeshore, but in summers the rising sun coming over the cascading mountains was beautiful with the air warm and fresh. The bridge replaced the ferry in November 1957. More traffic crossed it in summers as some Nelson residents, fortunate enough to have summer homes down the lake, would commute to work along with tourist traffic travelling the route. In 1959 I began selling papers on the bridge rather than delivering them to homes along the North Shore.

The first motorists were usually those arriving to work at McGavin's, a bakery located a block from where I stood a few feet from the bridge's toll station selling the newspapers. The bakery employees were the reason for the earlier rising for the paper sales. After the bakery workers day workers arrived for shift change at Kootenay Forest Products, a sawmill that operated then between Radio Avenue and Bealby Point Road, now replaced by a residential neighbourhood. The McGavin's Bakery was a large commercial outlet supplying bread to the Kootenay communities. My regular customers would never visit but make a quick stop to hand me a quarter for the paper and then drive off. After our move to Chatham Street, I rode my bike to the bridge toll station each day to resume my newspaper sales.

To entertain myself between sales, you'd find me performing from my location the "Top Parade of Hits" singing aloud each popular youth recording artist of the day entertaining passing customers and the toll both operators. I was likely heard by everyone in the neighbourhood while I sang those early mornings, but I didn't care. I was happy! When not singing aloud I would mimic news reporters, reading the news headlines and stories from the papers I was holding. Traffic was never that heavy. In fact, seldom were there more than three or four cars crossing the bridge during any given minute of the morning's rush hour. I had plenty of time to perform my repertoire.

"Nelson Daily News!"

I hollered at an unfamiliar passing motorist, from a sign fastened to a large truck tire and wheel that I stood on. The tires and signs had been positioned facing city bound traffic coming through the toll booth on the bridge approach. I selected one as my only protection from being hit by the motorists passing me on either side moving in both directions in and out of Nelson.

An automobile coming into Nelson braked and then backed up. The driver, a middle-aged man, poked his head out of the window and asked for directions to Blessed Sacrament Catholic Church. I told him that I would be leaving for there in half an hour, because I was an altar server at morning Mass and then I directed him to the Church.

"704 Fourth Street! You'll need to turn left at the Dairy Queen just

ahead. Can I sell you a paper too? That's what I do here?" I asked before he drove off.

"I'm sorry! Yes, I'll take one," he said as he handed me a dollar. "Oh, keep it!" He was a tourist and didn't expect any change, I calculated. Tourists always tipped.

"Where are you from?" I asked.

"Edmonton, I'm a Franciscan priest, Father Anthony Sebastian," he introduced himself.

"Oh, you're the priest that is interviewing me this afternoon for Saint. Anthony's College! I'm Paul Bickert, Father Anthony."

"It's nice to meet you, Paul. You have quite an enterprise here. I can tell you're a salesman and I like to see that. Talk to you later," he injected, after pulling his hand in from the handshake to check his rear- view mirror. He drove off to make way for two other vehicles lining up behind him for the newspaper.

It was in mid August during the summer of '61 and the arrival of the Franciscan Friar in Nelson made me a little nervous. I had already been approached by the Redemptorists to attend their Holy Redeemer Junior Seminary in Edmonton, but Father Lange, the resident Pastor of Blessed Sacrament Church, had told me that my failure in Latin, that school term, would put me on probation during the first three months at their school, so he suggested that I attempt admission to the Franciscan school that was more lenient. I immediately forgot my singing that morning and began to rehearse lines for the interview that I fretted about.

I had convinced my parents that I should be given the same opportunity to attend a school, away from Nelson, as my brother John had experienced and that I may be priestly material as well. John's academic record was better than mine, though.

Viewing photographs of John at St. Louis' College and then later hearing that he was then navigating foreign seaports was enough to convince me that I needed adventure too. My parents bought my convincing arguments and again were prepared to suffer through another year's tuition costs, while I obliged the Roman Catholic son role. answering a possible call from God to join the priesthood. Saint Anthony's and the Franciscans would now get to test that conviction, because the interview went well, and Father Anthony asked if I would come to Edmonton in two weeks for tenth grade. He liked that I played hockey and was a regular morning Mass altar server.

"You like to get out of bed in the morning and we Franciscans are early risers, Paul," said the Franciscan, as he handed me a brochure with a photo of the school on the front page. "Can I come over and meet your parents this evening, Paul?"

My adolescence was enough to temper my enthusiasm for Christ but not totally discourage it. Mass in the mornings was my way of saying to Christ that I had time for Him.

I was no different than most teenage boys, for the most part having little more than a scanty intellectual approach to my faith which lacked any real interior epiphany. Boys' faith at that age was mostly obscured by enthusiasm for sports and peer recognition, not unlike today, intrigued by what I was taught. Prayer was reserved for moments of worry or guilt. As for attendance at daily Mass, it was for accolades that I received from the priests I served, who were usually stellar role models and I enjoyed their recognition. After all, priests were special all through my childhood. Some of the exercises were beginning to impress me though. I was reminded of a special gift after nearly losing my life drowning at Kokanee Park beach.

I understood that my plan to leave home and live with the Franciscans in Edmonton may be overbearing and a burden to my parents, but I couldn't stop myself from it as something was driving me from inside. It was something I found necessary to follow, even though it was at the expense of what I felt was cheating myself of a life at home and ultimately shortchanging those closest to me.

Emotions began to take hold and for several days before my departure Mom and Dad's example, as honest hard-working people, living honourable, simple lives and imparting a real value system meant more than before to me. The fact that I was feeling compelled by an extravagant adventure made me resentful for the moment, but I had decided to leave home and my parents approved of it. Knowing what I realized later, about the importance of heading a family, it was likely a poor choice on my part; however, the compulsion to leave was likely a calling of sorts of just adventurism and I responded to it.

My father and mother stood by me when I boarded the bus. Dad grabbed my shoulder and within the shallow lines on his face smiled. I felt his love embrace me. Mom did that physically and with teary eyes.

When I climbed on the Greyhound bus at sixteen, I looked out the window and realized how endeared I was to my parents. Dad was forty-two and Mom thirty-nine. I was beginning to discover a new meaning to family and the value of good parents, enlightened on the day of my departure. The moment was enough to make me secure that home would always be a good place to return; however, not realizing how lonely I would be away from it or that I would spend little time at home again.

Chapter Twenty-four

Being greeted by two Franciscan Friars, after I climbed off the bus in Edmonton, was an uncomfortable reminder of the life I would be leading for the school term. I blamed my Catholic family heritage for my becoming attached to an order of religious mendicants who awaited my arrival at Edmonton's bus depot wearing bare footed sandals and clothed in twelfth century brown tunics.

"They looked strange to me in the crowd of onlookers awaiting passengers disembarking buses! Father Anthony's visit in Nelson was in street clothes, much less conspicuous to contemporary teenagers he was removing from British Columbia," I protested to myself.

I had never seen a Franciscan in full friar attire, except Brother John in the Robin Hood television series! Not only did I feel uncomfortable at the train station standing by these men, I wanted to move away from them.

I was surprised and chilled that the late summer air could be so cold in Alberta's capital city. British Columbia's winter equivalent had already arrived in Edmonton and when every tree should still be green, Edmonton's had already shed their leaves by that August's end.

It was obvious, that my order from the Eaton's catalogue of a trendy corduroy coat, off the backside of a catalogue model would be dreadfully inadequate for Edmonton's climate and it would be necessary to make a plea to my parents to spend more money on another coat in spite of

Mom's protest that the garment I had selected would be a little light for a Prairie winter. Her warning went ignored when I was given the liberty to purchase the garment along with socks, underwear, pants and a couple of shirts for my academic excursion to Canada's northernmost capital city.

"Welcome to Edmonton the land of the hardy, Paul," joked, Father Anthony.

Accompanying me in the back seat of the vehicle were two other boys who had arrived at Edmonton's bus depot coinciding with my arrival. They were both Southern Alberta farm boys and both smelled like they wore a peculiar brand of cologne. I would discover later that it wasn't cologne at all, it was Lifebuoy soap. Every Alberta farm boy used it during that period.

As we approached the structure at 6770-129th Avenue, I recognized the building from the photo on the St. Anthony's College brochure that had been given to me earlier that month in Nelson.

By the time of our arrival at the friary's school, I had grown more comfortable with my decision to attend. Father Anthony was humorous, and his mannerism warmed me to what was behind the habit he wore that day. The two fellows I was with in the back seat were full of talk about hockey season but didn't offer anything other than that to the drive's conversation.

"Yep, I play hockey." I volunteered

"Nope, I've never played basketball," I answered them and that seemed to end the attention the two gave me for the rest of that afternoon and the rest of the school term.

In the front wall of the brick building stood a statue of Saint Anthony, the youthful twelfth century priest of Padua, who changed his secular Roman collar to follow Assisi's Francis. I was directed to the third-floor dormitory by Father Anthony. He was definitely a St. Anthony look alike.

The large room was full of lockers and cots to accommodate the ninety or so students that would attend that school term. "You can have the pick of almost any bed and locker you choose." Father Anthony instructed. There were two other students that were present for the three of us to talk to as we unpacked. One was Steve Serenas, who arrived from Drayton Valley that morning. He would be attending tenth grade with me. Steve became a best friend that year as his friendship quickly warmed the strange surroundings for me.

As we headed down the stairs a handsome young Friar with a full head of dark brown hair greeted us. Father David Crosbie, the school's prefect, was described to us later that day as a hockey player who jilted the National Hockey League's Chicago Black Hawks that had attempted to draft him. He advised Black Hawk management that he had decided to become a priest. He would coach both the junior hockey and football teams that year at Saint Anthony's.

"What's he doing in here? He could have any woman he wanted," Serenas irreverently objected.

I had never had a friend that was as impressed as Steve by girls. I guess his hormones had kicked in earlier than mine, but that day his remarks were arousing an interest in me, that I should be noticing girls more, too. "So, why was I here?" I asked myself again.

Edmonton's streets were full of leaves blowing around along with dirt from the open field, planted with potatoes behind Saint Anthony's. It marked the end of the city in those days. The school was as far as you could put young boys from the action of the city and still be within its limits. The Franciscans couldn't have planned it better than what their frugal budget permitted them when they bought the land to erect the school and friary in 1925, thirty-six years prior to my arrival.

The only single females in the neighbourhood were four elderly Franciscan nuns that shared a house across the street from the school with the word 'CONVENT' engraved on a wooden plaque hanging above the door of the small home.

Serenas hopped up on a rock to see if he could spot any other offerings the neighbourhood had. "Nothing! The landscape was barren. Our exploring was interrupted by a loud bell that we had been warned would summon us to dinner hour. We abandoned our search and went to eat in the basement of the building that would be our home kitchen for the next nine months.

Meals would become very predictable in the institution. French fries and battered whitefish, along with canned corn, was Friday's evening meal offering for the duration of the school term. We could have contracted scurvy had we have spent longer than one school term in Saint Anthony's. Seldom was fresh salad or fruit offered with the meals, albeit most Canadians ate like that in those days filling themselves with canned or frozen fruit and boiled vegetables year around. The Prairie households were slower than British Columbians to convert to fresh from frozen and canned produce and fruit. The change came after more about proper diet became evident in the media in the Seventies. The nuns that cooked were pale and fat women who likely ate the same high carbohydrate diet that they served us.

Later that month, I got to help pick the Franciscans' potato crop. Meanwhile, the first couple of weeks away from home went fast, with new friendships being formed and gruelling athletic drills assigned for students to endure together. It wasn't until the end of September, that I began realizing that I wouldn't see my family or have the enjoyment of visitors like my fellow schoolmates who were frequently invited out on weekend visits with their families. Most were Alberta youth who had plenty of visitors. They often would leave for day trips to dinner with family. Initially, I would stay around and socialize with the few who were left behind and get a little homesick for my own family. I volunteered to help the nuns in the kitchen and spent some time visiting with Father Dave, the Prefect while working out in the gym during free time. Crosbie encouraged me in hockey, and I would occasionally go out on the ice on my own in order to improve my stick handling and skating, necessary to catch up with the Alberta students who were strong skaters and accustomed to the fast-natural outdoor ice.

It wasn't long before I was catching up to the boys that I played on the Saints team with. They were in a league with Alberta, Concordia, St John's and Holy Redeemer Colleges as well as Fort Saskatchewan Penitentiary's Inmates. It was a real challenge for a team of skinny young boys to compete with those inmates. Their brawn was enough to outsize our biggest teammates and the inmates liked to play rough. What the heck were the coaches thinking of by letting the guys from the joint join the league? I guess they figured we'd toughen up.

When we played at the penitentiary we always got to socialize for an hour over hot chocolate with inmates at the cafeteria. Of course, the prisoners that were otherwise not playing hockey were all in the lock-up while their hockey team players were allowed to fraternize. Our coach would go off and hear confessions of the inmates while we visited the team players.

KP duty was the punishment that we would get for our misdemeanours on the ice. Inmates got more time added to their sentences for bad behaviour. I recall one team-mate taking a swing at an inmate. Both were soon flopping through the food trays as they engaged one another in the cafeteria. Fortunately, the Saint player got a lucky punch in, enough to impress the inmate that he was healthy and fit too! Two burly guards promptly removed both from each other and that was it. It never happened again. I hate to think of what happened to the inmate. He was never seen on the ice again.

Our team won the league championship and we were all given nice jackets with pendants to wear home at the end of the school term.

Only once during the year did I end up involuntarily on kitchen patrol, punished for a couple of weeks as a result of a fight that I had with another student. He had the habit of placing his laundry, in a cloth bag, at the head end of my bed, rather than in his locker. The odour was annoying and when I suggested that he remove the laundry he refused, so, that was enough for me to remove it for him. I tossed it out the window and it landed in a garbage bin two floors below resulting in a fight breaking out between the two of us. The fight was broken up by a Friar.

Seven days a week the mornings began at six-thirty at St. Anthony's with a shower followed by morning Mass and prayers. Classes commenced at nine, followed by sports during afternoons, evenings and weekends. I played intramural football in addition to hockey that year, not excelling in either, but I managed to get a few goals in hockey and a number of assists. It was my last year to play hockey as I began to feel the sport was too physical and I objected to the injuries. As for prayer and my vocation to the priesthood, I was failing the Franciscan test. I had begun to recognize the world and wanted more of it instead for my future.

One Saturday per month the students were allowed an outing for four hours. Those outings usually involved visits to Jasper Avenue in downtown Edmonton where we would drink Cokes inside popular hangouts for teens. I was excited to be amongst girls and socializing with them, a rare occasion in my life.

On one of these few free outings during the year, Steve and I, along with a couple of other friends went to meet a girlfriend of Steve's, Marlene Ibbotson, of whom he had a photo pinned up in his dormitory locker. I always admired her photo when he would open the locker door which was adjacent to mine. But he was careful not to let me interrogate him too much about his friend. In the Jasper Avenue Blue Willow Restaurant, a regular haunt for teens, Marlene was waiting in a booth. In those days the facility was operated at the south side of Jasper Avenue just off of 100th Street. All four of us piled into the booth and Steve made the introductions. Marlene, who had just turned fifteen, was a quiet and attractive Red Deer visitor who had moved from Drayton

Valley, a year earlier after having a friendship with Steve during Junior High School. She was visiting her relatives in the city that weekend.

I sat across from Marlene and realized that she was far more attractive than the calendar model that stood beside a red and white 1961 Corvette automobile pasted up in my own school locker. I wanted to get to know her more; however, that opportunity wouldn't occur until a number of years later. In fact, I think she may have been a little annoyed that Steve brought his friends along for their visit together.

One weekend in late Autumn my second cousin, Peg (LaLonde) Hamlin, phoned and invited me to dinner. It was in March 1962 and I was excited to discover that family resided in Edmonton. Peg was the oldest daughter of Frank LaLonde, the youngest brother of my Grandpa John LaLonde. It was Peg's husband and family and her sister Dorothy and that family who convinced me by their warm visits on that and many subsequent outings during the balance of the school term, that I wasn't going to ever become a celibate priest. The Franciscans Friars were a happy group of men that I became endeared to in my time living adjacent to their friary, but the attraction to girls and longing for family during the year convinced me that I was not destined for the calling.

Archbishop Fulton Sheen, a provocative and beady eyed cleric telecast homilies to weekly audiences on CBS television. He was the celebrity of the day for church goers. His programs on Christian living mixed with the man's rants against lax values and the horrors of Communism provided timely spiritual council through a charisma that made the Church more necessary to youth that watched and were directed to Catholic universities and boarding schools. My parents felt that they were being obliging churchgoers by sending their sons away to continue their Catholic education. The paradox was that those schools made students want home and family more. In retrospect, both John and I benefited from the community life in the schools and I'm certain that the Catholic education received during our year at each institution enriched us. Something may have been sacrificed in the process; however, faith and sacrifice have always been partners.

Letters from my mother would bring me back to what really made sense, that God and family should be first. Every communication from home would advise me of that. It wasn't in the written words, but in the emotions that would surface inside me by the warmth and sincerity of my parents' felt in written communications. Most of all, my Mother's evangelizing from the home through her poetic dissertations about life were forceful. No Franciscan homily could match her ability to converse on matters of faith. She would mail me her most recent poems in letters written. She understood her role in life when she wrote:

> A poem within a mother grows
> For every child's a poem
> And lyrics wild and winsome
> Begin within the womb.
>
> And life a bloom unfolding
> God-fashioned, angel kissed,
> A wondrous love starts growing
> That before could not exist.
>
> Like poetry and music sung,
> So is each girl or boy,
> Each phase has added verses
> Of sadness and of joy.
>
> If we had not six children
> Who would we not have had?
> Oh God! To blot out even one
> Would make our hearts too sad.
>
> And so, they grow within the heart
> When they vacate the womb,
> To seal and magnify a love
> And make a house a home.

The most important lessons of love and life for youth are learned in family and one should not hurry away from those lessons. Those enriching years spent with a good family teach where we sit in God's family and how important we are to Him. Created in His image and likeness we long for one another. Any attempt to replace that experience was folly and today most of those institutions have closed down because they did not replace what families could best provide for their youth in the home.

For my part, I do not discard my experience at St. Anthony's, because I made life-long friendships and met my wife through one of those. Later, when presented with the choice of sending my own son to a distant private school, I rejected the idea because I knew he needed home and family and the lessons in love that those would provide him.

Chapter Twenty-five

A t the beginning of September 1962, I returned to Edmonton for the next school term feeling I was more prepared to handle another year away by the summer's recess end. Saint Anthony's non co-educational environment didn't appeal to me for a second year and my mother had suggested another option. She had spoken to the parents of a Nelson friend, Norman Boulet, whose family had moved to Edmonton and asked if it was possible for me to room and board with them while I attended school in Edmonton. The decision of not attending school in Nelson was mostly mine. I was happier with the Alberta curriculum in high school and was concerned over subject changes if I attended in Nelson.

They agreed, so it was arranged that I would attend O'Leary High School, a newly erected Catholic high school in the vicinity of Saint Anthony's, near Queen Elizabeth High School where Norm attended. Unfortunately, living with the Boulet's lasted for only three weeks because my friend's parents' marriage was breaking up. I advertised in the church Sunday bulletin and found another place to live.

Phil Newman, a quiet conservative banker, appeared pleased with my presence; however, his wife Carol had her hands full as homemaker. Two of their children were not yet school age and spent days in the house with their mother. It was through Carol Newman's body language, she exhibited that my presence during evenings was overbearing to her young family's privacy. I don't recall that anything was ever stated, but I had the impression that I was supposed to remain in my basement room and would only be tolerated for short intervals with the family each evening during the dinner hour.

I began to practice reading aloud to improve my oral reading skills to fill the loneliness. I wanted to develop a news broadcasting voice to emulate Edmonton's broadcast legend Walter Rutherford, who I listened to on a transistor radio each evening. At the time Rutherford was a young newsman at Edmonton's CJCA Radio. His authoritative delivery impressed me. Broadcasting had been an interest which I began to express while back in Nelson as I stood selling papers.

I had always been a poor oral reader in front of others. Nerves! It seemed the words never would come out coherently when I was asked to stand up in class at school to read. I stumbled through the reading exercises and resented ever being ordered to read by the nuns at St. Joseph's. Consequently, I became even more nervous after several embarrassing moments where they singled me out and made me attempt the ordeal. I guess that their demands were well intended, but the exercise never worked for me.

Broadcasters impressed me as I would listen to them on radio stations transmitted into Nelson on the airwaves during clear nights from the likes of Vancouver, Spokane and Seattle broadcast outlets. I envied their free-flowing authoritative style. Regretfully, in those years, Nelson's own CKLN radio had such a poor broadcast crew, monopolized by the station's infamous manager, A.R. Ramsden. Everyone in the community scorned the man's disappointing efforts announcing. For years, his lack of broadcast talent was imposed on the small community where he'd recite the news, commercials and commentaries, all in a monotonous monotone voice with endless streams of mispronunciations. His hopeless editorials and poor programming, confounded locals who wanted him off the air. Eventually in September 1966 the Board of Broadcast Governors canceled the station's broadcast license.

One well known mispronunciation of Ramsden's broadcast days was a news cast where he referred to nuclear war as "nucular wedding."

"Sounds almost as serious as a shotgun wedding," remarked my father.

Another notorious mispronunciation was the word 'realtor.' Ramsden would fumble the word using 'real-i-tor,' instead. To that my father would state, "See, the man's always reinventing the English language. There's no 'I' in the word realtor!"

There was no way to get rid of the Ramsden until the licence was cancelled by the BBG and the station's assets were sold.

"Paul Bickert, you're not paying attention. Are you in another world, over there?" Mr. Racette, an eleventh grade French teacher asked. I was daydreaming about my secure life back in Nelson. It was October 1963 and my musings provided a temporary escape from the subject matter mulling over the terrifying reality of a world crisis that was occurring. O'Leary High School had been going through many drills that week in preparation for the possibility of a Soviet nuclear attack directed at the USA. The horrifying thoughts that occupied my mind, were focused on American President, John Fitzgerald Kennedy's threatened nuclear exchange with Nikita Khrushchev's Soviet Union. The news had the effect of making me fear that I would never see my family in Nelson again. The "Red light in the sky" drills that occurred when I was a child didn't frighten me as much as what was going on in the world that month while I attended school six hundred miles away from my family. Hearing the shrill of air raid sirens blaring throughout Edmonton while the civil defence tested the city's warning system was relentlessly on my mind. Edmonton would be a First Strike Target with the American Air Force base located at Edmonton's Namao installation defending the northernmost reaches of the continent.

The 1950's and 1960's had brought a horrible reality to every living person on earth, that mankind's own self destruction, through the use of nuclear weapons, was a very real possibility. The suggestion that Russian nuclear armed missiles would be erected on Cuban soil, ninety miles from Florida, made the threat of an attack genuine.

Since I was in fifth grade, the certainty of a more serious war occurring than the last war my parents' generation went through was a concern for the whole world. As a child, I recall the occasional reminders that were delivered by Saint Joseph's nuns. They spoke of a supernatural event that occurred in Fatima, Portugal in 1917. The nuns told of the Blessed Virgin Mary appearing in an apparition to three young peasant children who were residents of the Portuguese village. Church officials were told by the young visionaries that the Virgin Mother of Christ asked them, eleven-year old Lucy Santos and her younger cousins, Jacinta and Francisco Marcos, to tell the world that Russia could become the instrument of God's Chastisement to mankind if the world did not turn back to God and live good holy lives that were faithful to Him. If not, then Russia would unleash its cruelty on the world through errs of the spread of Communism and War. "Was this the time Mary was referring to back in 1917?" I wondered.

The American Air Force, just north of the city was where nightly I could hear the rumble of Bombers warming up their engines and departing for the north in Canada guarding against Russia's threat. They were a constant reminder to all of the locals that lived in the north end of Edmonton, of the first strike capability that the menacing Communist enemy meant.

Eventually, both Kennedy and Khrushchev capitulated, then the Cuban Missile Crisis was over. Russia's nuclear weapons would not arrive in Cuba, in accordance with the Kennedys' demands and American missiles would leave Turkey in compliance with Khrushchev's request. The grave moment then became a record for the history books.

Not long after that event, I met local Edmonton radio celebrity, Don Lamb, at a remote broadcast at Edmonton's Peppermint Lounge, a small club where teenagers and young adults danced 'The Twist' a popular dance craze that I joined on weekends at the club. Lamb agreed to introduce me to Walter Rutherford at CJCA studios.

When I met Rutherford, he asked if I would be interested in performing an audition for the station after hearing of my interest in news broadcasting. It was arranged that I could do that whenever I felt prepared for it. I kept in touch with Rutherford and Lamb for the next month and frequently picked up teletype news stories from the station. Teletype was an electronic form of early newswire service that broadcasters used, before computers and the Internet came along. In addition, to rehearse, Lamb would offer me written commercial copy, composed by the station's writers. The two broadcast professionals' hospitality was very encouraging in the early development of my interest in broadcasting.

Unfortunately, the nightly visits to the station from the Newman's home, was difficult on my limited budget and school schedule. I had to catch a city bus to the station in the evenings when the familiar broadcasters' shifts commenced; hence, on a few occasions, I missed the last city bus home resulting in my having to walk the eight-mile trek which took most of the night. I recall stumbling in at five or six in the morning with legs and feet so sore that I couldn't get to sleep before being called for school by Carol Newman.

"I know you were out all night, Paul, but your parents wouldn't like that you were absent from school today," she'd remind.

I would force myself to get up and go out the door, acting as if I were going to attend classes. Instead, I'd take the bus to the public library where I'd sleep for a few more hours before waking and busying myself with reading for the rest of the day.

In a letter that I wrote to my parents, I mentioned my desire to purchase a tape recorder to rehearse my reading. For the next two months I read the Newman's discarded Edmonton Journals, nightly in my room.

Surprisingly, my parents sent me an early Christmas gift, in a letter that contained thirty dollars to purchase a tape recorder. Subsequently, I would playback my voice recordings and critique my own efforts at news delivery. Within a couple of months, I mustered the courage to phone Rutherford and arrange the audition session he volunteered. I was pretty nervous; however, managed to pull it off. After the audition, one annoying evaluation Rutherford made was that my presentation of the news sounded a little country like.

"You have a nasal twang to your voice, Paul," he remarked, "but you are a good reader, with lots of expression," he continued.

I couldn't believe it. Rutherford had complimented my reading! It was enough encouragement to make me want to persevere and succeed. He taught me how to breath from the diaphragm. Eventually, phonation and voice projection developed as I continuously rehearsed in front of my tape recorder and the occasional friend. Then, I made another trip to CJCA.

In May 1963, after my two-month interval away from the station, Rutherford sat me down at a microphone in the station's newsroom and handed me a newscast to read. Astonishing myself, I delivered the news error free with professional results while he recorded the audition. It was one of the most exhilarating days of my youth. I had succeeded in becoming a broadcaster and was complimented by both Lamb and Rutherford, who together prepared for me several additional recorded copies of that very important moment. They instructed me to send the recordings out to other stations. I eventually did that, but it would be several months before I received a response from one of the stations.

I never did feel that comfortable visiting upstairs at the Newman household. I began to avoid Sunday Mass and was beginning to lead a secular life during those remaining months of the school term. Carol Newman was interrogating me for my sudden loss of interest in church and I didn't like being pestered over my choice. She was being asked by her children why they had to go to church when I chose not to attend. It was all so typical of a home where older members take liberties affecting the younger ones. Unfortunately, my increased isolation added to my own loneliness that year.

The formal practice of my faith was now being replaced by new priorities. I wanted to be a broadcaster and began to make more frequent trips to Edmonton's downtown branch of the public library to read. I became interested in topics on journalism and reporting. I read editorials in the various North American newspapers that the library carried. I was convinced that I should conduct myself as a journalist and broadcaster, before even becoming employed as one.

One particular recurring news story that was being reported in the newspapers was Pope John XXIII's Second Vatican Council. It was a synod of all the Roman Catholic Church's bishops whom he assembled to clarify to the world the Church's teachings, with the goal of affecting ecumenism in Christianity. By defining the Church's mission to the modern world and to call all Christians to unity, the Church would promote and hopefully heal division. Every evening that I spent training my voice, reading the news orally, I took interest in the paper's articles that reported on various contemporary issues. The paper was full of editorials which commented on items such as birth control, sexual freedom, conscience, socialism, church divisions, etc. I recall how attractive the whole issue of faith as depicted in the press became to me. At the same time, I was feigning my prior convictions that were formed by my parents, the Sisters of Saint Joseph, at Saint Joseph's School and by the Franciscans, at Saint Anthony's. The convictions, that my conscience had been quite comfortable with in the past, were now beginning to become secularized as the media's editorials challenged my youthful thoughts on Church direction and my own personal freedom became emancipated.

I was becoming a liberal, or at least I thought so. Unfortunately, it would be a few years before I would eventually decide that the whole matter of faith was actually being suppressed by contemporary journalism's distorting the real message of the Church. For me, at that time in my life, Church and Christian life began to represent a paradox. I thought, "The Church doesn't have all the answers." Editorials and articles that I read along with the music I enjoyed aided in seducing my thoughts as I joined in on the moral revolution that was taking hold of society, duping me by explanations that I found in the world that were distracting me.

Becoming what was conveniently described as a neutral journalist, ignoring religion and by absorbing copious written material that aided in reshaping my views was enough to convince me that I had become more sophisticated. Unfortunately, I was abandoning my Catholic faith. Those new attitudes became for me the vehicle that would broadside my life and change me. I was experiencing a 'crisis of faith.'

For the balance of that school term I associated with a few friends, after school each day. Some were regulars at the Echo teens, an organization co-ordinated by Betty Grant, the mother of a female friend that I had met at the end of the prior school term. Mrs. Grant was one of those rare individuals who was popular with youth and worked hard organizing them. Her daughter, Cheryl has remained a friend to this day as I was still at an age where friendships with the opposite sex were joyful, platonic and uncomplicated.

Chapter Twenty-six

had expectations for my summer back in Nelson and the thought of going home reminded me of summers past where everything seemed right in my life. There I enjoyed the freedom to ride my bike along the refreshing lakeshore with my dog, Sambo, following me, or where I'd spend leisurely afternoons at Lakeside Park visiting with friends. Most weekday evenings were enjoyed at home with my family and on weekends I would go out to socialize. That summer, work would be my priority. I wanted to find suitable temporary employment to last until I secured a broadcasting job in response to the audition tapes I had mailed out from Edmonton.

In springtime 1962, my family moved to another house that my parents purchased on McHardy Street leaving the home they had spent time renovating three years earlier on Chatham Street. I was anxious to get back and see the new house when the school term ended. Carelessly, I ran out of money the week before and was short the bus fare home. With purchasing an O'Leary yearbook and frequenting the Peppermint Lounge to socialize, I burned through most of the money I had. Whatever supplemental income that I earned from my part time employment at Johnnie's Café on Jasper Avenue wasn't ample to cover bus fare that had already been provided for in a letter arriving from my parents.

Within walking distance of O'Leary High was Northland's Park where horse races commenced each June and ran throughout the summer season. The appeal of a visit to the park grew when I found myself down to only ten dollars. I made the decision to bet two dollars on a race, which seemed a worthwhile gamble if the horse I bet paid; otherwise, I would be forced to hitch-hike the six-hundred-mile trip back to Nelson.

On Friday afternoon, after finishing my final exams, I wandered over into Northlands and placed the bet on a long shot from Central Alberta, one listed in the park's program as never having won a race before. Adding to the excitement that day was an earlier discussion with a CJCA deejay that had won money the day before. The sound of the crowd's roar intensifying with each event as I approached on foot from O'Leary was so appealing. When I arrived, the horse I bet offered the best prize money and the fact that it resembled 'Black Beauty' convinced me. The height and appearance were the only credentials I used to qualify the horse for my wager, because the statistics presented on all of the horses listed in the program were too confusing for me.

"Two dollars to win on number six," I blurted to the man collecting bets from behind a wire screen. He returned, "Good luck, sir...er, young man." I tried to ignore the remark, so turned immediately away from the line-up after collecting my receipt. I was likely the youngest gambler at the track and it all seemed so sly to be resorting to gambling for my return bus fare that was presumed by my parents already paid for. Momentarily, I felt a little sheepish over the ordeal coinciding with my absence from home. Mom had written to advise that she intended to enter The British Columbia Vocational School under construction in Nelson and would enrol in a hair dressing course for the school's first term. Her latest letter spoke of the possibility of opening a hair salon in the basement of the family's new home, so that the extra income could assist in providing for the family. I wasn't feeling too comfortable with my excessiveness, nor with my gambling that day; however, was compelled by my situation. I recall rationalizing at the time that I deserved a little fun and my yearbook purchase wasn't that overindulgent. I think the gambling was more of a moral struggle for me as I couldn't imagine my father ever resorting to such behaviour.

The race was off as I watched intensely while standing in the noisy crowd and leaned on a fence rail at the edge of the track. My horse leapt out of the starting gate and never left the lead right up to the finish. I strained to see whether the horse had won or not from my location which was hampered. Within a few seconds the announcement came over the speakers, "Photo finish, one and six." I understood the broadcast, however, hated the monotone voice that provided it. "Damn!" I thought, as I stood clenching my wagering stub. The wait seemed an eternity for the track announcer's voice to come back on again. In the interim I gained a little perspective of my situation while looking around me realizing that I was amongst a crowd of pretty needy gamblers. They all appeared wanting and the surroundings drew an observation from me that I fit in. I attempted to ignore the scene as I grew anxious over the race's outcome.

"Number six wins," bellowed the announcer's unemotional voice. The delay lasted for about ten minutes, but was worth it as the horse I picked could thank its long nose for the win. I immediately forgot my momentary consternation when at once I forgave the broadcaster's voice who announced the outcome of the 'Photo Finish.' Intent on studying the lights that went on at the track's wagering board I realized that I had won thirty-two dollars and change!

Johnnie's restaurant paid me seventy-five cents an hour and my winnings had paid more than a week's full-time salary at Johnnie's. I was hooked! After collecting my winnings, I walked out of the park, but was compelled by the urge to bet on, so, immediately re-entered the park and placed two more bets with a higher wager on each horse I bet in the next race.

It was mid afternoon that I finally left the horse races again. By then, I had bet on four additional events, losing half of my earlier winnings. Selecting to bet a couple of horses in each subsequent race and by not winning any of the bets was costly. That was enough! I then decided that my departure was overdue and headed home to the Newman's house, resolved that I would keep the balance of my winnings deciding to hitch back to Nelson anyway.

That night I packed up my belongings offering my farewells to Edmonton friends by telephone. I made the decision to ship my possessions via Greyhound and ride a city bus the next morning to Edmonton's city limits where I would stand on the highway to thumb a ride home.

On Saturday morning, Phil Newman gave me a ride to the Greyhound depot and then to South Edmonton's city limits. Carol Newman had prepared a lunch for me that I placed on the ground at the edge of the highway as I proceeded to hang my thumb in the air for a ride. One came quickly, all the way to Calgary where, in that city, I rode a city bus to the south end of Macleod trail to attempt getting my second ride. Unfortunately, the lunch Carol gave me was left on roadside back at Edmonton.

I recall spending a few hours being ignored by Calgary's rush hour traffic and surmised that the mob of drivers in the city didn't like hitchhikers, so proceeded to walk until dusk which came a few hours later. I was a couple of miles north of Okotoks when I received my second ride, having walked almost twenty miles on shoe soles that were already thin that day when I left Edmonton.

Night had come when I arrived in a ride that dropped me off just outside of Fort Macleod. There I stood swatting mosquitoes in the dark until a Royal Canadian Mounted Police officer stopped and offered me a ride to a service station on the western edge of Macleod. He suggested it would be safer if I solicited rides from the service station's patrons. Since breakfast I had only eaten a couple of chocolate bars that I bought while I was going through Calgary and by then was so famished that I went into a fast-food outlet by the Fort MacLeod service station to buy myself a burger. After I ate, I found a ride which provided transportation to the small town of Michel, in the Crowsnest Pass, where no one seemed to be on the highway at the hour I arrived.

Michel and Natal were unsightly coal mining villages that the British Columbia Provincial Government decided were an eyesore to border British Columbia's eastern boundary. The dilapidated remains of the communities existing since the 1870's, were bulldozed in 1967 with the inhabitants relocated to newly erected housing in the town of Sparwood, which would become BC's newest community located a few kilometres west of the original villages.

When I arrived at Michel after midnight, there was construction on the highway where I became stranded with no travellers on the road for the remainder of the night. It is likely that the highway construction discouraged travellers from using the route that night. I recall the frustrating task of making my way through the construction zone while dodging earth movers and other large equipment that were rebuilding the section. After leaving the lit construction zone, I continued to stumble along the highway for miles in the dark, in an area of British Columbia that is well known for its Big Game and remoteness.

Around dawn, the next morning, I managed to flag down a Greyhound bus and inquired about the fare on to Nelson. "Seven dollars from Fernie," the driver advised and then added, "I'll let you on for that." I was content enough with the savings that I had made and settled for riding the carrier the rest of the way over to Nelson.

When I arrived in the door at my family's new home, I expected to be greeted by my dog, Sambo. He was usually the occupant that exhibited the most excitement to see me home. It was Sunday afternoon and I was advised by my mother that my pet was no longer with the family. The dog that was a gift from a newspaper customer that I delivered to in 1958 was evicted. Subsequent to my departure in September, Sambo had developed the habit of rolling in any object he found had an unpleasant odour, I believe to attract attention. Subsequently, the dog would be kicked out of the house, eventually becoming so dejected that he spent most of his time at another house down Chatham Street where he was more welcome. Soon Sambo no longer had a home down the street either, as that family moved prior to my family's own relocation up to McHardy Street. Mom offered me the explanation that Sambo was given to a kennel owner, nine miles north of Nelson. Of course, I was upset over the loss of my dog and continued to think about the betrayal for a lengthy period afterwards, while simultaneously, I continued to wrestle interiorly with my youth and the independence I had taken.

Sambo was quickly replaced with a German Shepherd pup, Duchess, when my parents gave in to my younger siblings' demands to get another dog. For my part, I had grown enough to keep silent my hurt over the loss of Sambo. Home was no longer comfortable. It had changed during my time away and the changes seemed unwelcoming.

During that period Alberta high school students completed matriculation a year earlier than British Columbians and I was content that I had made up for the year that I lost in third grade. I was eighteen and it appeared that I was would be burden on the household, so I felt more than ever that it was time for me to use my broadcast training to support myself.

I announced confidently that I would become a broadcaster to my parents. They welcomed my pronouncement. To discontinue my education for what I assured them was a good career choice was acceptable to my parents. Dad believed that the radio experience that his younger siblings, Jeanne and Edward had embarked on was an important launch to their future.

Earlier that year Dad had been appointed service manager at the Central Truck dealership and his salary improved when the promotion came. My father's prayerful devotion to Saint Joseph, foster father of the Lord, a saint venerated by the Catholic Church throughout her history as 'Patron of Workers' had always been given credit for helping my father's enduring role as head of the family. He revered the saint's example with the Holy Family and included him in his prayer life for Joseph's intercessions before The Lord during turbulent Bickert family times. Dad would frequently announce when Novenas would commence and when they were successful.

My father's daily arrival home from working at Central Truck and Equipment was highlighted by the purr of his black 1956 A-90 Austin Westminster Sedan. The larger and newer Austin provided the characteristic squeal of its British brakes when it entered into the home's carport at five-forty-five each afternoon. He babied the vehicle like his own child, calling it, Bertha. I believe it's the only car he ever gave a name since his "Tin Lizzy" that preceded the gifting of Grandpa LaLonde's Oldsmobile. In Lumby, the old Ford wore an international handle given it by drivers worldwide.

The second occurrence was that at the top of the front entry steps Dad would always hammer out his pipe on the veranda rail to discard the remaining smouldering contents of the pipe prior to entering the house.

"Hello, I-izz home!" he would squeeze out of his mouth, mimicking, a man that had slaved all day to provide for his family. Occasionally, his face would be covered with patches of grease and then his heavy eyebrows would appear extra thick if dirt and grease had filled the brows while he inspected work under trucks. When he carried groceries, picked up for Mom on the way home, he'd slap them on the counter quipping, "Present for yah, Mammy," and move closer to kiss her, offering a peck on the cheek, while for the benefit of the family, distancing himself at the waist.

After his greeting Dad would always escape to the home's only bathroom, located just off the kitchen and clean up before dinner. Minutes later, he would come out, leaving the bath in spotless order, with the only hint of his being in there, the lingering odour of grease that he had rinsed out of the sink that he left immaculate. His re-appearance would start with a broad smile and a short monologue, usually consisting of some yarn from the shop, enough to set the tone with Mom each evening. Sometimes for relaxation, he would place a jazz recording on the stereo while Mom finished preparing the evening meal.

The few days that I spent at home that summer have etched only a few memories of my youth with my family at home, because we didn't have a lot of time together after my departure from Nelson at the end of ninth grade. I do recall some changes that had occurred in my sister, Janice, that year. She was nine years old and quite competitive with her younger brother, Patrick, who was seven. Patrick was about to enter second grade while Geoffrey had just finished fifth. Both of my younger brothers were advanced enough to recognize Janice had the social disadvantage and they respected her for that. The burden of Janice's disabilities, physical and mental, required more of both my parents' attention, always at young Patrick's expense. Even though he was the youngest he was often ignored while Janice received considerable attention from both my parents. Mom and Dad's unintentional neglect of Patrick, due to Janice's demands, was something we may all have been somewhat ignored over, but likely to a lesser degree. I'm certain it was tiring for youngest sibling Patrick.

At dinner hour Janice was usually a fixture around the kitchen table where she fidgeted and twisted on her swivel chair until Dad would arrive home. She always anticipated the special attention that our father would assign to her and jealously guarded her territory and the moment. Dad regarded it as a period for the rest of the family to step back, while he was attentive to Janice's needs. After bestowing the first honours on our mother, his attention usually shifted to Janice.

Geoff was beginning to show his personality and I recall how very definite he was in his opinions, exhibiting a characteristic directness that grew from when he was much younger. At four years of age, he was asked by his Grandpa Bickert if he was an Irishman.

"Nope, I'm a human bean!" The humorous remark and mispronunciation, was Geoff's attempt to emphasize that he had a penchant for the exact. Later in life, when I was in sixth grade, I would accompany Geoff to his first year in school. I was astounded how well my younger brother could defend himself on the city bus when he rode with older kids that would deride him. "Yah know, I'm going to be big someday, too. What are yah going to say to me then?"

At an early age Geoff had developed the habit of interrogating everyone about their life, including questions about their preferences on politics and religion. He liked to determine how well-read people were. As a boy he always had his head in a book, reading volumes of classics and commenting on them.

As boys, Patrick and Geoffrey were an intense combination to view together. By then, Patrick was easily exasperated by Geoff's ability to verbally assault him, with endless deliberations on his younger brother's lack of social grace. In turn, Patrick was clever enough to respond with a pantomime of facial slurs, sufficient to horrify Geoff.

"What, my brother's a chimpanzee, now?"

The verbal assaults would continue on and on, for years afterwards and then eventually the two would begin to work in concert, attempting to use their developing debating skills and humour on others. It became a convenient distraction for both to direct their attacks toward John and me. Ultimately, their efforts to out manoeuvre their older brothers would trigger a response of a theological nature.

It's like half the family was Jewish and the other half Irish! We'd become a peculiar progeny, destined to make for interesting future gatherings together, always full of debate.

At the beginning of summer 1963, John was somewhere in the middle of an ocean living in the hull of the HMCS Saskatchewan, operating sonar for the Royal Canadian Navy. I missed his presence at home that year. During the prior year his ship and its crew were at sea in the Caribbean assisting the Americans in that country's boycott against Haiti's notorious leader, Papa Doc Duvalier, a deranged dictator who professed to have Voodoo powers over his nation and anyone who disagreed with him. At one point, John was ordered to prepare to enter the country, bayoneted along with a small brigade of Canadians, to re-establish the rebelling nation's peace by quelling rioting. In the course of the uprising my brother had written home with his Last Will and

Testament. It was accompanied with salutations, given to the family in order to prepare all of us for the worst.

For a couple of weeks, at the beginning of summer, I associated with a friend that asked me to assist his father's roofing crew that operated in Nelson. At the same time another friend inquired if I would be interested in accompanying him over to the Okanagan city of Penticton, to search for summer employment. Prior to the invitation I agreed to working with the crew roofing commercial buildings. The operation involved hoisting hot buckets of melted tar up a ladder onto the roves of the buildings. Still today, I have scars on my arms from burns received in the work, that I would painfully pick the tar off of that had adhered deeply into my flesh.

Years later, when I took my professional degree in Iowa, I recall hearing stories of American students, from the South, who admitted their involvement in the Ku Klux Klan. They'd describe 'Tar and Feather Rituals' that they claimed to have been part of. I could relate to the pain that their African American victims experienced in those inhumane and horrifying rituals. Soon, I had the excuse I needed to leave the work when the other friend had a ride with his dad to Penticton.

Before leaving Nelson for Penticton, I made an attempt to locate my dog Sambo. I went to the Kennel operation to ask if the owner could advise me of the location that he had found for Sambo's new home. He didn't give me an answer; so, disappointed, I left and returned to the property later to snoop around for answers. I recall wandering by a shack that had one large window exposing the man's makeshift surgical theatre, where he performed animal dissections. Lying on a tilted surgical table was a black Cocker Spaniel dog opened and gutted with its four legs tied and stretched outward, exposing an empty abdominal cavity. Horrified, I hoped that the dead animal was not my pet. Years later, as an adult, I was told by my younger brothers that Mom had eventually admitted to them that the dog had been destroyed by the kennel operator and not given to the man for the purpose of finding a new home.

In Penticton, I found work at a gas station as a gas pump jockey. The frustrating part of the position was that I had little knowledge of the design of each vehicle of the day. Cars were large and full of chrome fixtures, around head and taillight assemblies. The manufacturers prided themselves on how they hid the gas tank access. It was all quite disconcerting. Customers would disappear into a washroom after leaving me with their vehicle and then reappear to discover that I was still looking for the gas tank access. You can thank those very automobile manufacturers that we have self serve re-fueling stations today! I quit the job and found another in a restaurant. Chris quit his job at a fast-food outlet and returned to Nelson that first week.

At the end of my third week in Penticton, toward the end of August, I received a telephone call from my mother who asked if I would be interested in travelling to Marquis, Saskatchewan to work as a farmhand that autumn for her cousin. Harry Cannon operated the farm that was the homestead property of James and Anna LaLonde, parents of my Grandfather John Joseph LaLonde. Harry was my mother's first cousin, son of Lucy LaLonde, Grandpa's sister and her husband Charlie Cannon. I accepted the invitation and left Penticton. After my return to Nelson and a short visit with my family, I boarded a train to travel to Saskatchewan.

Chapter Twenty-seven

Initially, I was uninspired by the prairie landscape around Marquis. Still too early for harvest, the crops were just beginning to ripen. The Cannon's farmland, had numerous elevations and depressions on it with the turn of the century dwelling built by J.S LaLonde my great grandfather. It had a few outbuildings perched on a high part of its homestead quarter. The homestead farm was positioned three miles northwest of Marquis, a village located near the northernmost part of the Qu'Appelle Valley, an area left over from the receding glaciers of the last ice age. Its mural appeared bleak to me on that mid-summer arrival.

Importing an eighteen-year-old from a small city in British Columbia's Interior was a risky undertaking for my second cousin, Harry Cannon. For my part, I had little more life skills than how to cut the lawn, turn on a radio station microphone and play hockey and I'd discard any one of those for Rock and Roll music and racetrack betting or whatever other distraction the world offered in my late teens.

The man was a hardy farm businessman, the eldest son of John Joseph LaLonde's younger sister Lucy and her husband Charlie who expected performance from the kid he invited to work with him. He misjudged his ability to recruit farmhands by transplanting on his British Columbia second cousin what he knew of the area's youths that were raised in Marquis's culture giving them the basics of the farming trade. I didn't even understand how to shut farm gates properly behind me and continue to require my wife today to remind me to close doors and turn off lights in our home. I'm accident prone and oblivious to the world around making for a poor mix for farming where accidents have taken limb and life from many who have attempted it and been more aware than I will ever be of the precarious occupation.

I had never before driven a vehicle, other than to operate peddles on Grandpa LaLonde's truck for my four-year-old brother, John. I must have appeared useless to Harry on my arrival that summer; however, the man revered Grandpa LaLonde and needed help in a province where other young men were being employed on oil rigs in a booming and more generous petrochemical industry. The room and board included with a seventy-five-dollar monthly salary was too much pay for me to be his assistant.

Harry had been enlisted in the Royal Canadian Air Force during the World War II and conducted himself with a disciplined demeanour that somewhat intimidated me at first.

After spending my first day on the job weeding his wife Hazel's one-acre garden, I was being sunburnt from the day's sun for refusing protection or to wear a hat because my hair was more important. It was a hilarious picture to the Cannons as they watched me weed the patch in beige pants, with both white shirt and runners on, clothes that were of little use to farmhands. I arrived dressed for Penticton's beach city. By the end of the day, it was only out of respect for my mother's LaLonde family roots that I continued working another day. I hated the taunts and corrections given while I displayed total disregard for my new position. Weeds and vegetables appeared the same and were uprooted together.

Begrudgingly, I consented to another unpleasant chore the next day while I contemplated returning to Penticton as soon as I could muster the courage to make the announcement to the Cannons. Harry handed me a broom and a garden hose and ordered me to clean a truck that he had transported a bull to market the day before. He explained that the animal had been encouraged onto the vehicle with a pail of flaxseed and consequently it had transformed the vehicle into a septic tank. I was so humiliated and filthy at the end of the job that I could have strangled my own mother for sending me to Marquis.

That evening Harry attempted to humour me and laughed during dinner. "Paul, I gave you the worst of the jobs first. Are you sticking around to find out why farmers really like their work here in Marquis?" His timing was impeccable. I would have otherwise, left the home of my LaLonde ancestors the next morning.

As I lay in bed with my painful sunburnt upper torso and aching muscles, with a hint of manure still remaining in my nostrils that night, I considered the efforts I had made during the past year preparing myself for a radio broadcasting career. While I stayed in Marquis, my life was a contradiction to what I had planned. I asked, "What possible good can it be for me to waste time as a farmhand while I wait to become an employed broadcaster?" I was so perplexed, but quickly fell asleep out of exhaustion.

By the end of the first week, I had begun to adjust to the farm and was amused with the work and what farmyard peculiarities I observed. Cows were curious-animals, gophers had no sense at all and farmers themselves were never satisfied with the weather. As my muscles, flesh and determination adjusted, I began to look at it all as a learning experience necessary for me to discover my roots.

The Marquis residents remembered me from my childhood and seemed entertained by my presence. "What's John LaLonde thinking now?" they'd question. I recall that many of the area's folk had familiar names. They were people my mother had shared stories about over the years, people whom I otherwise would not have known about.

"If you're as good a worker as your Granddad, you'll be a real asset to Harry," they'd remark. Their assessment of me was too generous as my efforts were a disaster for the farm operation, but Harry never let on to them.

At the end of the first week the Cannons arranged an outing to Buffalo Pond where locals spend their weekends in July and August each year. It was Sunday and I was asked to feed the dozen or so head of cattle that Harry kept in a corral, adjacent to the farmhouse. I did my chores that morning before Sunday Mass, but I failed to properly secure the gate. By evening, on our return home from the day's outing at the lake we discovered that all of the cattle were next door in the neighbour's barley field. Now, if you know what barley does to animals, you'll understand that Harry had a crisis on his hands! Some of the cows were belly up as a result of bloating on the barley.

The mistake cost Harry three cows, a twenty-five percent reduction in the small herd he was raising to supplement his dry land farming income. In addition, he paid a huge veterinarian bill that I expect John LaLonde would have written a cheque for, if he were alive, but the costs just kept escalating for Harry!

Other additional benefits of the job were driving instructions. Harry offered, which resulted in my earning a vehicle operator's permit for Saskatchewan's highways. It was not a spectacular event by motor vehicle operator's standards, though. Really! My impression of the Saskatchewan Motor Vehicle's Branch has been blemished by it allowing me the right to drive so easily. With all due respect to my Saskatchewan relatives and the rest of the province's citizens, I wonder if that province has since improved motor vehicle operator testing and driver preparation?

My examination amounted to driving around the block and turning off the ignition, before I followed the instructor out of the car. "You passed," the examiner remarked as he walked ahead of me into the office. I laughed at the man's casual approach to his work. "What, you're serious?" I responded, with a chuckle.

For the next two weeks after the driver's test Harry would combine the wheat, barley and oat fields alongside the grain truck that I operated. When the truck was loaded, I would drive off to a granary at a distant quarter and unload its contents into an auger that would deliver the grain up into a storage facility.

Learning to swath the crops prior to Harry combining them was quite an ordeal for an inexperienced driver. The routine would require that I drive the tractor in a straight line down the quarter of land, with my head turned backward, while watching the height of the swather blades to keep them from digging into the ground as the tractor moved along pulling the swather behind. The blades would cut the grain stalks just above the surface of the ground. Today swathers have blades in front of the tractor. No doubt, I'm the one written into the provinces history books of being the reason the farm implement manufacturers were required to change the design of the swathing equipment!

The first several swaths were pretty irregular and resulted in my receiving a lecture from Harry about my not being 'up to the task.' Soon, I smartened up and did a pretty good job, but the work resulted in my running over a family of skunks when I was just finishing up my last swath on the first quarter. The critters moved in to the centre of the quarter section as I swathed around the perimeter, moving closer to the centre of the field with each swath. The death and smell of the farmyard pedestrians was terrible. Five skunks were mangled in the blades of the machine. Harry was left to clean up the mess and I had to live outdoors for a few days while taking tomato juice baths. I don't believe that the tomato juice did any good at all other than to entertain those around me as the Cannon family and any visitor coming to the property took turns pouring the juice over my head.

In the end, I nearly destroyed Harry's only swather, by running the machine into the side of a granary at the end of the third week. It was the only granary on that quarter of land and the mishap should never have happened, but I was careless and parked the tractor and swather too close to the granary without looking behind to see how near the swather was. I've since damaged a couple of recreational vehicles doing the same.

When the piece of equipment was repaired, I continued with the swather to prepare the last quarter for Harry's combine work. The land was planted with oats and the elevation over the rest of the area of Marquis offered a special view of all its surroundings. The feelings I experienced that day could have almost changed my life's direction. I was becoming convinced that, one day, I too, may be interested in becoming a dry land farmer. It was as if John LaLonde had spent the day with me while I operated the tractor swathing. It seemed as though he was teaching me about the peace and goodness of his life's work. I felt moved by every wisp of wind that swept through my hair cooling my brow. The mature oat crop's fragrance aroused my spirit as I looked over the expanse of the fields from the rise on the LaLonde homestead quarter and then became kindred to the Marquis farmers that were going through the same experience as I. Their tractors, operating in distant fields that I could see from my vantage point, helped me to understand that I too could belong there and become an area farmer. John LaLonde's gift to me of a nearby quarter of land that was to be turned over from his estate when I turned twenty-one could be my start. Perhaps he had hoped that one day a grandson of his would return to Marquis, to experience the life that he had loved since he was a child. The experience helped me know my grandfather and mother better.

For a time that day I belonged to Marquis, forgetting all about the manure wagon, the skunks and the physical pain and taunting that I endured early in my visit to the Cannons. I began to understand the area's people who lived a quiet, undisturbed life. Imagining the years my relatives worked the fields, became easy and I was happy that I had re-visited my mother's home at that time and connected with my heritage that I otherwise would have never known. Marquis enriched me with a unique earthy spirit.

In mid September, as I washed up in a sink outside Harry and Hazel's home, I examined my healthy tanned face in the mirror above the sink and I suddenly felt something was leading me away from Marquis. It was a sentiment that the visit was a mere stepping-stone on the path that I was treading in life.

I was young and every sense that I possessed was then, possessing me. One moment, I was in love with a day, the next, in love with a place and then, a face. Everything I did in life then came with an uncontrollable compulsion to be liberated from my reserve, unleashed from whatever in me was quiet and reticent, whether it be my resolve to uphold my past allegiances or by moving ahead to an uncharted future. I wanted to be free to experience everything that I needed to, to find me and who I was.

My musings were interrupted by Harry opening the door to the kitchen and making an announcement, "Paul, you have a telephone call from Walter Jones, Station Manager of CFJC Radio in Kamloops." By then, I had all but forgotten my broadcast training and had to think before realizing that I had submitted an audition tape to the man's station that spring.

Jones told me that Kamloops' CFJC radio, the CBC regional affiliate for the Interior of British Columbia, wanted me to come to work as a broadcaster there. He offered me the position to be evening news announcer for the station. The audition tapes that I had submitted, recorded earlier at Edmonton's CJCA Radio, succeeded in impressing the station's management that I possessed the ability to broadcast the two major newscasts each evening from the network outlet. Initially, both newscasts would prove to be gruelling half hour ordeals that would scare any newcomer to the newsroom.

Chapter Twenty-eight

I already possessed enough vanity prior to that telephone call inviting me to join CFJC's broadcast staff. Now, I had the career to accompany it. The train trip from Moose Jaw allowed plenty enough time for me to socialize with strangers and boast, promoting my sense of celebrity while indulging in any accolade the various coaches' occupants offered. From the moment I boarded the train I immediately began my campaign to inform strangers of the position I acquired at Kamloops. I was pumped!

"Congratulations, we heard about your assignment!" Passengers offered as they passed by my seat on the train. Their compliments were likely intended as goodwill gestures for the purpose of assisting my youthful self esteem, but my shallowness and self-indulgence became vain companions, inflating me while I rode the Canadian Pacific rail line to Kamloops. I recall being so inflated with hot air before my arrival in Kamloops that I could have easily been named the cause of any Prairie Chinook had it been winter that I travelled the Rockies rather than late summer.

Greeting me in Kamloops were my father's youngest sister, Jeanne and her husband, Lory Rodrigue. They quickly helped me to regain some perspective with their genuine offerings about life.

"So, you were a Saskatchewan dirt farmer and now you want to be a radio announcer?" prodded Lory.

Lawrence Rodrique is one of the most forward people I've known. He has an ability to bring anyone down to earth with his reviews that are usually candid and always timely. I can't imagine how he must have felt about his nephew arriving, wearing white pants and shoes to match, highlighted with a pink shirt. I expect that my uncle felt I needed a little ribbing, but he politely restrained himself to one comment.

"Well as long as you don't mind living with the lousy pay that these stations are notorious for, Paul! They usually give you about two thirds the salary that a grunt earns at my sawmill." Lory didn't mind letting me know that the career I was embarking on was full of glory and often returned little financial reward. I was unaware that those broadcasting careers were notorious for making men pompous, loud and full of themselves on incomes that were usually standard. I tried to ignore the remark, realizing I didn't inquire of Jones what I'd be getting paid for the work.

It was the first time I had seen Jeanne in seven years since her honeymoon when she surprised our household in Nelson on a visit while she was returning from her escape with Lory. The pair had eloped to Idaho after they both agreed not to put Grandma and Grandpa Bickert to the cumbersome expense of a large family wedding. Harry Bickert's income couldn't handle that and Jeanne and Lory's unpretentious type didn't want to impose on their parents. The Bickerts both approved of Lory, a respected sawmill worker, employed in management, who could teach you anything you ever wanted to know about loyalty to wife and family. He also had a penchant for building anything mechanical, including sawmills, hydraulics and steam engines.

While Lory was occupied dawn to dusk at the mill north of Kamloops, my father's youngest sister, Jeanne was leading a very busy life homemaking and caring for her three pre-school children, Kathy, Guy and Lincoln.

They offered me a bed in their basement family room for three weeks until I received my first paycheque and found alternate accommodations. Meanwhile, I could always count on Lory's early morning rising when he'd begin his day at four-thirty. I usually awoke and listened to his activity from my bed below while he prepared to go off to work

My shift at the radio station commenced each day at four o'clock in the afternoon and it ran until midnight, so I was almost ready for a nap by the time I arrived at work after my short night's rest at the Rodrigues. It seemed impossible for me to get back to sleep after Lory's departure, because at six-thirty Jeanne began her day which would coincide with the awakening of the Rodrique children. That's when I'd give up trying to sleep. It was always a happy rising though as I enjoyed visiting my twenty-seven-year old aunt and her children during the daytime before I went off to work.

Jeanne's gift for adding humour into what could otherwise have been a stressful homemaking life, rearing young children, was so much like I had imagined my Grandma Helen Bickert when she would have been young raising my father and his siblings. Jeanne would put a smile into every bit of inconvenience she encountered, exemplifying her mother's joy in her own maternal role. She'd correct the children with a word or two and then laugh. They'd immediately return the chuckle and seemed not to resent their mother directing them. Jeanne always sang as she worked at home. Throughout her life she'd entertain in various music groups. One group that she had been affiliated with for several years was Vancouver's renowned Maple Leaf Singers. Much later she beat the odds by competing against hundreds of other Canadian senior citizens and won the National Seniors Star Award at a contest held in Toronto in autumn 2009. The contest allowed seniors to show off their talents in front of both critics and a national television audience.

Prior to my leaving Jeanne and Lory's home I was advised that Lory was looking for another car for Jeanne. He offered me the use of my aunt's 1953 Ford sedan to drive to and from work.

"Better yet, I'll give you a deal. I'll sell it to you for two hundred dollars and you can even make payments on it after you start getting your salary at the station," offered Lory. It was a great buy and the terms worked, so the new vehicle acquisition coincided with my new career!

At the end of my third week at the Rodrigues I moved into a two-room suite at the back of a Kamloops family home at 366 - 6th Avenue. I was eighteen, a bachelor and had a Ford car while broadcasting for one hundred and ninety-five dollars a month. I was on top of the world, except for the odd stressful day during the early weeks while I attempted to fit into the work.

Following my Aunt Jeanne into CFJC Radio, which in those days had the studios located in a small building at the northeast corner of St Paul and Fourth Avenue, brought some expectations on the part of CFJC management. They surmised from my audition tape that I had Jeanne's experience and talent and that I would be a positive addition to the operation. Jeanne, who was now enjoying her homemaking role, was sorely missed by the station's management. Her experience certainly had influenced Walter Jones's decision to hire me and I believe it took a few weeks before he finally began to accept that he hadn't made a mistake with his latest recruit. While I fumbled my way through the position, I received a few reminders from Jones that I was still in my probationary period.

At the end of each shift, I could not sleep at night as I was so wound up from the work. I felt like Nelson's broadcaster owner, Ramsden, at CKLN, when the phone would ring, and listeners would straighten me out on various mispronunciations that I had made during my own broadcasts. Usually I erred with the names of European hockey players during the sports broadcasts and sports fans were always unforgiving.

I was unprepared for being the only person in the station for the duration of each evening shift. There I spent most of my working evenings preparing for the two lengthy newscasts. In between programs, I'd provide station breaks announcing, "This is CFJC Radio, your CBC Regional Network affiliate in Kamloops, British Columbia." That's all I initially had to do in the eight-hour shift. The perception of celebrity soon fizzled as I became bored with my responsibilities before Remembrance Day Weekend arrived. I was two months into the job.

In early December, I was asked to do a two-week afternoon shift for another broadcaster who was on a honeymoon. That work gave me the opportunity to do his music program reading commercial copy and selecting and announcing music introductions. The years of listening to Edmonton, Vancouver and Spokane deejays paid off. I had the act down perfectly and the phones rang for a full week afterwards as Kamloops youth demanded more of me. Shortly afterwards, the station held a contest for the public to vote their favourite announcer. I was voted number one! That annoyed Jones, because I was the lowest paid broadcaster at the station. Eventually he permitted me do additional disc jockey work on Saturday afternoons allowing me free rein to do my own programming.

Even though I became happier afterwards, I felt that I needed friends, missing the social life that I had enjoyed in Edmonton and Nelson. Living alone for so long without family and friends made me feel isolated from the world while for the six nights a week I worked. Others my age socialized at night, but I socialized with a microphone in a lonely quiet studio.

In the daytime, when I wasn't working, I continued to immerse myself in books. First, I read Charles Dickens' Great Expectations, a novel about a young man in search of love in the absence of family. The book wasn't a good read for me as it offered a tasteless approach toward love, but the character, Pip amused me by his resilience accompanied by his ability to overcome dispossession and hardship, all resulting in his personal success, unknowingly financed by a stranger Pip helped save as a young man.

Somerset Maughan's Of Human Bondage, which provided some healthy perspective toward my own life impressed me as well. I realized that my state was not so deprived as those characters in Maughan's book, whilst I lived on my own helping me to feel better when I compared my life to the book's characters. Both authors' works aroused a need for me to find a female friend. I wasn't dating anyone, but I dreamed of finding someone to console me as my senses quickened in my solitude.

Exploring the North Thompson area from behind the green hood of my 1953 Ford sedan provided a scenic repose for my eyes which were uninspired by the pallid desert around Kamloops. Between Kamloops and Clearwater there's a transition as the Thompson River winds and mountainous peaks provide numerous streams enriching that valley's foliage. It was before the Yellowhead Route was completed and the gravelled segment had few motorists. A middle aged First Nations woman stood in the middle of the road waving down my vehicle, so I stopped the car thinking something serious may be wrong.

"Mister will you give me a ride?" asked the woman. After I reluctantly agreed to do that, she then seated herself in the back seat and hollered from her opened door at a male partner who stepped out of the bush to join her in my vehicle.

He opened the front door and sat in the passenger seat beside me.

By then I was thinking this day may not continue as well as it had begun! I attempted to be my normal cheerful self; however, neither of the passengers spoke a word. Both reeked of liquor and whatever other odours accompanied their imbibement.

A few miles down the road the woman from behind had her arm around my neck and was screaming, "Kill him, just Kill him! Kill him quick!"

I wrestled with her and attempted to control my car which by then was at full highway speed. I braked while she was pulling me backwards in her stranglehold. Meanwhile, her partner seated beside me just stared into space not speaking a word ignoring his lady's behaviour that also succeeded in making me weak with fear. He suddenly swung his left out which I thought was aimed at me, but his fist connected with the woman who screamed more while hanging on to my neck.

"You were going to kill him. Why don't you kill him?" Then he spoke.

"I have to pee, so shut up!" Can we stop, I have to pee!"

I didn't give myself a moment to question his intention, so braked the vehicle to a full stop. Then she sat back and loudly ordered, "I have to pee, too, so stay here!" She got out of the car and followed her companion into the brush to join him to do her business.

It was my moment to escape and I took advantage of it! I drove off as my heart continued to race while I checked and re-checked my rear-view mirror in astonishment. I was alive! I suspect her male companion either had a moment of trepidation about taking my life because my erratic driving would kill us all or simply, he realized a stronger call from his bladder. I haven't picked up a hitch hiker since.

While visiting in the couple's home who owned the small suite I resided in, on the morning of November 22, 1963, I was introduced to Karen, a friend of my landlord's daughter. She was new to Kamloops and had made a friendship at work with the girl who was enrolled in the same hair stylist program. Shortly after our introduction and in the middle of my conversing with her, the Barrett's' phone rang. It was Walter Jones from the station.

"Paul, have you heard the news?" asked Walter Jones.

"Ah, no. What's up?" I asked

"Kennedy has been shot in Dallas, Texas and we're having a National Emergency Broadcast briefing in twenty minutes. Can you get right over here? Jones was referring to John Fitzgerald Kennedy, the President of the United States and the event was an international emergency that could possibly require that all announcers work extended hours in our respective broadcast duties.

I was emotionally shocked by Jones's announcement as I expect were most people about the news headlines that aired throughout the world. John Kennedy was loved in the West and with the gravity of his condition coupled with the assassination attempt itself the world faced possible grave consequences if the ordeal happened to be the result of Russian or Cuban involvement?

The announcement came when I arrived at the studios. Kennedy had succumbed, but the assassin, Lee Harvey Oswald, was an American that had been tracked to a theatre in Dallas where he was apprehended after the man apparently gunned down a Dallas police officer before entering the building. Some of the pressure was off the world for the rest of that day.

It was an incredible moment for me to remain composed. I was a novice broadcaster and had to deliver two major emotionally gripping newscasts that night. By the end of the evening I was fully captivated as I contemplated the role I was experiencing, broadcasting news history with the Interior's public glued to each newscast as the day's historical events unfolded. Every precaution that I had read, about being an emotionally detached reporter, was impossible to observe. Kennedy had captivated my youth just as he had succeeded in doing to most of the youth of the Free World. People of all ages had placed their hope in his leadership, to pull the world through the menace of Communism. He was gone now, and an older Vice President Lyndon Johnson was left to continue his work.

Before I departed the station that night, I studied a piece of paper that I had pulled out of my pocket. On it was written a telephone number that Karen handed to me that morning when I rushed out the door from the Barrett home to the emergency briefing. Before leaving I had asked her for her number suggesting that we continue our conversation at another time. She wrote down her contact information, handing it to me. That evening from the studio I phoned her to arrange for us to meet after my shift ended.

The next morning as I contemplated my visit with the attractive woman, I decided the visit was good, but worried. Was I ready for this to continue? True, I had found a friend, but she was three years older than I and that was troubling. So, I contented myself with the fact she was there if ever I decided to call again and chose to give myself time before getting more involved.

For a short time, I continued my life, dedicated to improving my broadcast skills. On weekends and the occasional weekday evening, on my one day off, I joined Walter Jones as statistician to his play-by-play hockey broadcasts. The work allowed me into area hockey games free of charge and took me to other interior cities as Jones and I accompanied the Kamloops Chiefs to the various hockey outings. For me, the opportunity meant gaining knowledge, so I could improve my delivery on sportscasts and Jones liked that.

That year I recall making numerous trips to the Kamloops library where I continued reading current affairs and sports magazines while having only limited engagement with people other than those in the broadcast business. I had to work both Christmas Week and New Years that winter unable to visit with my family in Nelson. At eighteen it was a difficult effort and the full effect of that came when I was almost in tears behind the microphone during a Christmas night music program I hosted.

Not long afterwards I opened my wallet and pulled out Karen's phone number and called her. I had a suspicion before the conversation and asked myself should I call? My own interior passions were being stirred about engaging a female friend at such a time. It was in the middle of January and we drove around Kamloops stopping to visit with each other at various locations. It was early morning, after work and not much was going on in the city; however, we only talked. Karen had to be at work at eight in the morning.

By March, my resolve for Karen had weakened and that vulnerability was no match for her womanhood. As detached as I upheld myself to be from my passions, her affection melted me. She was a powerful companion to encounter during my loneliness and I only measured her warmth and attractiveness, ignoring both her and my dignity, succumbing to my instincts which required that I take anything she offered me. Immediately, I felt the mistake in our relationship, but it was too late as my infatuation was too strong to set aside.

After becoming physically involved our friendship became strained when Karen announced she was going to Winnipeg to straighten up personal matters that she advised involved an unfinished relationship with a man friend there. What annoyed me most was that she then advised that her friend fathered a baby she had when residing in Manitoba. She had given that baby up for adoption. The pronouncement made me feel foolish for becoming involved.

Sometime in April she phoned announcing, "I believe I'm pregnant, Paul."

I was flabbergasted! At just eighteen years I realized that I might be the father. My life had become terribly complicated! I admitted to myself that I didn't love Karen, nor did I completely trust her during that period. She couldn't have loved me either, for both our reactions were now a bit calloused toward the other. By that time in my life, I hadn't even calculated the possibility of her getting pregnant. How naïve was I?

"Paul, it's yours!" she insisted in a response to my coolness over the subject.

Out of obligation to the relationship, afterwards I did date Karen a few times. I really wanted to run away from whatever was going on in my life rather than patronizing a relationship that had gone so very wrong. Later the impact of my actions became clearer as I contemplated the life of a child being orphaned and that I may have been the one responsible.

I guess my immaturity could be blamed for my behaviour, but in retrospect, I think I can lay more blame on the fact that I chose to spend a couple of years away from my faith which presented a more ordered life. I had blindfolded myself and although I was just eighteen, I understood my actions. Truthfully, it was in a period of my life that I enjoyed testing and sampling every freedom that I cared to and by giving licence to my passions I allowed a tempest to take control. But self control was not parallel to my heartiness and my generation's youthful standards and the enjoyment received from them. Although my enthusiasm had to encounter all that life offered while I enjoyed testing my own persuasion, deep down I still possessed a standard that was above that which I had slipped to. Those novels I read had assisted in moving me to abandon my respect for the lady friend and in less than two years I had become completely indifferent to my true conscientious hope that I should live a dignified life.

In April I found another place to live. It seemed that Karen's friendship with the Barrett's resulted in her sharing the secret of her condition with them, so I moved in with an Anglican Priest who had advertised for a roommate while he was in Kamloops on sabbatical from the Central Alberta Diocese. He had several months left to vacation before he would return there and needed a tenant to help with his rent. We did all right together, but the man had all sorts of theology to offer me. His devotionals, grace before each meal, Mass and the rosary each morning, made me uncomfortable because he usually asked me to join in. It was peculiar for an Anglican to have a Marian devotion then, but he did.

Unfortunately, the man may have offered some advice to me; however, I didn't want to talk to anyone about my predicament. I felt any amount of prayer in my current spiritual state was overbearing. For the moment what I needed was a Roman Catholic confessional to expiate my sins before I attempted any devotional with another Christian. I did make a confession and it helped the state I was in mentally as well.

In early May my brother John announced by phone that he was spending the night in Cache Creek before continuing his way to Prince George with his new employer. He had taken employment with a siding company after receiving an early discharge from the Canadian Navy. The Canadian Government had decided to scale down its military and

John saw that occasion as an opportunity to get out of the five-year contract he had signed when enlisting three years earlier. His request for a release was accepted by the military and he had begun working as a civilian.

John's telephone call came at the radio station and couldn't have come at a better time emotionally for me, but my Ford was in a garage having its engine replaced. I had to arrange for another friend to transport me over to see John at Cache Creek where he was overnighting fifty miles west of Kamloops.

John was full of news about his service years and during the visit I was equally compelled to offer stories about my life and career. My brother's employment in siding sales gave him plenty of yarn to share about his sales successes. He had developed the ability to get his foot inside prospective customers' doors with a sales trick he used, and his sales record was apparently rewarded remarkably as a result. My brother would always go to a customer's back door if he happened to be first rejected by the homeowner at the front door.

"Pardon me, but somebody was very rude to me at the front door and slammed it on my foot. Could I talk to you about how my company can refinish your house?" That was John's retort to any coolness he received at the front door. That second approach often resulted in his humouring the owner and making the sale.

It was great to see him, but the visit lasted only one evening before he continued with his work in Northern British Columbia. He advised that he planned to return to Kamloops within a couple of weeks. I was pleased to hear that as the two of us had rarely connected for the past three years. Although I wanted to talk more to my brother about the specific events that had transpired in my own life, I decided to take up that discussion much later.

Shortly after John left, I contracted Infectious Mononucleosis which left me quite ill. I couldn't face food and was bedridden for two weeks. By then my friendship with Karen had ended. She advised that she was going to stay with her sister in Blue River where she intended to work until closer to her due date which was estimated to be around the middle of December 1964. She still planned to give the baby up for adoption.

Internally, I was changing as the impact of my actions began to have their full effect on me. I promised myself never to allow such a situation to occur in my life again. Although the effort to be Catholic had temporarily seemed contrary to my freedoms, those practices were better than the disorder I had encountered since. Through the whole experience I discovered that the old recognizable path returned where those familiar structures of my youth affirmed ideals that taught why I should live more of a contradiction to the vain life the world offered.

When John returned to Kamloops, I had already handed in my resignation to Walter Jones. I hoped that once I recovered from the Mono, I could find a new broadcast position elsewhere that would offer more variety. I intended to look in cities in Alberta, British Columbia and Washington State, but first I would return to my family in Nelson and take time to recover from my illness.

Chapter Twenty-nine

My brother never did get to hear about my secret that summer. It was a few years before anyone in the family got the news, or so I thought.

I hadn't lived at home for three years other than for a few short weeks, so it was good to be with family even though Mom and Dad had planned a trip east. Mom's brother, Patrick was in Thunder Bay and her mother had relocated with her son, Charlie, to Pefferlaw after the death of Charlie's father several years earlier. Dad's youngest brother, Edward, had been in Toronto and resided in Scarborough with his wife Madeline and children while Edward enjoyed a successful career as a Jazz guitarist. In Mom's case, she had not seen her mother or brother, Patrick, for twenty years, nor Dad, his brother, Edward, for ten. On the other hand, Mom's brother, John who was stationed in Moncton, New Brunswick, had been seen a couple of years earlier when he was assigned to Moose Jaw's airbase as flight commander with the Royal Canadian Air Force. He and his family had made a trip to Nelson in 1959.

The return of my brother John from the navy and me from Kamloops was after the family had already planned the excursion eastward. Neither John nor I minded the departure of our family from Nelson, as we were grown enough to allow them a vacation away while we watched the family home. Geoffrey, Janice and Patrick went along on one of the few vacations our parents ever enjoyed having together while they had children at home.

For a period that summer, I had lost confidence in myself. Interiorly, I continued to be a little troubled by emotions that occasionally erupted as I struggled facing my actions head on, feeling that I had betrayed both faith and family. Through it all, I felt that I needed to make some sort of restitution but couldn't. First, I had to figure out where I fit in the amends process and what role I should play to effect healing. In order to do that, I needed to understand whether I was the father of Karen's baby. My involvement at the time all seemed so, complex as I lived the interior life of the Dickens' novel characters I read about. My whole being was affected while I experienced extreme sentiments about every thought I faced, and shadows lingered in my mind while I mentally visited my past and thought about Karen and the baby's future.

While living at home telephone conversations could not occur with Karen and when they could, she had moved and was no longer in contact with me. I had no success in determining her whereabouts, so I waited. She hadn't called nor written, except for one letter and that communication arrived in the middle of July providing an address at her sister's home in Merritt; however, when I attempted to contact her, she was gone and her sister and family would not let me know of her whereabouts.

In November, I received a letter from the government agency in charge of her case, asking if I would be willing to support the child. Subsequently, I phoned the agent who had written and stated that I would first like to clarify that the expected child was mine. In that conversation I explained about the circumstances of Karen's visit to her Winnipeg man friend, stating that I needed convincing there was no involvement with him, and they should ask her questions about that visit. Something within me advised that I was being an ass, but I felt I had the right to ask since the pregnancy coincided with her Manitoba visit. After writing a letter expressing my involvement with her, I never heard from the Ministry again and presumed that Karen had made some admissions to them that she had not made to me.

Meanwhile, within a few weeks of my arrival back in Nelson, I was unsettled about being unemployed, so went down to CKLN Radio, met with the owner, Ramsden and offered my service. At first, he appeared taken aback that I would suggest I could improve his broadcast operation, but then he capitulated and told me that he may actually be willing to hire a broadcaster, deciding first that he wanted to talk to CFJC's management and inquire if I was as capable as I had boasted. That night he came over to my parents' house and offered that I could come to work at the station, but that my salary would be the same as the one I had left in Kamloops. His reason for the low salary was that his station could not afford to pay more. I doubted his sincerity and rejected his offer, so went down to Spokane to look for work there.

In Spokane a new station was opening. It was KUDY Radio and the management immediately offered me the position of News Director, a position that would also pay for my continued education at Gonzaga University while I worked for the station. Unfortunately, for me the position had one drawback. The station manager announced while he poured a beer for me out of a larger container in a pub that he was a homosexual. At the time we were celebrating my newly acquired employment at the trendy establishment located near Gonzaga.

"Pardon me, Paul, but do you mind if I ask you a very personal question?"

"Ah, no, go ahead," I replied.

"Are you a homosexual?

"No, of course not," I retorted.

"Well, I am, so don't be offended as I find you very attractive, but I would still like you to come to work for me anyway."

I was irked that he was so attracted to me that he would consider propositioning me after my successful interview that afternoon. That pretty much wrapped up my job search in Spokane. I took no time in making my decision. I didn't want a homosexual as a boss, nor, at that time, did I believe that his homosexuality was something I should be apologetic for feeling objectionable. I got up and walked out of the bar leaving the poor man on his own to pay the bar bill and to ponder his preamble to what otherwise was likely going to be a proposition.

My two-day stay in Spokane had cost me every cent I had, so I was desperate to find work when I returned to Nelson. Fortunately, a men's clothier, Frank and Stan's on Baker Street in Nelson, was in the middle of a closing out sale and Frank Beresford, the owner had heard from my folks that I was in town. He phoned and asked if I could come to work until the store's inventory was sold off. He was an acquaintance that I had always enjoyed visiting in his store and the offer of temporary employment seemed a suitable alternative while I awaited something better for my future. The position remunerated more than Ramsden's CKLN offer and I had nothing to go to otherwise. The store's inventory quickly sold out, so I was out of work again by September. Tragically, Beresford died shortly afterwards in a private plane that crashed while he piloted it.

KUDY Radio's university offer opened my mind to the possibility of commencing my first year that September at Notre Dame University in Nelson, although I was apprehensive over the continuing my education, since I really wanted broadcast employment instead. The broadcast jobs were scarce as the field had little or no movement. Usually, when there was work, it was quickly taken. I needed money, so decided to attend Notre Dame that fall while I took temporary employment driving a delivery truck.

The university was operated by the Catholic Diocese of Nelson during that time period and needed students, so admission for me was easy. I had no program of study in mind but enrolled in three courses while I worked making grocery deliveries for the Allied moving agent.

My return to Nelson led me back to my Catholic faith. It seems that my confession in Kamloops and the grace that it offered made me feel a compulsion for my return to Blessed Sacrament Church and my former pastor, Redemptorist Father Lange's Masses. I continued to use him as confessor and Parish Priest while my parents and the rest of the family attended Monsignor Monaghan's Masses at the Cathedral. Lange asked me to be reader at Sunday Masses. I was always comfortable with the priest who enjoyed a special connection with youth in his parish.

I have one perilous anecdote to pass on about my parttime work, regarding the difficulty I had in making deliveries to the many Chinese restaurants, grocery stores and hotel pubs that lined the hilly streets of the small city. Their owners all wanted restocking orders brought to the businesses' back doors that were frequently located up several exterior stairs that were exposed to the elements. Snow, that year, commenced just after Halloween. After injuring myself, a couple of times, while I packed heavy loads and tumbled down the slippery staircases, I resorted to leaving the deliveries in the main entrance of the respective establishments that refused to shovel their snow at their rear doors. I recall chucking a snowball at a cranky restaurant owner to remind him that he hadn't cleared a path up the stairs for a second time that snowy week. He had told me to "live with it" and his remark infuriated me. My boss at West Transfer laughed off the incident, while defending my obstinacy when he responded to a telephoned in complaint from the businessman. "Shovel your damn snow and you won't get snowballs!" responded my boss.

On the evening of December 14th, 1964, I received a telephone call that came during the middle of dinner hour at my family's residence while I sat at the table during mealtime.

"Paul, you have a son." It was Karen on the other end of the line.

I had very little to say in return. "Oh! Hi, how are you doing?" I asked in a sheepish tone.

"I'm okay and so is YOUR baby. He was born in Blue River and he looks just like you," she proclaimed. I wondered about her trip to Manitoba, but suspected the baby was mine while I was in denial.

The conversation ended as abruptly as it had started. Karen was evasive from her hospital bedside where the conversation apparently originated from and so was I. I didn't want the ears around me to know what the phone call was about.

The next day, I attempted to call the Blue River hospital and there was no hospital in the town. I would have to wait thirty-seven years before I would find out the truth about Karen's birth and the whereabouts of my son.

That evening after I hung up from the call and returned to the dinner table, my parents asked where it originated from. I successfully diverted their attention from their question by lying.

British Columbia continued to seal birth and adoption records for the next thirty-six years and I would not have any more information other than what was delivered to me over the phone by Karen that evening. Deep down inside I believed her that the baby was mine but resented the situation regarding the Winnipeg visit and her man friend.

After completing that autumn semester at Notre Dame, I decided not to continue courses in the next semester as a result of a conversation I had with a Nelson friend. Richard Joyce told me there was work at Cominco in Trail where the salary was paying union scale. In February 1965, I was hired on in Cominco's Zinc plant where I worked for a month before being transferred over to the plumbing department. Both jobs were awful! Fortunately, I was rescued by a telephone call that came from CJAT Radio of Trail. The management hired me on as a news reporter and broadcaster. My salary was three hundred and seventy-five dollars per month for my work which involved city council, school district and police reporting along with some disc jockey work.

While in Trail, I lived in a suite upstairs from Richard at 93 Rossland Avenue that I shared with two other Nelson acquaintances. Once, alone in the apartment at night, I awoke to what felt like a hammer tapping me on the head.

"Get out of bed!" ordered a familiar voice. I flicked the light switch on above me to discover my neighbour, a man near my age, from across the hallway had a revolver held to my forehead. By his breath I knew that he had been drinking.

"Come and celebrate my birthday with me or you're dead! It's loaded," he added, and I assumed he meant the gun.

I got up and followed him into his apartment as he backed out of my doorway and pointed with his gun to his door as if to say go in. He pushed me on to his sofa and began to tell me the storey of his life while frequently ordering me at gunpoint to imbibe with him. I did, but cautiously sipped my drink one drink to four of his. Eventually, he passed out and I removed the loaded gun from his hands.

The young man, whose name I can't remember, claimed that he was the illegitimate son of well known Canadian Federal politician and British Columbia Supreme Court Judge, Davey Fulton. His complaint was that his personal life was a disaster because his mother was hurt by the scandalous relationship with his estranged father. I doubted that was the real reason for the inebriated neighbour wanting company and endangering my life, but suspected alcohol was.

Afterwards, I moved in with an eighty-year old Italian widow that spoke little English. Her cooking was incredible, friendship congenial, but until I started my own study of correspondence Italian there was little verbal communication between us. We initially resorted to smiles and hand signals. Over time, I learned enough conversational Italian and have since continued to refresh my Italian on occasions throughout life for five separate journeys that I've made to Italy.

On July 17, 1965, my sister, Sherry, married Leonard Hackett a Vancouver lumber grader. They had begun dating when Sherry attended psychiatric nursing school in Essondale. Len's favourite pastime outings were fishing and camping which became his signature vacation with the family. John and I were both home for the wedding that was at the Cathedral of Mary Immaculate in Nelson.

Dave McCrady, the broadcaster who was responsible for my being hired on at CJAT, left to take on a News Director's position in Lethbridge, Alberta for CHEC Radio. He had called me a couple of times at Trail after leaving CJAT to encourage me to come to work in Lethbridge. Initially, I was quite happy with CJAT; however, that changed when my friend, Steve Serenas of Drayton Valley, Alberta, whom I met at St. Anthony's College called and subsequently the two of us made arrangements to go off to California in August for a two- week vacation. I had been given the time off by the station, but that offer was revoked when the provincial government called an election. I was told that I couldn't have the time off until after the election. Steve was going to California and I had no intention of cancelling my plan to do the same. I phoned McCrady and he told me I was welcome to come over to CHEC as management had agreed to hire me on his recommendation, but first he told me to take the vacation I planned. With no allegiance to Trail's CJAT, I left for California returning to Trail only for the purpose of picking up my paycheque.

The radio market in Trail was limited. Alberta's mid-sized cities offered more diversity and broadcast opportunity than the sleepy little cities of British Columbia's interior, so McCrady's encouragement won me over with a little help from my Alberta buddy, Steve Serenas. Steve was working in Drayton Valley for a pipeline company at the time.

After spending two weeks travelling down the West Coast with Steve on a whirlwind tour that took us all the way to Tijuana, Mexico, while we slept on beaches, in olive, almond and orange groves, I returned to Trail and then took the train to Lethbridge after selling my car to my brother John, who had been working for a few months by then at Trail's daily newspaper in advertising sales.

Before staying in Lethbridge, I first made a Greyhound trip up to Red Deer where another offer had come from CKRD Radio in that city. I wanted to investigate the opportunity before starting the position in Lethbridge. In the end, Lethbridge paid more, so that was where I continued my broadcast work.

At CHEC, I co-hosted a live call-in show along with the News broadcasting assignment. The position paid a fair salary which included a company automobile. CHEC had an excellent manager, Bob Wilson, who treated me very well and appreciated my work. He had the knack of bringing the best out of his announcers as the man was an excellent broadcaster himself. I learned a great deal from him and had his respect that made me want to perform for him.

The radio station was working to keep any competitor station from opening a broadcast outlet in Taber, a small city that is located fifteen miles east of Lethbridge. That effort involved CHEC placing a remote studio in downtown Taber. The remote outlet amounted to a mobile trailer being setup where I was assigned to co-host Taber's open line segments hearing residents' complaints and accolades regarding local issues. Meanwhile, CHEC's, Dave McCrady did the same from that studio.

One major distraction while broadcasting in the mobile trailer, was that there were always a number pedestrians passing by waving and looking in on me through the large studio window, while I broadcasted. I got one complaint made to the elderly woman I had roomed and boarded with while I resided in Taber. Some of her elderly friends would stop and expect me to chat with them and I didn't do that as I was usually preoccupied by studio work. It resulted in them calling me a stuffed shirt for ignoring them. True, but unavoidable when I was managing open line callers that required my attention on air.

By then I had developed a talent for delivering extemporaneous garble over the telephone through a microphone on my radio program with an ad lib that was both pleasing to listeners and station management. The program was called 'Beefs and Bouquets.' The program enjoyed the number one position in ranking in the broadcast census ratings. In addition to that responsibility I did an early morning show from the Lethbridge studios on weekends. That program was largely a music program with interviews and the occasional remote broadcast.

In June the station manager, Wilson called me into his office to ask if I would be interested in taking over the morning show on weekdays. I told him that the offer was a real compliment, understanding that the assignment was usually given to one of the station's senior broadcasters; however, I doubted my ability to get out of bed each morning at four-thirty, necessary because I needed to be at the station in time to sign-on with the Farm Report at six. Previously, on a couple of weekend stints, after driving a girlfriend, home to Taber from a movie or outing in Lethbridge, I would immediately return to Lethbridge and settle down for the next few hours in the staff coffee room, reclining on its couch to sleep the balance of the night in order to be at the station on time to sign-on at six. I once overslept and awoke to the station's telephone lines ringing from perturbed farmers phoning to enquire why their beef, hog and sugar beet reports had not aired yet. It was more of an embarrassment to me than my station manager, Wilson, who laughed off the late sign-on incident. The morning man position paid sufficient income to live well but not enough to convince me to stay. I wanted better than the station could offer.

Chapter Thirty

Each year the early summer landscape of Central Alberta greens as a result of the arrival of the warm sun and rains during May. In July a redecoration of the emerald rolling geography occurs while the canola crops mature displaying their yellow floral hues as prairie winds cause them to wave as if greeting motorists travelling along Highway 2.

While nature renews itself in Central Alberta's corridor the spirit of the locals is energized with the commencement of summer's solstice and each night's most spectacular event, the luminescence of the sky by the Northern Light's aurora borealis usually present until late autumn. Under Alberta's endless heavens that unmatched spectacle captivates every eye positioned below the brilliant Milky Way. Spectators the feel as though they're almost touching the galaxy while gathered at lakesides huddled around campfires or at city gatherings during seasonal events, the likes of Edmonton's Klondike Days, Eskimos' football matches or in backyards enjoying every minute of the short season which is characteristic of the region.

For me, returning to Edmonton in summer 1966 meant renewal as well. I needed to revisit my teens and be refreshed by the joy of re-connecting with old friends, because I craved Edmonton's spirit of vitality where friends resided that I recall meeting in my two years spent there from 1961-1963. I was driven by the excitement of the region that exuded opportunity, wealth and growth.

In early July as I motored along the highway toward Red Deer, I became momentarily distracted by thoughts of Marlene Ibbotson, the girl that had once dated my friend, Steve Serenas. That prior year while Steve and I vacationed in California, he told me that Marlene was living in Red Deer, so stopping there I attempted to speak to her by telephone, but succeeded only in reaching her father, who didn't volunteer her whereabouts. That had happened to me once before when I attempted reaching her after departing Edmonton when returning to Nelson at the end of eleventh grade. Instead of motoring on to Edmonton I decided to make a detour over to Drayton Valley to visit Steve Serenas where I hoped to get his co-operation in providing me Marlene's contact information.

"Bickert, you always did have a thing for her," replied Steve. "Okay here it is," he capitulated as he wrote her telephone number on a piece of paper and handed it to me. She had moved to Edmonton.

I don't know why I was so compelled to meet Marlene at that time, other than I felt she would be receptive to my call and something told me our meeting would be good. I recalled the warmth I felt from her when she was first introduced to me by Steve in 1962. Now, it was over four years since our brief encounter at Jasper Avenue's Blue Willow Restaurant and the first meeting's effect on me was still fixed in my mind.

Steve was mildly annoyed by my insistence that he hand over her number, but his compliance was to oblige our friendship and as a result that the two were no longer dating one another. It seemed that his youthful crush on Marlene was over, so I was ultimately rewarded by my detour to Drayton that day.

My arrival in Edmonton was early the next morning, because I overstayed with Steve the day before. That made it very late for me to search for hotel accommodations. The city was overbooked due to the commencement of its annual summer Klondike Days festivities, a time when Edmonton celebrates the arrival of the 1890's Gold Rush and that period's influence on the region. I resorted to attempt to contact my old chum, Norm Boulet, hoping to stay with him, but he had left the city being enlisted in the Canadian Navy. Persisting until six in the morning I was eventually given a room key by a sympathetic front desk clerk at the King Edward Hotel on 101st Street off Jasper Avenue. The room had been rented during the night to a businessman who left early that morning, so I wasn't charged for the room. The clerk advised that I would have to be out by eleven as the room was booked. I was happy to take it.

When I got up, I phoned my friend, Cheryl Grant and her mother invited me to stay with them until I found a place to live. There I stayed for two nights before relocating again to a hotel in downtown Edmonton.

Cheryl had been sick with infectious hepatitis throughout her eleventh grade and had just finished repeating the year at Edmonton's Queen Elizabeth High School and enrolled to enter grade twelve that autumn. Betty Grant's daughter dating a Mormon horrified Cheryl's mother, who wanted me to run interference on the friendship. I only managed to squeeze in an outing for coffee with Cheryl which provided enough time for me to understand that my friend was going through a sort of religious epiphany, a result of the Mormon's evangelization. I was barely strong enough in my own faith by then to tackle Mrs. Grant's objections to her daughter's freedom of inquiry about The Latter-Day Saints.

Once I was over my auditions at CBC, CJCA and CFRN Radio Stations, I waited for a response to those attempts to secure broadcast employment and within a week was offered a position at CJCA as announcer and Program Manager for their new FM station. Unfortunately, a pending decision on the application for licensure by the Canadian Radio and Television Commission was denied delaying the availability of the position making it impractical for me to wait the additional three-months the CRTC reapplication would take.

Shortly afterwards, CBC Radio hired me on as a news announcer and then that same day revoked the offer by telephone when upper management advised the station manager that it wanted a female announcer instead, in order to facilitate a rebalancing of the network's staffing. Of course, I was disappointed and was forced to become more intent on finding any temporary employment to hold me over until a broadcast position opened. CFRN did advise they expected an opening by January and would likely hire me on then.

My hotel accommodation was near city center, the Park Hotel, an old and risky establishment, well known for the seedy crowd that frequented it. I only needed a bed at night and seldom would want to be there in the daytime, so until I had work in the city and found an apartment to move into, I made do with the place.

It was toward the end of the Klondike Days festivities before I called Marlene Ibbotson, who agreed to a date that Saturday. For some reason I had been nervous about making the call prior to that.

On meeting Marlene, I found she was everything and more than I remembered her to be. At twenty she had matured and appeared confident. Her blue eyes, smile and mannerism totally captivated me. I was smitten!

It was the purity that I saw in her, along with the quiet simplicity, unpretentious mannerism and looks that made me swoon. I was unglued and she seemed to enjoy me too! The comfort I felt in her presence made visits together delightful. I could totally respect Marlene. I wanted her for life! The trouble was that she had several suitors and that posed a temporary problem; nevertheless, I was on a mission to win her loyalty which would take three months to do. The lady was busy enjoying her independence away from her home in Red Deer along with the attention that Edmonton's males were giving her.

After a couple of weeks in the Hotel I found a suite in an older house on 105th Street, south of Jasper Avenue and spent August and September there while working at a new selling position with Federated Investments, a mutual fund that hired me. The job required that I travel out of town to see prospective clients that were not so hounded by investment advisors as their city counterparts. It was a commission enterprise that offered a five-hundred-dollar monthly draw, but barely paid my expenses during the first couple of months but I persisted. I was learning something from the work. Unfortunately, I wasn't so available to hound the girl that I was attracted to then leaving her free to date others in my absence. I had to do something drastic!

I used a little trick to give Marlene time to think about me. It was a risk I took, but the results proved successful. I disclosed that my intentions were serious for her, telling her that I was leaving town for awhile and gave her time to consider where I stood in her life.

Following that conversation, I took a trip back to Nelson for a few weeks, but before doing so volunteered to take her winter coat out to the dry cleaner for cleaning. In doing that, I planned not to re-deliver the garment to her until it was good and cold in the city. A month later, in mid October, when snow was about to fall on Central Alberta, a phone call came from Marlene asking if I would like to deliver the coat over and visit with her for the evening. I was intentionally evasive about the offer but asked if she wanted to go out for the evening instead. She stated that she was doing laundry and had her hair in curlers, so it was not a good night for her to leave her apartment. I responded by telling her I would find someone else to spend the evening with. After returning to Edmonton from the visit with my folks, I had joined a church young-adults group and started dating others while I intentionally avoided calling Marlene

It was later during that week Marlene phoned to get her winter coat and made a peace offering. She realized that I was perturbed with her but felt one of her delicious chocolate cakes would win me over. I couldn't resist the invite and let the relationship warm again suspecting that she had tired of the others by then.

My gamble on the strategy worked. We immediately resumed dating again, this time, on an exclusive basis and by the ninth of November she was wearing an engagement ring. I had found the person who completed me and was in love. By then she understood about Kamloops and my past.

While my timing for a proposal was not the best as I was not working in permanent employment yet, I felt confident that that would be easy to rectify. What was difficult were the efforts I made to convince my parents on the matter of my readiness for marriage at twenty-one. Additionally, Marlene's parents were not easy to win over.

We had privately set the wedding date to be September 1967 but decided to move it to February knowing waiting was only to accommodate our parents who were objecting to what was inevitable. My parents objected that travel to Alberta was hazardous in winter. Marlene's mother remarked, "Engagements can be broken," while her father refused to speak to me. Marlene was twenty and I twenty-one. Who could believe we would ever make it?

I had money that I had inherited to get Marlene a diamond ring, make a down payment on a new home, buy furniture, a new Ford automobile and pay for the wedding. This annoyed Marlene's father who complained, "Where does he get his money?" He didn't know that his future son-in-law was nearly broke by then. I can certainly understand why my parents were concerned over my intent to marry from the proceeds of my inheritance. They must have wondered, "How long would the party last?"

Marlene and I made two trips in early winter, one over to Nelson for my prospective bride to meet my parents and then to Vancouver for my sister, Sherry and her husband, Len, to meet Marlene as well. That seemed to be the turning point in convincing my side of the family that I had picked a good mate. Both Mom and Dad liked Marlene as did Sherry and Len.

After our return from the British Columbia visits to family, I then needed to decide for a priest to marry us, so resorted to contacting my Franciscan friend, Father David Crosbie, the former Prefect at Saint Anthony's College. He consented to perform the ceremony and enrolled Marlene in a marriage preparation course taught by him in the Franciscan friary. During that winter while she attended the classes, I continued to grow my Mutual Fund clientele which still was not too financially rewarding. Marlene worked at the Toronto Dominion Bank on Jasper Avenue, located between 103rd and 104th Streets in those days where she was sexually harassed by a married manager. She had moved to an improved salary at the TD Bank, but its manager was on to my lady's good looks and was overlooking that he was a married man.

I didn't have to attend the classes Friar Crosbie taught Marlene surmising that the Church had it figured out we Catholics knew all there was to know about faith and marriage. For years afterwards I felt the Church failed to teach the many complexities of Christian mixed marriage and what it meant for one to be partnered for life as God's witness in that mission. I thought the Church could have better contributed to an improved union through marriage preparation that involved both partners, like the way it does today. I don't believe that my dear Franciscan friend's discussions with Marlene, at the exclusion of me, succeeded in doing that. Some lessons for the two of us would have provided a better footing for the rest of our married life by directing us to grow together in Christ undivided as he prayed for us to do at the Last Supper. For years our marriage struggled while divided in faith, which had its basis rooted in family history, that was to blame.

Paul Bickert and Marlene Ibbotson engagement photo Dec. 1966

Chapter Thirty-one

Most who know me will have one thing to say, "He smiles a lot!" I can't imagine that any one person doesn't deserve that as an opener. That's the best side of me that I can give out when meeting people for the first time. Some might say it's a nervous tic. There are only two people that I can remember where my smile was nervously displayed. I wanted so much to please Marlene's parents and the first encounter has left lasting impressions.

In autumn 1966 while I courted Marlene, her mother, at the age of forty-two, delivered her fifth child, a daughter they named Bernadine, born on September 23rd. During a torrent of financial difficulties for Alleyne and Leonie Ibbotson the baby was likely a joyful blessing.

Originally, at our first introduction, I felt that my future mother-in-law had lost composure in my presence, surmising I was likely responsible for her nervousness. She fidgeted with her hair and her apron, annoyingly cleaning up in front of me and then rearranging household effects behind me. I couldn't believe that any woman could be so agitated in my presence. For my part, I overlooked the unsettling introduction of my wife's mother and became extra nervous for her as she fumbled around me.

I didn't understand why Leonie was the way she was until Marlene let me in on her mother's past with a story that went back to childhood. Apparently, her obsession with cleaning and self-conscious attempts to rearrange her own appearance resulted from living an impoverished life with the loss of her mother at a very young age. Afterwards, she bore the brunt of the psychological effects by being the oldest child in a family of six siblings while she continued to attend to order. Living in different homes she was assigned to throughout life while struggling to have a semblance of dignity and orderliness caused her acquired behaviour becoming obsessed by cleanliness. The nervousness was a result of another predicament.

Most regard mothers as special people understanding each has her own degree of influence on her family. Although the ability to mother is an instinctive call to womanhood, for one to do it with dignity, without any proper preparation, requires more than just a natural summoning. It requires a special gift.

Leonie, the childhood name of the woman who was destined to be my mother-in-law, will always be regarded by me as having been an extraordinarily graced soul. Born into hardship, she endured every measure of her situation with dignity and later in her role as a mother carried herself with a considerable poise for her personal hurts and trials. She had little preparation for the role after losing her own mother to being first institutionalized with tuberculosis when Leonie was seven and then her mother's death occurred when her daughter was fifteen. Never did she let her personal plight destroy her.

According to Louise L'Heureux Dombrowsky, a L'Heureau family historian and biographer, Onezime L'Heureux was born in Pontuneuf County, Quebec on April 19, 1862. The family lived in Quebec prior to relocating to the Eastern USA for a short period prior to moving to Manitoba, a five-hundred-and-eighty-mile journey where they were carried in covered wagons pulled by oxen. Prairie grass fires nearly destroyed the travelling caravan. Onezime and others were severely burnt on the hands and legs while fighting to control the oxen and wagons in the fires while releasing the animal from the wagons. The oxen were rounded up the following day. They first settled at the St. Jean Baptiste Settlement sixty kilometers south of Winnipeg. Onezime married his wife Oxanna Arcand in 1883 in Winnipeg's St. Mary's

Catholic Church. He then homesteaded property in North Battleford area, where he built a log and sod hut for a residence on the land situated on the banks of the North Saskatchewan River near Battleford. Not long afterwards they were asked by the Northwest Mounted Police to take refuge in Fort Battleford as the natives were on the warpath. By 1900, the couple had lost five of their children including triplet girls and two others. Afterwards the couple relocated to Duck Lake where Onezime was the baker for the Duck Lake Indian School.

By 1904 Onezime's health was failing him and he returned with the family on the homestead near Battleford. An eleven-room house was built by his older children on the property for the expanding family. The home became the first Catholic Church for Sunday masses for the area where friends and neighbours would gather for the Sunday liturgy. There were five sons that assisted Onezime until his death at sixty-nine in 1931, followed by Oxanna in 1932. They lost one more child to meningitis however, two daughters and seven sons survived the six babies that died. Eldest son, Leon married Matilda Mercier who were parents to Leonie Ibbotson, Marlene's mother.

I made a very astute observation when I met Leonie Ibbotson, calculating, that if my wife's mom could look so good to me when she was middle aged, it was likely that if I married her daughter, I would still be attracted to Marlene when she was much older as well. At that time, I had no idea that I would one day feel so much love and appreciation for my mother-in-law in the future.

Leonie's father had his legs amputated by a train running over him rendering the man unable to care for his children. That resulted in a painful separation of Leonie and her five siblings from one another, except she was not apart from her baby sister, Stella. First, she endured a stay with an austere order of nuns, living in a convent and then afterwards with cruel relatives. Both events were likely responsible for the woman forever being apprehensive about people. Additionally, she endured the insensitivity of an aunt and sexually aggressive uncle who punished her harshly for the most trivial of mistakes, making her kiss a hot stove top or walk to school without shoes as forms of punishment.

I expect that the cruellest hurt she encountered was the treatment given her by her insensitive Roman Catholic parish priest after she complained to him about her uncle's sexually explicit advances toward her. That led to the priest being hostile toward Leonie culminating in a lifelong distrust that the woman held toward the Roman Catholic clergy.

At fifteen Leonie found compassion and friendship in an Anglican home at Frenchman's Butte, a small hamlet in north western Saskatchewan, located on the eastern banks of the North Saskatchewan River before the waters work their way south to North Battleford. Margaret Ibbotson, whose husband Wilfred (Bill) had gone off to Europe to be a foot soldier during World War II, hired Leonie to care for her household while she managed the town's general store that the Ibbotson's owned.

Immediately, the Ibbotson's' oldest son, Alleyne Charles, was attracted to the young housekeeper despite his one-year disadvantage in age. The two were married in early 1942 when Alleyne was eighteen and Leonie nineteen. It was then that Leonie took the more common name Leona until old age when she reverted to her given name.

Alleyne's mother, Margaret Ibbotson was born of one quarter Cree Indian descent. She was a thrifty, intelligent and determined woman, well liked by townspeople who frequented her business. Fairness regarding credit issues, the portions she served, and service given earned her that respect. She ran the business with a disability that resulted from a birth defect that left her with a stub right arm. Margaret used the deformed stub as if it were a club to raise her four sons and daughter in the absence of their father, but her humour was enough to let any one of her five children know she was fun and deserved respect. They all loved her dearly. Three of her children were still teenagers while her husband was enlisted.

I met Alleyne Ibbotson, at dinnertime in the Ibbotson residence in Red Deer, later that afternoon after the encounter with Marlene's mother.

He came in the door and without greeting any member of the family went into the basement and re-appeared after several minutes lapsed to plunk himself on a dining room chair for dinner. Marlene made the introduction to which he nodded without saying a word.

The dinner was quiet until Marlene's older brother, Rupert, broke the ice asking his fourteen-year old sister, "Brenda, why don't you tell Marlene's boyfriend about the essay you wrote at school about your grandfather fighting in the Frenchman's Butte Massacre?

"Okay, I will," responded Brenda, proudly. "Well grandpa was one of the men who as a brave soldier shot at some men in the war at Frenchman's Butte and it is an historic event in Canadian history."

"But the trouble is, Brenda, that you didn't tell Paul which side your grandfather fought on," reminded Rupert. "Well, Paul, our grandfather was really an Indian Brave, not just a brave soldier." Rupert continued,

"Brenda forgets to tell that part, as it upsets her to the point of always crying. So, we have since given her a new name, Little Running Tap," finished Rupert with his summary of the historical event.

"Oh! Which side of the family is the Indian on?" I inquired?"

"That would be on my father's side," volunteered Rupert.

Leonie attempted to interrupt the direction of the conversation by interjecting, "Alleyne are those Rupert's pants you have on today?"

"Yes, they are," answered Alleyne.

"Looks like a heap big chief in a young buck's pants," I interjected hoping to thaw the course of the conversation that was going nowhere for Marlene's father.

Alleyne did squeeze out a few heaves from his chest and half a grin but withheld open laughter at the remark. I had succeeded to make the man emotional for the first time that evening. It would be a few years before he'd laugh again with me.

He was different than the other Ibbotson brothers. They were happy, but Alleyne was the sober one of the four surviving sons. His quiet and restrained manner seemed to persecute his family that could laugh easily without him.

He seemed a sincere and honest man in his dealings and a hard worker that provided well for a family that he seemed to suffer in. I don't know why? There is seldom a joke told about fathers-in-law. That day I made one and it may have been a mistake to do so.

Immediately after their marriage, both Alleyne and Leonie carved out a living in the neighbouring small communities that dotted the narrow dusty road between North Battleford and Frenchman's Butte. He drove trucks for operators. The first child, Rupert Alleyne, was born two and a half years before Wilfred Ibbotson returned from Europe, but by then, Leonie and Alleyne followed others that had relocated to the larger centre, North Battleford, to enjoy the CCF Government's free hospital and health care services.

Later, only a few years after his return from Europe, Wilfred Ibbotson died, leaving Margaret a widow in 1950. She soon remarried a much older man, Jimmy Manson, a Spruce Lake farmer that had homesteaded the land nearby Frenchmen's Butte. He had farmed since coming, at the turn of the century to Saskatchewan from North Dakota. I recall one conversation with Jimmy when he leaned over to me in 1967 and asked,

"Have you ever been to a lynching?"

"No, I can't say that I have. Have you?" I inquired.

"Yes, I have, once in North Dakota! My neighbours and me hung a man. That's how we took care of horse thieves in those days." Responded the ninety-year-old American who came north at the turn of the century to homestead in Saskatchewan.

"That's how I'd like to deal with Premier Tommy Douglas and the CCF, too!" Jimmy Manson didn't like a Socialist government! He lived to almost a hundred years and refereed his last hockey game at ninety-one on speed skates.

After Margaret sold the store the Manson couple resided in North Battleford during the winter months preferring the larger community after farm duties ended each autumn.

Alleyne's work continued to be mostly in trucking while the family resided there. The work paid well enabling him to purchase new vehicles and gave the family a comfortable yet humble home. Throughout life he was a thoroughly organized individual that liked that his wife catered to that quirk encouraging her to keep herself and their home meticulous. One other whim the man exhibited was his aspiration to be out of bed early in the morning, three hours before he had to be at work. He would sit drinking coffee, chewing on a toothpick and a stick of gum and at the same time he chain-smoked cigarettes while checking his timepiece to pass the hours before he'd finally leave the house to go off to work.

Known as A. C., the man had a quiet disposition, enough for Leonie to know she was best to allow him to his silence rather than to demand a lot of conversation from him. Chatter was reserved for her own friends and children. From early on in her marriage, instead of expecting verbal communication from Alleyne, Leonie busied herself with housecleaning and found humour was her best tool to draw her husband out.

On March 3, 1946 Marlene Margaret Ibbotson was born. Her large blue eyes, quiet, shy and hesitant smile would portray the person she would eventually become. For the rest of her mother's life Marlene came to provide comfort to her mother who needed the gift of this daughter to sustain her even until Leonie's death.

Rupert, at three, travelled around the neighbourhood of the Ibbotson family home in Battleford, inviting people to come and see his little sister. From those early years onward Marlene and Rupert were the best of friends until darkness would eventually befall her brother's life and that change affected their closeness. I recall that when I first met Rupert in 1966 that he acted extremely proud of his sister and can easily reflect on how the two enjoyed one another's company together.

Eventually, Alleyne moved his family over to Lloydminster and then in 1949, south of Edmonton to Calmar, after news of the discovery of oil from a drilling success at Leduc occurred and he found work on rigs, eventually being promoted to Tool Push.

The family moved into Edmonton when Rupert was eight and Marlene five where the family took up residence near the University of Alberta, just off One Hundred and Fourteenth Street on Seventy-Ninth Avenue. Marlene commenced primary school and Rupert resumed in his fourth grade in classes at the University of Alberta campus. Incredibly, Marlene and her brother would walk to school in the congested university area.

Until the oil discovery and the Ibbotson's arrival at Edmonton the city had largely been a military base and acted as a service centre for the North. Its population was just shy of a hundred thousand residents occupying predominantly just ten to fifteen city blocks of residences, sprawled along either side of the North and South banks of the North Saskatchewan River Valley providing a nice community to raise the young family.

Brenda, the third child, was born while the family resided in Edmonton and a couple of years later, son, Dwayne. In 1956 the family moved on to Drayton Valley where Alleyne operated oil well service trucks along with his three brothers Owen, John and Garvin. Alleyne's family resided in a skid house on the east side of the highway below the town Centre until Marlene completed tenth grade at Drayton's Frank Maddock High School.

Prior to entering High School, Marlene dated Steve Serenas, the friend I would meet in tenth grade at Saint Anthony's College. In her free time during winter months she would carve edges with her figure skates on the community's outdoor ice facility while on winter weekends and during summer months, Steve Serenas, whose parents owned the sole movie theatre in town, sat next to his sweetheart, Marlene, for free movies. At the end of tenth grade Marlene's family moved to Red Deer.

In Red Deer, Alleyne started a supply company that provided silica sand and crushed walnuts to the drilling rigs. The business supplied those products for the drillers assisting in the oil extraction process. It eventually underwent hardship when new suppliers began to compete, becoming a serious strain on Alleyne's health. He seldom took a holiday and worked relentlessly to save the company for relatives and friends that had invested in it.

My introduction to the Ibbotson's occurred when the family business was failing. Both Alleyne and Rupert were employees of the small company and anything a potential son-in-law had to offer the family in the form of friendship was overbearing. Meanwhile, Leonie Ibbotson, for her part, offered what she could to accommodate for the lack of enthusiasm her husband had for my presence in their daughter's life and to make me feel welcomed into the home. This was the way she always was, working to please her family and those her children brought in.

I guess Marlene's mother had her hands full at the time juggling the wedding plans, their newborn daughter and her husband's emotions and the sensitive issue of their daughter's impending marriage. Apparently, there were objections that were being raised by Alleyne who thought Marlene was far too young and the marriage needed both parents' legal consent, due to Marlene's age being under Alberta's legal age of twenty-one.

Alleyne's disregard for me came to a head a few minutes before the wedding ceremony when I showed up in my new tailor-made wedding suit to see if I could help with any last-minute pre-ceremonial preparations and my future father-in-law handed me a paper bag full of bows to decorate two cars. "You called on this show. Get decorating!" he ordered with a contempt that was likely displayed for his having to sign the document that authorized the government to allow me to marry his underage daughter. Nobody really needed me at the house that morning; however, Alleyne wasn't in the decorating mood to participate in the event's preparation and wanted me to know that.

It was my wedding day and I wasn't going to let the man destroy the joy of it, so I did the decorating of the cars and then went off to Red Deer's Sacred Heart Catholic Church to be married. As I was leaving, Marlene's mother stuck her head out the screen door and asked, "Are you okay?" Perhaps she was trying to appease the effect of Alleyne's scorn that she had known about after his reappearance into the house.

"I'm terrific! I'm marrying your daughter, today!" I responded.

Chapter Thirty-two

The year we married would turn out to be a remarkable year in the life of any Canadian, humankind and for me. It was 1967 and the nuclear arms race was at its pinnacle with the Soviets and Americans being the most significant players frequently detonating weapons into the atmosphere, from deserted islands or deep below the Nevada Desert and at Siberian outposts reminding each opposing force of the military might it possessed. Before the year ended China too, became a nuclear nation joining with the United States, Russia, Britain and France. It always seemed so insane to me!

Meanwhile, the small nation of Israel engaged its neighbours in its own Six Day War. At the same time a conflict was being waged in Southeast Asia expanding from Vietnam to Cambodia and Laos. Despite American bombings of Hanoi and Haiphong that war was spreading. Yemen, Bangladesh, Nigeria and Biafra fought and oppression in South Africa and Eastern Europe regularly reminded Westerners that the world was a keg of dynamite.

Royal weddings, world expositions, lunar landings and historic signature baseball careers earning 'Five Hundred Home Runs' pennants all provided only temporary distraction to the public of the upsetting headlines about the state of the planet, though hope was on the horizon for weary humankind.

That year Pope Paul VI appointed twenty-seven new Cardinals, including Karol Wojtyla, Archbishop of Krakow, a man who was destined to transform the Church, befriending Christians, Muslims and Jews while effecting a new level of unity in both the Church and throughout the world dismantling barriers between religions and nations that had existed for years. It was a faint glimmer of God's goodness and a prevailing light that would, effect a healing on earth for future generations to contemplate.

In January, as Marlene and I were preparing for our own wedding feeling secure in our love, we watched on television while Princess Margaret, sister of Queen Elizabeth II, married Peter van Vollenhoven in a ceremony which prompted most sceptical Canadians, including ourselves, to comment that the royal nuptial would likely end in disaster, because the phoney affair was typically overbearing like the lives that were led by most of Britain's Royals who lived out their existence symbolizing the Empire's harmony while ignoring good conduct toward one another. It was true that that marriage would eventually continue the litany of failed unions in the Royal Family as had many in the house of Windsor since Henry the Eighth. The Church of England, marvellous in its Royal wedding ceremonies, would also influence our own married lives for the next forty-two years.

At 11:20 on February 4th, Alleyne Charles Ibbotson handed his oldest daughter over to me while offering a grin to appease his earlier behaviour that morning when he left me alone to decorate the cars while I stood dumfounded suited for a wedding ceremony in his driveway. Stepping over to the front pew at the left side of the church he sat down beside Marlene's mother. He had done his duty and for the rest of the ceremony wiped his teary eyes with a white handkerchief lamenting that his daughter was grown and had found love.

My family had arrived in Edmonton the day prior to the wedding; however, they were not in the church on time for the ceremony. Father Dave Crosbie, O.F.M, who had come down to Red Deer to witness the nuptial was being hurried by the regular Parish Priest at the church in order to get the ceremony underway, because the venue was booked for another ceremony immediately following ours. My parents and brothers,

Geoffrey and Patrick, along with our, sister, Janice, were all missing for the commencement of our wedding. Could they have misunderstood the directions that I had given them?

"Kay it looks like your fur coat just flew out of the trunk of the car, across the freeway," Dad blurted while driving his black A90 Austin Westminster Sedan down the freeway north of Red Deer. He had just caught the image of a large brown furry object in orbit sailing across the freeway reflected in the driver's rear-view mirror. The car's loaded trunk opened on the snowy Number 2 Highway near Red Deer.

"Bick, I need that coat! I'll freeze if it gets any colder!" Mom shrieked, realizing that the overstuffed trunk contents were being sucked out by the vehicle's turbulence into the chilly winter air.

"Can you believe it? I told you we'd never make it!" laughed Patrick, "What else could go wrong?" he continued.

Patrick, at eleven, had already begun to find humour in such events. Nobody could keep a straight face as he joked more about the predicament.

"Okay Dad let's see you get yourself out of this mess. Why don't you just take a shortcut across that median to test how much hairspray Mom put in her hair this morning?" suggested Patrick

"And we'll all spend the next three hours freezing our asses off while you dig us out of the snow. You're a big help!" Geoffrey chided.

Janice loved the word asses, "Geoff! No way, not my ass!"

It was several miles before the freeway's next exit ramp permitted them to turn around and head north to collect the contents from the highway's snow covered median adding an additional twenty minutes to the trip that was already behind schedule as a result of my mother's holdup before departing Edmonton. She had insisted that she be given time before leaving to redo a failed hairstyling attempt performed by an unfamiliar Edmonton stylist earlier that morning.

Halfway through the ceremony my mother's smoker's cough echoed throughout the church signalling to me and the rest of the wedding party that the family had arrived and was being directed into the building's front pew by Gary Haughian, Marlene's cousin, an appointed usher who was the son of Marian, Leonie Ibbotson's sister.

It had become sort of a tradition for my mother to be late for family weddings. First, my sister Sherry's and then mine. A year afterwards my brother, John, told Mom that his wedding was an hour earlier than the actual ceremony was scheduled to commence. His lie succeeded in having her on time for that occasion; however, a few years later, at my brother Patrick's wedding, John commenced serenading the full church from his church pew with an out of tune rendition of 'Beautiful Katy.' That ceremony was delayed for twenty minutes while the congregation awaited our mother's arrival and laughed at my older brother's entertainment. Again, Mom had overstayed at an Edmonton beauty salon.

The rest of our wedding day went as planned. The ceremony was attended by sixty friends and family members. My good Franciscan Friar friend gave the toast to the groom and notified the attendees that I was his first discipline problem when I attended Saint Anthony's College while, during the same year, I had additionally impressed him with my attraction to the opposite sex more than I had toward becoming a priest.

Mutual friend, Steve Serenas, was Best Man and my brother, John, Groom's Attendant. Marlene's Maid of Honour was her first cousin, Marguerite, daughter of her mother's sister, Marian and Marlene's sister, Brenda, her bridesmaid.

To give one a perspective of some of the costs related to the ceremony during that period, the wedding meal was a dollar and a quarter per plate and the three-tiered wedding cake twenty-seven dollars. Sterling silver cufflinks given as gifts to the Best Man and Groom's Attendant were two dollars. It all seemed so expensive then but pales in comparison to the costs for a wedding today. The ceremony was followed by a reception and meal catered to by the Anglican Women's League at Red Deer's Anglican Church Hall.

For the wedding night, I had ordered a special bright orange pair of pyjamas intending to look quite dapper in front of my bride. The staff at the men's store that sold me the pyjamas offered to custom fit the outfit to my personal measurements. Of course, until I attempted to put on the pyjamas on the wedding night, I didn't clue into the fact that they would stitch up both the fly and pant legs. Our first night was spent in a honeymoon suite at a hotel that stood across from the Chinook Shopping Mall on Calgary's MacLeod Trail.

The next day we travelled to Kimberley for skiing. Marlene had never skied so I did my best to impress her on the slopes and make her forever afterwards lecture me about the audaciousness of my attempt to have her become advanced in the sport all in one outing. Her retort was, "You're really trying to end this honeymoon in a hurry!" After Kimberly we were on to Coeur d'Alene, Idaho for another ski outing. Of course, I skied that day on my own! Within a week we returned to Edmonton after a layover in Nelson.

I recall, for the remainder of that winter and springtime witnessing nightly television news of Canada's Liberal leader, Prime Minister Lester Pearson, working to influence a divided Canadian Parliament to vote against the forces of John Diefenbaker's Conservatives to declare the country's unofficial anthem 'O Canada' as our new official anthem replacing 'God Save The Queen.' At the same time a new Maple Leaf Flag signifying our independence from Britain was about to be elevated above Parliament, because the Liberals had invoked closure on a debate in the House of Commons a few years earlier approving the new flag. Our nation's one hundredth birthday celebration at the Montreal World's Fair site, Expo 67 needed a national flag for Canada's twenty million residents to be proud of.

1966 Alleyne and Leonie Ibbotson - Red Deer, AB

February 4, 1967 Wedding Day Lt. to Rt. Steve Serenas, Brenda
Ibbotson, Marlene & Paul, Marguerite Haughian and John Bickert Jr.

Diefenbaker opposed all of that too! He seemed quite offended that the country should want its own distinctiveness to separate from Great Britain.

Simultaneously, the Beatles provided a great influence on the behaviour of the youth of our day promoting a contra culture utilizing as tools peace and love adorned with beads, long hair, music and Eastern religion to formulate a rebellion against the establishment. Group member Lennon's love-ins, in Western hotels in front of television cameras along with visits to Indian Gurus, while challenging Western society's bias toward Christian values, shocked traditionalists as the four young men inferred that meditation could replace prayer and flowery ballads, theology. Youth loved the charade and joined in by the masses culminating in enormous rock concerts the likes the world had never seen before as the rebellion grew to include consumption of mind-altering drugs which provided an escape from reality. Other Pop groups that followed the Beatles out of England would offer equal support to the cause. The Rolling Stones were one such group who spirited more outlandish behaviour with their own 'Bad Boy' image further challenging compliance of youth toward the day's moral standards.

I was too busy with my own new life and the responsibility of marriage while earning a living in Edmonton, outside of the familiar broadcasting work I once enjoyed, to ever become absorbed with the changing mentality of youth. I had experienced enough rebellion in prior years to feign the concept and the eventual repercussions such rebellion might exact. Subsequently, that autumn I voted for my first-time supporting Alberta's preacher-politician, Ernest Manning, a man who appeared sensitive to traditional moral values and who would ultimately lead his Social Credit Party to its ninth consecutive win that year to control the legislative assembly. Simultaneously, while Manning celebrated his victory, the nation's Justice Minister, Pierre Elliot Trudeau, who in the next year was to become Prime Minister, brought forward what appeared to conservatives as an appalling motion in Parliament. Supported by his own majority Liberal party he voted to legalize homosexual acts in

Canada. He was a Roman Catholic, but his liberal attitudes collided with Catholic values.

When the law was enacted it reminded Alberta's religious right that the Federal Government had an obvious difference of opinion to Albertans. To emphasize what sociological madness was taking place that year New York and London Broadway shows, for the first time in recent Western civilization, in a segment featured a nude cast member in the Broadway Play 'Hair,' a farce on the youthful contra culture's behaviour driving home the point that times were changing and so were the morals of the world.

We spent our first year of marriage residing in the house at 5002 – 92nd Avenue in Edmonton, a new three-bedroom home, bought for the sum of sixteen thousand dollars with fifteen hundred dollars down payment and assumed my first mortgage in life. We did what newlyweds do, enjoyed our own love-in. Unfortunately, the love-in ended within three months when my brother John moved in with us after relocating to Edmonton from Vancouver. Strains on my bride and her regard toward marrying two Bickert brothers began to show when she eventually revolted against our leaning on her feminine domestic credentials. The honeymoon was over, because we would mess up the house and she would invariably end up having to clean up behind us. She never threw a pot or pan, but a hairbrush grazed my right ear when she once became quite perturbed. It was enough to warn me that I could take her just so far before being required to ask John to find his own living quarters.

Marlene's income from her bank employment wasn't enough to support the two of us while I trained in financial sales, so, by May I felt it was time to look for more gainful means and found work with Capitol Records of Canada. The job I secured was as a marketing representative calling on radio stations and accounts. It required periodic travel, to other centres of Alberta north of Red Deer and over to Saskatchewan to service clients there throughout that province promoting the company's recording talent. It was a giant leap from broadcaster salaries that I had earned in the past. In fact, the salary more than tripled plus I was provided a company car.

Capitol Records had acquired convention facilities at the city of Montreal for the World's Fair. In July, that event provided an opportunity for me to see my Eastern relatives while enroute. Grandma LaLonde and her son, Charlie, lived in Pefferlaw, Ontario, as well as my Dad's brother, Edward and his family resided in Scarborough. I visited both on a three-day layover in Toronto. It was my first re-acquaintance with Grandma since I was two and a half. Charlie, my mother's half brother, was now nineteen and still residing with his mother. His father had passed a few years earlier.

Ed Bickert was booked to play at the Canadian Pavilion at the World's Fair. I managed to take in one of the concerts and for the balance of the week, Ed and I spent evenings touring Montreal Jazz clubs together.

Within eight months of my employment with Capitol Records, Columbia Records offered me a move over to that company providing better remuneration and an improved working environment. With Columbia I wouldn't have management looking over me and that meant some freedom to discover my own potential in managing the territory I serviced. Immediately, Columbia would move me to Regina to clean up Saskatchewan distributor problems as the territory had no representation for several years and account customers were complaining. In February 1968 we sold the house on 92nd Avenue and relocated renting a half duplex on the south side of Regina near its legislative buildings. Marlene had quit her job in Edmonton to follow me and for a time she was content to make road trips back to Alberta and throughout Saskatchewan travelling with me. After a few months she found work with an optometrist in Regina. That year Columbia sent me off to the Bahamas to their product convention and shows. I stopped over again in Toronto and was met at the Airport by Madeline Bickert, Edward's wife and stayed overnight at the Bickert home in Scarborough. Madeline was a wonderful hostess.

In April 1968 my brother, John, married Gail Davidson, a girl he had started to date while he worked selling furniture for Sears Department store in Edmonton. We attended the wedding in Vancouver travelling from Regina. After the wedding John found temporary employment in Vancouver as a cab driver providing some interesting anecdotes to his life while spending nights 'hacking.' One story he relates is of picking up a sorry female who in turn related to John that she had failed to end her life that night.

"See I can't succeed at anything, not even suicide," she complained as she pointed to the dented rooftop on a vehicle she apparently had collided with after jumping out of an adjacent high-rise apartment a few minutes earlier.

John slept in his cab at nights in between customers often taking watches and other forms of payment in kind for fares he'd exact from rides provided while Gail trembled at home in the seedy Vancouver apartment they had rented, awaiting John's arrival from the precarious life he led at work.

By late summer Columbia transferred me back to Edmonton; however, I would be required to travel to Saskatoon and Prince Albert occasionally.

Immediately, we began looking for a new residence in Edmonton and subsequently bought a house at 14507-81st Street. It happened to be under construction at the time; so, we first rented until the building was completed moving in just in time for Christmas 1968 which we spent at home with Marlene's family.

Marlene and I were discussing the idea of our first child when we returned to Edmonton and were both supportive of the idea as the two-year period that we had spent together was void of what most couples seek when they marry, wanting to enjoy family.

Chapter Thirty-three

The first two years our married life was about us and the sweetness of one another's affection. There were few other distractions. I went off on excursions to call on clients for Columbia Records in Saskatchewan and Alberta, periodically leaving Marlene who worked at a steel company in Edmonton where she did receptionist work and bookkeeping. She had tired of the bank work where the middle age manager was making passes.

Changing times were reflecting on me as I was being reminded by customers that I looked a little too trendy with near shoulder length hair and Nehru suits that were introduced to my generation by the Beatles who were influenced by regular visits to Maharishi Mahesh Yogi of India, a guru for their millions to be wasted on.

Once while returning from Saskatoon during a hot summer afternoon I picked up a mangy young hitchhiker who stood on Highway 16 west of North Battleford asking him if he'd care to join me for a beer at the next town if we could find a pub. We found a local hangout located in a small hamlet east of Lloydminster with a venue that resembled a service station made over to function as a bar. The town offered little else for locals, so we made do wanting 'cool ones.'

Immediately after entering the establishment, I left my hitchhiker companion and went into the men's room. When I came out the associate had disappeared. As I sat waiting at my table in my Nehru suit feeling a little overdressed for the location growing impatient, I finally inquired of the bartender where the guy had disappeared to.

"Well young man, I instructed him to leave. We don't like any of them Beatle maniacs in this place," he retorted.

"You're joking!" I laughed.

"Nope and come to think of it, your hair's too shabby too, so get yourself out of here!" pointedly deriding with his finger aimed at the door.

I was out the door in a hurry as the man turned his head nodding at three other patrons as if to let them know they had his permission to help me out of the place if I didn't leave without resistance.

Small towns hadn't grown accustomed to the changes that the rest of the country had. Capitol and then later Columbia's recording artists had temporarily influenced me, but before ever returning to Saskatchewan again, I had my hair cut. I continued to let it grow over my ears and still do today, a mark of the era I grew up in.

I met many recording artists and some of them I'd look after while they toured. Some of the more prominent artists that I would get to know during those years will be remembered years into the future. They are: Bob Dylan, Paul Simon and Art Garfunkel, Janis Joplin, Dave Brubeck, Johnny Cash, Alice Cooper, Stan Getz, Stevie Wonder, Dizzy Gillespie Carlos Santana, Leonard Cohen, Pink Floyd, The Byrds, Sly and the Family Stone, Bobby Vinton, The Jacksons including Michael, as well as comedian Bill Cosby who recorded comedy albums with Columbia, He was a very likeable man, but later notoriously became a deceitful criminally prosecuted rapist.

———◆———

I had forgotten about the odours that would emit from the stockyards in North Edmonton. That autumn the air stunk from what was Northeast Edmonton's signature landscape, the stockyards. The hot summer lingered into autumn in 1968 and one was constantly reminded of the stockyards that lined Sixty-Sixth Street and the Fort Road. They hid their stench until after I made a down payment on the new house, we would move into at nearby Londonderry district.

Any visitor to Edmonton would wonder why anyone would choose to live within twenty miles of a stockyard. It had always been a matter of cost for housing. The north end had stockyards and industry that made housing more affordable for the working man. Where we purchased the odours were never so prevalent.

Central Trucking in Nelson had been sold to new owners who decided the position my father held with the dealership would be manned by one of the purchasers. They wanted dad to stay on but as a mechanic. Dad would have no part of that at his age. He felt his health would not do well with working under trucks and 'swinging wrenches' particularly during winter months. He moved the family to Vancouver where he commenced looking for work and I soon got word that his job search was not going well, so asked him to come over to Edmonton where Alberta's economy was vibrant. It was late autumn when the family arrived all seeming a little perturbed by the circumstance of being forced to settle for Alberta's chilly winter that had already arrived.

In advance Marlene and I had done a search for living quarters for the family finding them what appeared to be a reasonably attractive turn of the century home located near central Calgary. Unknown to us at the time was the fact that the residence was very poorly insulated. That winter we were reminded continuously by the family that even the dog refused to sleep on the floor of the building as temperatures plummeted to record lows freezing unattended water in the house's kitchen's sink, plumbing fixtures and the dog's water dish.

Dad found work as a service manager at a Ford car dealership in downtown Edmonton, but the owner attempted to force him to sell service that was not required for customers' vehicles. My father would have no part of the dishonesty, so he moved on to a tractor trailer manufacturing firm within weeks. That company's employees voted to join a union which placed dad between both union and management resulting in him being fired for the first time since back in the tomato patch when he and his dad commenced work in the Okanagan Valley during the Thirties.

Eventually, he began talking about a complete career change from vehicular companies opting to make the move after his employment was terminated by the tractor trailer manufacturing firm. The new sales career for my father was equally perilous though. First, he found work at an office furniture company and subsequently, sold furniture to the businesses that were occupying the newly erected high-rise buildings constructed in Edmonton's Seventies building boom. His sales for that company were good, but as his commission cheques grew the company began cheating him.

Watching all the turmoil in my father's life, the toll that it exacted and financial along with emotional stresses he endured began to arouse concerns about my own future. I felt vulnerable having not continued my education and began to take correspondence courses to upgrade with the intent of some day re-enrolling in a university degree program. Although I wasn't certain what that program would be at the time.

Dad's precarious career in sales was having a different effect on my youngest brother, Patrick. At thirteen Pat created a ventriloquist act with a manikin he made developing a humorous skit that picked at my father's work life.

"So, you don't suppose you'd like to buy a steel desk," the dummy mimicked my father's sales efforts. Patrick would respond acting out the customer's role.

"Nope, I don't suppose I would!"

In early September 1969, Marlene experienced several nights of premature contractions as she approached full term in her pregnancy. The Royal Alexandria Hospital's maternity ward staff became quite acquainted with the two of us as the contractions usually ceased within minutes of our near daily arrival. Finally, on the night of September 23rd things were different; the contractions persisted and by 5:30 on the morning of the twenty-fourth she gave birth to our seven-pound daughter, Natalie Carmen (Christmas Song), given the name as a result of her being conceived at Christmas.

It was a protected delivery process. Likely for the sake of the doctors in those days, men were not permitted to be present during birthing. I thought it a saving grace for me. Women complained of struggling alone while their partners were absent and most men were insensitive to the process. Women would eventually win their husband's participation in the birth event by the time our next child arrived. I would miss that birth too! For our first, I slept on a vinyl hospital lounge, while Marlene fought the contractions alone in the deliver room. Finally, that doctor resorted to forceps.

Our poor daughter was bruised, forehead and crown from the forceps. Marlene looked horrible. I awoke from my night's sleep on a vinyl padded bench in the waiting room to a telephone ringing on the wall. It was the obstetrician who announced on the phone that I was a father to a seven-pound six-ounce daughter. For me, like most men, it was sort of a blissful co-parenting event.

It was one of the most emotional mornings of my life, to stand in front of the nursery ward's window looking at my newborn daughter in the arms of a nurse. I couldn't wait to hold her. Being reunited with my wife at her bedside with our daughter was immensely touching. Within four days we drove home with our baby feeling things to be normal.

Weeks before the birth, Marlene had been given a book by my mother, authored by paediatrician, Dr. Benjamin Spock. It volunteered all sorts of contemporary advice to new mothers reforming past concepts on childbearing and rearing. One piece of advice that influenced us was that parents should keep the baby distant from them. Excessive contact time between parent and newborn was taboo according to Spock. Although painful to follow, we obliged the author and placed Natalie in a bedroom on the other side of the house and peered in on her waving toys above her crib rather than picking her up to cuddle her. Poor child! She would become the product of inexperienced parents and modern paediatrics.

In addition, Natalie went through readmission to the hospital for an umbilical cord infection that occurred within days of her arrival home. It got quite carried away before we realized our daughter's life was in peril. In the hospital she was placed on intravenous antibiotic injections for seven days, all terrifically upsetting to us! When Natalie returned home her blackened and bruised brow was now shaven where the intravenous needle had been inserted and she had lost, to a nurse's razor, the full head of beautiful hair she came into the world with.

Within a few months of our baby's arrival back home we grew sceptical of Spock's recommendations reading in papers that the paediatric reformer's advice had decimated the emotions of thousands of newborns and children throughout North America and that his recommendations were judged cruel.

In autumn 1969 my folks moved into the Edmonton community of Steele Heights; into a new home they had built which was located a mile from our home. Geoff attended O'Leary High where I had attended. Patrick attended St. Francis next to St. Anthony's College and the Franciscan Friary.

The next summer my Grandmother LaLonde, made a trip west after Mom purchased an airline ticket for her mother. It was a visit that offered an occasion to see my sister Sherry and her family who came out from Vancouver. By then, Sherry and Len had three boys, Dwayne, Stephen and Gary, all under school age. John and Gail were at the reunion as well having returned to Edmonton the prior autumn after he finally gave up on Vancouver cab work. They had Charmaine who was two.

John entertained the visitors by bringing out his photo collection. He had spent most of his free time over the years, since leaving the navy, flying or filming aircraft. It had become a custom to compete to see who could stay awake the longest during John's slide presentations which consisted of airplanes, landings and air shows. For John, each slide had its own story. There were few baby photos shown of John's year-old daughter, just airplanes. Geoff and Patrick always disappeared when our older brother commenced setting up his slide projector. Every adult smoked in those days, including Grandma LaLonde and the house filled with smoke as the audience puffed on smokes to ease the monotony. Most smokers still had not given up the habit in response to the growing warnings by doctors that now recommended we all quit the addiction.

Smoking was part of the culture that formed back in the first half of the century when cigarette ads promoted it as a healthy choice, vogue and necessary to calm nerves. "You'll live longer and lead more productive lives," some ads suggested. Back in Nelson children were indoctrinated subtly where candy stores like The Sugar Bowl, across the street from Saint Joseph's School enticed us with candied cigarettes sold from the shelves. Cigarette manufacturers continued to advertise their tobacco products in the Mass Media and governments hiked taxes on the products for years to rake in the billions from the addicted public.

Marlene's family was gathering around Edmonton as well. Brenda had graduated and was working as receptionist for a chiropractic office in an office building on Jasper Avenue. Her brother, Rupert, had been working as a sales rep for Johnson Wax and then moved over to Budget Rent-a-Car to be transferred on to Victoria and later Kelowna. Marlene's parents and Bernadine had moved from Red Deer to Lloydminster where Alleyne, after his company closed its doors, was employed with Husky Oil as drilling boss.

In the spring of 1970, my wife developed a painful shoulder bursitis from hoisting Natalie around. I took her off to hospital emergency at three one morning and watched while doctors scratched their heads prescribing sedatives along with pain killers for my wife.

"Nuts to that," I said and phoned a chiropractor who had his home number listed in the Yellow Pages of Edmonton's Directory.

The doctor met us at his office at 4:30 AM and adjusted Marlene's neck alleviating the irritated nerve that led to the bursitis in her shoulder. At the same time, I had been fighting a bout of bronchitis, something that had plagued me since I was a child.

"Looks like I should take a look at you too!" volunteered the chiropractor.

"What's that got to do with it?" I wondered but didn't garner the courage to ask.

"You've got a subluxation. Ever injure your thoracic spine?" he asked.

"A what? My what?" I asked?

"You don't understand. Let me explain. Nerves regulate function and if you have an irritated nerve supply in your thoracic spine you get symptoms and in your case that could be the cause of your bronchitis. Any injuries?"

"Ah, yeah, I fell off a stool when I was four and suffered a compression fracture up there somewhere."

"I'd be willing to bet my chiropractic degree that that is your problem. Let me have a look."

I was a bit sceptical as I had forgotten that Dr. Murphy in Nelson helped me after I had bouts of bronchitis and after the double pneumonia in ninth grade.

The Sherwood Park chiropractor referred Marlene to a chiropractor on the other side of town to a more convenient clinic location, so I told him that I would see the referral doctor the next day along with my wife.

"Great! Do it! Chiropractic works!" he affirmed.

The next day we both went to the new chiropractor and commenced a program of care which solved the bronchitis problem and Marlene's bursitis never returned. Prior to that I would always get infected and the MD`s resorted to antibiotics. I was so impressed that I picked up a brochure from the chiropractor's office containing information about the Canadian Memorial Chiropractic School in Toronto, but I placed it in a dresser drawer at home and left it there forgetting about it.

Dad was fired again as his commissions were so high in office furnishing sales.

My Nelson friend, Richard Joyce, was in Edmonton studying at the University of Alberta taking a one-year teacher's certification program after having completed his undergraduate degree at Notre Dame in Nelson. The two of us would get together and Richard would always be dismayed over the hardships my dad experienced from unscrupulous employers.

"Paul recall when we were boys how your father paid us for our huckleberries?"

"Uh, you mean the butter?"

Richard was referring to how dad always wanted huckleberries for my mother's huckleberry pies, a frequent dessert during those summers back in Nelson. He would pay us for the berries. Richard occasionally joined in on our huckleberry expeditions as my brother, John and I made it part of each summer's activity. We'd pick the fruit in a patch located in Kokanee Park, near our home and store located at ten-mile on the North Shore. My father's method of weighing the berries in exchange for payment always impressed Richard.

"He was so scrupulous and fair. He'd take a pound of butter out of the fridge and hold the berries in one hand with the butter in the other," continued Richard while discussing my father with admiration and sipping at his beer. "Remember? Then he'd ask us if the weight felt the same in our own judgement while he handed the items to us to scale with our own arms."

Richard admired my dad and that admiration continued when dad eventually hired my friend on at Central Trucks for summer employment while Richard was vacationing from high school. Dad had a mutual respect for my friend, too.

"I'm not letting that ruthlessness happen to me!" I angrily asserted at home to Marlene in a later conversation. Simultaneously while my father experienced work employer moral challenges, Columbia Records was troublesome for me as some of the label's rock and country recording talent expected that I be equally unscrupulous by providing every service to them from that of a pimp to a pusher to please their whims. I never co-operated, resulting in the artists grumbling all the way back to New York.

Some entertainers would be 'shooting up' in dressing rooms, behind stage or attempting to so in my car while I was required to chauffeur them to airports, hotels, restaurants and performances. Others that I had difficulty with would phone my home attempting to arrange hookers or ask if I could find suppliers for their drugs. Even more troubling was that others would let young girls into their hotel rooms and fondle them and talk to me of it. Breaking the law was what some artists did when touring. I resented the risk of being associated with that element and would attempt to lecture them. That didn't sit well with upper management. Record representatives throughout North America were fulfilling the immoral demands of the artists as the industry skidded downhill along with the rest of the decaying morals of many North Americans. Simultaneously, my New York boss, Clive Davis, President of Columbia was indicted for supposedly having crime boss connections and for misuse of company funds, but charges were subsequently dropped, but only after he lost his position with Columbia and the Past President, Goddard Leiberson, returned to the company to replace him.

I did the 'payola thing' as Canada tolerated it at the time. The bribes encouraged deejays and account managers paid by reps with gifts of television sets or boxes of albums to move the product. For me, finding hookers and looking for pushers was out of the question.

My desire to leave the record business seemed a good decision as news stories implied what was going on in Canada closely paralleled the American activities. The work requirements as a record representative challenged my value system while other reps were vying for my position. My choice to leave was further precipitated by a threatened roll back of all the reps' bonuses. I wasn't happy as the company advised in a written memo of coming changes. By then, I had grown accustomed to a pretty good standard of living and the new bonus changes meant my income would be leaner in the future.

I found the Canadian Memorial Chiropractic College brochure and phoned to see if the school had openings. Their classes were full, so I went to Dr. Swartz's office and talked to the chiropractor about the career choice that I was now quite interested in.

"Go to Palmer, Paul. There's no school like it and there's a better chance that they'll accept you!" he encouraged telling me that he'd have some admissions material in my hands within in a week and he'd attempt to get me into that October's class if I would be prepared.

Along with the correspondence courses that I had taken that year, I was engaged in some extensive reading becoming a fan of the classics helping to develop and prepare me for the reading comprehension section of the testing. By April 1971, I wrote the tests and managed to perform well in all of them. The rest was history. In July Palmer College of Chiropractic in Davenport, Iowa approved my application on the condition that I prepare to complete a pre-chiropractic curriculum if I didn't perform well on some admissions tests that that school would have me write. I spoke to Swartz about that and he suggested additional reading material to have me prepare for those tests. I was determined not to have to spend any more time in Chiropractic studies than the four-year degree program would normally require, so I prepared myself for more tests with reading what my friend, Richard had suggested.

In October 1970 I decided to leave Columbia as my mind was fixed on making as much money as I could in order to finance my intended education at Palmer. I found work with Willowbrook Homes, an Edmonton home builder. The company offered a salaried plus commission sales position selling new homes. I resigned my position with Columbia.

Willowbrook had a huge inventory of pre-built housing that wasn't moving in the current market and I felt that the situation was an advantage for me. I knocked on hotel and motel room doors offering breakfast to the prospects as enticement for accompanying me on home tours arguing that I could put them into a house at discount prices. To me interest rates should not be a factor to their monthly mortgage commitment. I was convincing enough with the approach that the couples followed my advice after I had filled their stomachs with bacon and eggs prior to each morning's new home tour. I was required to sit in the show home from one to seven and nobody came while I waited unless they were customers that I went out and dragged in.

Rather than the company facing ruin by hanging on to inventory that was costing its owners dollars to sit on, I convinced them to accept what offers I brought them. My pitch was convincing to both customers and the company owners and within seven months I sold forty-two homes. While doing so, I made history for the company and it had a record year in sales while its competition was simultaneously shutting down.

That October Marlene, Natalie and I flew to Davenport, Iowa, as I embarked on again another career change at twenty-six. While I was off to chiropractic studies, my brother, John enrolled at U of A in a Bachelor of Education program and Geoffrey commenced his pre-law at U of A. Patrick was in O'Leary and Janice attended private school for the challenged. Mom embarked on a career in cosmetic sales at the Bay that autumn and my father replaced me at Willowbrook Homes.

Chapter Thirty-four

I expect that life had a way of positioning me where I belonged by moulding and then providing direction to where I could best serve.

Suffering bronchial asthma, the reoccurring pneumonias and later radio broadcasting work taught me to perform with convincing vocal presentations evoking a confidence that was further honed in sales. These all became the tools that provided buoyancy for my developing chiropractic career.

I enrolled in Palmer's four-year course of study to become a member of what was then thought to be a questionable healing profession. The fringe healers struggled to earn respect at a time when few believed they offered value to the public's health. Only a small percentage of the population enjoyed what chiropractors offered and the profession required forward and courageous individuals that would move its science, philosophy and art into the mainstream of every North American's thinking.

I was primed to swim upstream against a false current of public opinion and prepared for the next twenty-two years of professional service in a work that would require I encounter and challenge every patient to assist them back to health awakening in them the idea that health does not come from a pill bottle but is inherent within a body that is functioning properly. What I'd offer those I cared for with my chiropractic knowledge after earning the Doctor of Chiropractic degree would be a tremendous gift freeing them from the fear of the necessity many had to rely on unnecessary drugs in order to discover health.

Davenport, Iowa is located on the northern banks of the Mississippi River opposite from Rock Island and Moline, Illinois, cities located on the south banks which face Davenport and Bettendorf, Iowa. The Mississippi travels south and then bends west as it approaches what is known as the Quad Cities Area all having in those years a combined population of four hundred thousand inhabitants. The River's grey waters are blackened when they pass the charred nineteenth century brick structures of the cities that line its riverbanks.

Overlooking Davenport's centre is Palmer University's campus crowning Brady Street hill. The University's Chiropractic College is domiciled in several structures that make up most of the institution including clinics, research facilities, libraries, auditoriums and various classroom buildings.

The school was opened shortly after Port Perry, Ontario native, Daniel David Palmer, made his discovery of the profession back in 1895. Palmer who practiced a form of magnetic healing, in September that year examined the deaf janitor in the healer's office. Harvey Lillard experienced his hearing loss nineteen years earlier after lifting a heavy object. The patient gave Palmer permission to use his hands to reposition what Palmer expected was a misaligned fourth thoracic vertebra. Within minutes Lillard could hear again. Since then, that same result has been duplicated many times on other patients with the aid of chiropractic adjustments to the spine. Much later this was explained to be the result of the peripheral nerve injuries causing altered vasomotor responses that affected the auditory canals and constricted the Eustachian tubes in such patients. Similar repeated results led to more interest in the subject and investigation by both early Twentieth Century medical and chiropractic researchers. More recently joint medical and chiropractic research done in Milan, Italy has demonstrated adjustments can give positive outcomes to patients with Meniere's Syndrome, a disorder where patients experience equilibrium problems and persistent ringing of the ears from labyrinthitis (inflammation) of the inner ear. My own children along with patients' children always responded quickly to adjustments if they had an earache.

Palmer began teaching the method after his early success on Lillard. Today, in addition to Palmer, there are twenty-four other Chiropractic schools throughout the world including two in Canada. Today a course of study in chiropractic takes eight academic years including undergraduate work as chiropractors work to improve a scientific approach to the healing art.

I was fortunate not having to spend so many years to prepare. For me the next four years were gruelling enough. I can easily imagine what a hardship professional preparation inflicts on students today. Marlene and I only got to reacquaint with one another during semester breaks, when we made rushed trips home for Christmas and summertime, usually driving the sixteen hundred miles in a thirty-six-hour stretch.

America has a penchant for the history of its wars fought both at home and abroad. Trips through the Midwest easily reminded tourists of the nation's military history. In many towns the only tourist attraction was what battle was fought or what army general lived or died there. Most had little more to share. If it wasn't wars it was gunslingers' stories that marked the map where historic sites were erected. Besides General Robert E. Lee, you had MacArthur, Custer and others. But the gunslingers were many including Jessie James, Billy the Kid, Hitchcock and Doc Holiday to name a few.

The corn states of Iowa and Illinois and the wheat states of the Dakota's, Montana and Wyoming had dreadfully boring landscapes. Rows of corn and acres of wheat or ranching along with the site of the occasional tornado provided for scenery and entertainment along the I-80 Highway. You got a lot of gunslinger history and a big rock with four heads of presidents where dust storms replaced the prairie tornadoes. It was hard to keep awake while driving the Midwest states, other than when a tornado was bearing down on you. After arriving in Canada, you had Saskatchewan and that's all there was between Edmonton and Davenport to keep one awake for the drive. Twice we flew to Davenport, but Ozark Airlines was the principal carrier into the Quad Cities Airport. Over the years it had gained a horrible record for incidents as a result of pilot error. I had a classmate at Palmer who was a pilot for the Airline. His lifestyle was enough to convince me never to use Ozark again.

Iowans pronounced Iowa, I-o-way. Men wore what they referred to as 'Flat Top' hairstyle we Canadians referred to as 'Crew Cuts' having abandoned the hairdo in the 1960's. Iowans were friendly until summertime when the heat and humidity made everyone miserable. Mississippi rats the size of the Canadian Beaver ate all the family pets in Davenport, so you never heard a dog bark. Instead you could hear the termites eat away houses and the occasional pet yelp as another one was devoured by a pack of rodents. I exaggerate of course, but just a little.

For a period, during my second year, I was encouraged to take over as a Webelo's Pack leader. WEBELOS meaning "we be loyal scouts." They are non-varsity boy scouts and under-age. A Palmer student was graduating and required a replacement as den leader. I reluctantly accepted the position feeling I would enjoy what I recalled of Cubs from when I was a child. Webelo's is something that is popular in the USA for kids that are too old for cubs and too young for scouts that have not participated in Cubs nor earned the badges required for Scouts.

Now there are two things you should never ask me to do. The first is to paint for you. The second is be your basketball coach. I can't hang on to a paint brush or a basketball, nor keep track of either. It was a crazy experience that took place in a poor African American neighbourhood and the kids had only one play interest, bazzz-kut-ball, they called it, but I had to take them through the hoops of earning three badges. Those were in science, art and sports, in order to give them the requisites for scouting. Other badges would have sufficed but the programs I chose to develop my pack in they resisted most in participating in two of them. The boys wanted only the sports. Eventually I got their attention by deflating the ball prior to teaching them tumbling instead. That was something I had been good at ten years earlier in high school. It was required that two at a time spot for the others including myself during part of the tumbling routines. Teenage boys spotting a one hundred-and-eighty-five pound grown man is a recipe for someone getting hurt. I hurt my neck so bad in the tumbling class when the boys knocked the horse out from under me as a joke. I still suffer from that injury today. We did make it through the year, and everyone was given their badges in time to progress to Scouts. That was the end of Webelo's for me!

Marlene's sister, Brenda and her husband Lloyd Esak, moved to Davenport after Lloyd's father was helped with his Multiple Sclerosis disorder by a chiropractor during my first summer's recess. We had returned in the first year's summer break for Brenda and Lloyd's wedding in Edmonton. Instead of attending medical school at the University of Alberta, I convinced him to enroll at Palmer.

Soon Brenda and Marlene were both expecting babies. Our son, Taylor Christian was born in Edmonton on January 27, 1973. Marlene and Natalie stayed over in Edmonton after Christmas for the birth of our second child while I returned to Davenport to continue my studies. I missed Taylor's birth but got several views of what women got to go through in a series of Obstetrics classes. I didn't ever care to partake afterwards.

Our son was born on January 27, 1973. Two weeks after the birth, I met my expanded family at Chicago's O'Hare Airport. We crowded ourselves into a two bedroom six hundred square foot apartment to remain in it for the remainder of our stay in Davenport. I couldn't study at home afterwards, so spent most of my evenings and weekends either in the library or sitting in the corner of a restaurant sipping on coffee while I studied.

When I think about the time we spent in Davenport, it was all about my studies. If I hadn't such a wonderful wife and she wasn't so, devoted to her role both as wife and mother, I would never have succeeded in becoming a chiropractor. I needed her loyalty and stability while I worked to achieve what I otherwise would not have completed on my own. Marlene spent many hours assisting me in the early semesters, preparing notes from textbooks she'd be required to read to help me get ahead of what I found daunting from the beginning. Then she spent many lonely hours at home musing over the hardships I imposed by taking her away from her secure and comfortable home in Edmonton near family. I will be forever grateful for her support.

Marlene's father, who had suffered a heart ailment for a few years after the closing of his business in Red Deer, suddenly passed away on March 13, 1973, just weeks after my family's return to Davenport and Marlene giving birth to our son. Alleyne was on the road working for a friend's company in an enterprise related to oil rig servicing. His death was an immense sadness to Marlene and worrisome while she stressed over her mother's loneliness of being widowed and attending to my wife's six-year-old sister, Bernadine, back in Alberta. We along with the Esak's returned to Edmonton for the funeral.

Chiropractic's acceptance was rapidly improving while I was a student at Palmer. Chiropractor Dr. Lou Heard, a member of the Alberta Legislative Assembly and father of my Palmer classmate, Stanley Heard, introduced and successfully passed a Private Member's Bill in the Alberta Legislature permitting the inclusion of Chiropractic services under the new Alberta Health Care Act.

Heard's work was the launch to a revolution in healthcare insurance throughout North America resulting in chiropractic inclusion in many other private and public health insurance schemes including Medicare, Medicaid, Workers' Compensation and most motor vehicle insurance.

His son, Stanley eventually went on to practice in Arkansas becoming a friend of the Clintons, Bill and Hillary when Bill was Governor of that State. Eventually, after Bill became President, Stanley was instrumental in assisting the Clinton Administration in effecting Chiropractic's full inclusion in the nation's Medicare and Medicaid programs. Shortly thereafter and tragically, Dr Stanley Heard along with Dr. Stanley Heard along with his lawyer, were both killed in a private plane crash while returning home from Washington D.C. The accident transpired during the notorious Savings and Loans crisis that rocked financial markets during Clinton's tenure in the nation's capital. It left questions in the publics' minds over what was the cause of the accident.

My friend, Stan was not the first chiropractor affiliated with the White House. In 1931, after graduation from college, Ronald Reagan, who was to eventually become the fortieth president of the United States, went to work as a sports broadcaster for Palmer Broadcasting's WOC. Reagan was a friend of Dr. Bartholomew Joshua Palmer (B.J), son of Daniel David Palmer, chiropractic's founder. B.J. Palmer who is attributed the title, 'Developer of Chiropractic,' simultaneously built a broadcast empire to promote the developing profession. Palmer attributed the call letters that he selected for two of his radio stations, WOC of Davenport, Iowa and WHO of Des Moines, Iowa, call letters abbreviated to mean 'Wonders of Chiropractic' and 'With Hands Only.' Eventually Palmer's broadcast empire included television stations too. Reagan's broadcast career with Palmer ended in 1937 when he screen tested and was awarded a Hollywood motion picture contract, subsequently, appearing in fifty-three major motion pictures prior to entering politics to become Governor of the State of California. Reagan visited Palmer on occasions when he was in the Oval Office as he continued his friendship with chiropractic and WOC.

It was always an important part of my profession's development for chiropractors to have their own lobbyists to influence decision makers in government and the subsequent connection with Washington D.C. was of great importance to the US Medicare and Medicaid funding.

B. J. Palmer's part in the development of Chiropractic often involved televised exhibitions on his broadcast network of stations. One infamous moment that captured the attention of both friend and foe of the chiropractic profession was performed in front of live television cameras as his stations telecast a chiropractic adjustment being delivered to a retired and lame circus elephant. Palmer himself delivered the adjustment after hoisting up onto the placoderm's back straddling it and then thrusting on the misaligned segment moving the vertebra sufficiently enough for the elephant to recover and return to work. Palmer's theatrics were often an annoyance to both chiropractors and others during his era. Today there is a special program for graduate chiropractors and veterinarians certifying both fields to work on animals through the American Association of Veterinarian Chiropractors,' a fifteen-hundred-member body, many of whom care exclusively for animals.

My hair had grown to shoulder length while I studied. While not being so involved in book study I had found time for my personal musings, because I had successfully passed the sittings of the American and Canadian Board exams prior to graduation. A source of relaxation and enjoyment was contemplative reading again, so I read classics such as Teilhard de Jardin's Future of Man and The Phenomenon of Man in addition to several eastern contributors as well. Those of Ghandi and Baha 'u' llah were consumed along with Christian literature and the Bible.

In October 1974, I graduated, in a spectacular graduation exercise attended by my mother who travelled from Edmonton. I wanted to return to British Columbia to practice, but I could not because that Province had a rule prohibiting licensing for graduates that had studied during summer semesters. It was a stupid and political rule initiated by members of the profession that had graduated from the Canadian school that didn't offer summer sessions. I felt it was not the time to object so I decided on returning to live in Alberta and set up practice in Calgary. The summer before graduation I found a location to practice in the north end of the city where a friend had opened his clinic the prior summer after his graduation. His wife was an American and both had subsequently decided to relocate to Spokane and advertised the developing practice for sale. I purchased it and we moved into a house in Calgary that October after selling the additional house we had purchased in Sherwood Park prior to departing Edmonton.

When the four of us returned to Alberta our families had changed. Mom and Dad were now both busy and successful realtors who had relocated to a new home in Castle Downs area of Edmonton. Youngest brother, Patrick had married Mary Anderson after graduation from O'Leary High School. Geoffrey had completed his law degree and was about to commence articling. John had completed his Bachelor of Education degree and would teach in Edmonton. Gail had given birth to a son, Michael, now three. Marlene's mother had moved from the Fort Saskatchewan area of Edmonton to Leduc where Bernadine was now in her third grade and enrolled in figure skating while Rupert had divorced his wife, Susan, moved to Kelowna and since returned to Edmonton where he managed a Ford car dealership. My sister Sherry, along with Len and their three boys continued to reside in Vancouver.

Chapter Thirty-five

There's a Norwegian saying that a soul is kissed by God before it is united with a body. That kiss lasts a lifetime and always leads you back to what is good.

People of God are always led in what they do if they listen to that inner voice that keeps them honest and loving. My parents helped me to understand that summoning and told me to work hard and follow true and sincere conviction holding fast to my conscience and the inner voice that leads.

Mom and Dad had aged while we were in Davenport and I sensed they were worn by life even though their finances and security were going better for them by the time we returned to Alberta. Their life's effort was carved on faces and the weight of their toils was carried by a resignation that only good honest people could earn. I recall how it frightened me to think that life could wear down people who once seemed so youthful and unaffected by it.

My father stood alone watching while my brothers Geoffrey and Patrick organized a crew of friends to assist erecting a double car garage on the back of my parents' property in Castle Downs area of Edmonton. Dad stood looking on as the building was assembled by youthful exuberance. I had never seen him idle while such projects took place. He had always been the worker. Realizing, at that moment, how quick the years had passed and how I had taken for granted his vitality, I could see his stamina was nearly spent at fifty-five.

Today, when I travel to Alberta I'm reminded of my own prime and a time of my life when I exuded energy, confidence and commitment resourceful enough to carry myself as a professional to serve the thousands of patients I'd assist annually. I had become extra confident during my chiropractic training and internship, but the responsibility was maturing and required commitment and dedication which exacted a toll on me, too.

"You're here! I was expecting you any day." Dave Winsor, a tall lanky Scot, greeted us at the door and directed us to his living room sofa in the small Marlborough Park house located in Northeast Calgary.

"Paul, did I ever tell you that my father is an Osteopath in Edinburgh, Scotland. He looks after the Royal Family, Queen and all."

"No, you didn't," I responded.

"You got me so excited about Chiropractic when you were here in July that I decided to go back to the University of Alberta for my pre-chiropractic and then enrol in a chiropractic college myself," Winsor announced.

"What does your dad have to say about that?" I inquired.

"In fact, he recommended it to me when I told him about selling the house to a chiropractor"

Osteopathy was America's early equivalent of chiropractic founded by Andrew Still, the son of a Missouri preacher. Initially, Still miscalculated the early Science of Osteopathy when his attempts to teach it failed and he subsequently described the work as "impossible to teach." Later in 1893, the osteopath claimed Daniel David Palmer sought treatment from him and from that one visit to Still, Palmer went on to develop chiropractic; hence, accusing Palmer of stealing the work.

Palmer defended himself by claiming that his teaching method was a more precise form of spinal realignment utilizing the spinous and transverse processes of the vertebrae, as levers, to realign the spine. By the time Still had his school up and running in Kirksville, Missouri, Palmer was already graduating chiropractors that eventually outnumbered osteopaths ten to one. Eventually, Still's followers were swallowed up by allopathic medicine while chiropractic itself remained a separate and distinct healing science researching and developing the field.

Winsor had been told by his father that chiropractic would be a better place for him to go for his future. Six years after that conversation he graduated from Life University in Atlanta, Georgia with his Doctor of Chiropractic degree and later ran a busy practice in Florida.

Thomas Edison is attributed with saying: "The doctor of the future will give us no medicine, but will interest his patients in the care of human frame, in diet and in the cause and prevention of disease," and Winsor's excitement over Chiropractic was typical as chiropractic's health care alternative approach swept throughout North America with renewed vigour in the 1970's while people migrated from allopathic medicine to the services chiropractors offered.

Chiropractic was the contradiction of modern medicine and my profession's system of educating patients to the cause and prevention of disease and restoring nerve function, hence restoring health at least partially fulfilled Edison's prophecy. I was being carried on the wave of change in public attitude toward my work and I could sense it! Public utilization of chiropractic services was increasing exponentially as the results became more pronounced with government and insurance funding along with public acceptance of the alternative approach increasing.

We moved into the house in Marlborough that Winsor had sold us, and I commenced practice in Northwest Calgary at Simon's Valley Mall, a small building located on Centre Street and 62nd.

At the risk of the public perceiving me as being a little evangelical, I proceeded to hold talks on Monday nights in my clinic and at noon hour in clubs, church halls, on television radio as well as wherever I was invited to speak about my work. I had engagements at Alcoholics Anonymous, the University of Calgary Medical School, U of C's Faculty of Law, the Calgary Law Society and Mount Royal College as well as on several open line radio shows throughout Calgary informing and educating the public about the benefits my profession had to offer. I built a very busy practice, not just for myself, but for many other chiropractors in Calgary that would attend my lectures and commence doing the same themselves. It was all part of who I was. My broadcasting past was being utilized to educate the public about chiropractic!

Shortly after our arrival in Calgary we received news that my grandfather, Harry Bickert, was ill with bowel cancer. Grandpa's condition was terminal, and the man rebelled against his impending death just as he would resist against any obstruction to his freedom earlier in life.

"What are you doing here? The funeral's not for a couple of weeks," he blurted at the door to my brothers John and Patrick who had driven five hundred miles to see him. Then he proceeded to let them in for a visit after Grandma objected to his abrupt greeting.

The wide-open grin that usually divided his face whether he was joyful or angry was his most outstanding attribute. Throughout life the man had a way of notifying friend or opponent with his mouth and furry brow how he would receive them. Whether pleased or disgusted his eyes penetrated souls while a grin beamed his content or a smirk of discontent, but that had all changed. He was spent and the visit from family exhausted him. Our grandfather was anxious for his end to come, so he could get to "those pearly gates." Harry Bickert passed on October 26th, 1975 and was buried at the Coldstream cemetery, east of Vernon.

Life was full of excitement that year as we watched Natalie go off to kindergarten. Taylor was growing from being a baby into a busy boy speaking complete sentences at two and a half years.

"Mom are you going to have a baby?" asked our son from Marlene's lap in August 1975.

"I don't think so?" responded my wife looking over at me with a confused expression on her face. "Unless you know something that I don't, Taylor?"

Then in a peculiar fashion, while holding his little hands up to her forehead and speaking into them, he pronounced, "I think you are!" The eeriness of the moment left both of us unnerved that evening.

Within a couple of weeks Marlene's medical doctor advised her that she was pregnant with our third child. That pregnancy would be her most difficult, because at the end of the sixth month she fell down the home's basement stairs and injured her pelvis. Subsequently, premature contractions continued each night until full term requiring that I adjust her pelvis in order that the peculiar early labour cease. The adjustments didn't hold well as a result of the stress on the pelvis from the pregnancy. Her hip injury could have been much more tragic had she not, just a couple of days earlier than the accident, placed a soft suitcase at the foot of the narrow stairwell. Marlene feared someone falling down the hazardous staircase which ended abruptly with both a concrete floor and wall at its base.

Charity Marie was born May 1, 1976, from a delivery that I attended. Again, I was required to adjust Marlene in the course of the birthing procedure as my wife suffered severe back pain. It was the only birth I attended with her and as I watched the Obstetrician, I was convinced that chiropractic was where I belonged, not in obstetrics.

On one trip to the hospital after the birth to visit Marlene and our newborn daughter I brought along Natalie and Taylor. I had been told by the babysitter that Taylor had experienced a bout of diarrhea that afternoon advising that I should be certain to get him to a toilet before taking him off to the hospital. When we arrived at Marlene's bedside Taylor wanted me to hoist him up onto the bed so he could examine his baby sister. First, his mother requested that I remove Taylor's cowboy boots before placing him on the bed. When I had taken the boots off it became immediately apparent that my son's earlier episode with the trots had resulted in him partially filling the boots with poop.

By then, Marlene had grown used to my parenting and housekeeping skills and while the other ladies in the adjacent beds laughed to the point of hurting their recovering bellies, Marlene was not at all surprised at my oversight.

Charity had eyes as large and blue as Marlene's and they would always be a lasting feature of our youngest that was so shy as a child, but who would later grow in life to be an outgoing woman displaying stature and confidence. The name given Charity Marie means "gift exalted" as she was never planned when she was conceived.

Prior to our second daughter's birth Marlene had spent many days in my office, training and assisting staff to do clerical and receptionist work, but the responsibility of caring for the baby at home temporarily ended my wife's work outside the home.

Unfortunately, staff problems persisted as help tired of the demanding clerical workload, they managed appointments and the insurance claims while I served such a large volume of patients. Consequently, after Charity was past nine months, again Marlene resumed assisting several months each year training and filling in for help that was quitting moving on to oil companies that offered higher wages and benefits in Calgary's booming petroleum industry. Those corporations had limitless resources to pay staff stealing the best from other employers that couldn't possibly compete. In the second year alone, we hired twenty-six different assistants as most moved on. Some that didn't were fired. It was a wearing experience on both Marlene and me.

Meanwhile, back in Edmonton my brother Patrick had entered a two-year pre-optometry curriculum at the University of Alberta, but would eventually enrol at the Canadian Memorial Chiropractic College in Toronto to commence his Chiropractic studies after he finished at the U of A. His wife, Mary, had given birth to a son, Sean, their first child.

Geoffrey had gone on to criminal defence law after articling with an Edmonton law firm and then worked in criminal defence and soon switched to becoming a Crown Prosecutor for the Federal Government at Yellowknife. Eventually, he would become the youngest Director of Justice installed in the Northwest Territories by Ottawa and earned his Q.C. in that capacity. Much later he became the Assistant Deputy Attorney General of Canada.

After Lloyd's graduation at Palmer in October 1975, he and Brenda returned to Edmonton with daughter, Brandy, who was the same age as our son, Taylor. Lloyd practiced in Edmonton for a year prior to moving on to Vermillion where the Esak's settled. They had two more children, son, Dustin, first and much later daughter, Jordan.

Rupert had moved on to Kelowna and then back to Leduc to spend time with his mother and sister, Bernadine, who had a home there after Alleyne's death. Eventually, Rupert remarried a neighbour and a young widowed girlfriend of his mother. He and his new wife, Linda, had a daughter, Tracy and then a son, Ryan. They all moved on to Medicine Hat, sometime in the late Seventies and were followed by Marlene's mother and Bernadine. Bernadine was about eleven when that move occurred. Both Rupert and his family and Marlene's mother and Bernadine continued to reside in Medicine Hat for several years afterwards.

In the spring of 1978, we purchased a cabin on the Westside of Okanagan Lake at ten-mile, near Whiteman's Creek on the Okanagan Indian Reserve near Vernon. The cabin was located on leased land and affordable enough to be enjoyable. That first summer, I booked six weeks off after the kid's school term ended and at the end of June loaded the family in our station wagon along with bikes, beach toys and cabin effects in a trailer that we towed to our Vernon destination. We spent until the third week of August each summer at the cabin for the next four years while I had other chiropractors perform locums in my office caring for my patients.

The Hackett's' visit to the cabin became an annual event where they spent three weeks of Len's annual vacation time together with our family. It was good for the cousins to be there each summer with our children while we enjoyed Sherry and Len, a very relaxed and congenial pair. They slept in their own tent trailer with another tent for the boys both pitched alongside our cabin. Each summer provided its own humorous moments when we'd gather. Leonard would organize the trunk of his vehicle in such a way that everything was available for use while they camped. He'd back it up against the tent trailer, so Sherry didn't have too many steps to make as she continued to suffer from her ailing heart.

Meanwhile, next door to Sherry and Len our cabin had a mouse problem. Every year when we would return and move into the cabin the mice would suffer so much harassment that they'd move next door to the Hackett's' car trunk where there was always plenty of grub. On one occasion the mice set up bedding in their tea kettle using the stuffing of a discarded cabin mattress. Eventually, the Hackett's brought their cat from Vancouver to rid the area of mice. When the mice were gone their pesky cousins, the moles, moved into the neighbourhood carving holes in the landscape and filling up the outhouse hole with dirt forcing me to re-dig the facility annually.

For me, the Seventies, after Davenport, went so fast. What left a lasting impression on my life about that period were two events that occurred in 1979. First, while I stood behind a patient in my Calgary office examining the patient's cervical spine, I began to feel like I was about to pass out. I had an irregular heartbeat in my chest. I dismissed the patient and went and sat down for a minute. There was no strain in my chest, and I was not in any discomfort, but when I attempted to stand again, I almost fell on my face, so I sat down again and checked my pulse. My heart rate was 200 and I was in atrial fibrillation. Within minutes the event was over.

I had a medical doctor friend in the same building, Dr. Francis Chan, who I went over to visit as soon as I could empty the patients out of my reception area. Chan prescribed Digitalis to regulate my heartbeat, but I rejected his prescription. The episode didn't occur again for eight years.

A second event that comes to mind is that shortly after the atrial fibrillation episode I quit the sixteen-year habit of smoking cigarettes. The addiction had accompanied me since I was seventeen while in high school. It was a gruelling exercise to quit, accompanied by emotional changes and insecurities about many aspects of my own life, marriage and career. I was completely unglued during the process of withdrawal. To be smoking while I was encouraging healthy lifestyles to my patients was an obvious contradiction of my value system and disturbing as the compulsion to smoke cigarettes continued despite my inner disapproval.

When I started consuming tobacco in 1963 when in Edmonton, I'd go to CJCA Radio to visit and train for broadcasting. I'd socialize with the staff at the station that were mostly smokers as was most of the adult population of Canada. I understood the issues and fought the dependency while attempting to quit on several occasions over the years. Quitting cigarettes was always an easy decision for me; nevertheless, the process was daunting as it became both an emotional and physical battle in my persona. Once it was over, I felt so free! It was like I had wings and I never wanted to smoke again. I have never craved the substance in the forty years since.

I had taken up skiing again after returning to Alberta. As family we would ski weekends together at Mount Norquay, Lake Louise, Kananaskis or Sunshine Basin. The kids would follow Marlene down the easier runs while I'd go off and ski the moguls. When the family wouldn't ski, I would be off on my own for a day during weekends with friends, Jack Clouse or Richard Monaghan. Richard was married to my cousin, Jan Griffin, both teachers who settled in Calgary. Jack was my banker.

Eventually the intrigue of warm summers and milder winters took its toll on my disdain for Alberta's climate. I wanted to move back to British Columbia and Marlene and the kids agreed with the idea. By

1982, I had convinced the British Columbia College of Chiropractors to drop their rule of restricting American graduates attempting to enter the province who had finished studies in accelerated summer sessions. I had become involved in chiropractic politics in Alberta and that assisted with meeting and twisting the arms of my British Columbia political colleagues. Subsequently, they welcomed me to sit the province's Chiropractic Board Exams which I successfully passed, finally giving me a license to return to my home province to live and practice.

In June 1982, I drove Marlene and the kids along with our Wire-Haired Fox Terrier, Scooter, to the cabin after school recessed at the end of June and then two weeks later returned to Calgary to greet movers.

Two inches of snow had fallen in Calgary on the departure morning of July 16, 1982 when I headed for Kelowna. I was thirty-seven and had spent more than half my life away from B.C. Southern Alberta's July winter day convinced me that I was going where I belonged.

Chapter Thirty-six

I sense the spirit of my childhood resurging when I motor toward the Okanagan passing by Mara Lake on Highway 97. The trip through Sicamous rekindles sentiments I have for the Shuswap region with solemn images surfacing of Grandpa LaLonde's final departure by train from Sicamous in dreary December 1953. After leaving that area my emotions are warmed as I approach Enderby, where recollections of my Great Grandparents Johann and Agatha Dyck resurface with the joyful childhood remembrance I have of visits to their home. In Vernon my heart is cradled with a sense of endearment to my father, John Bickert, his parents and the childhood home he provided us, twenty-six kilometres east of Vernon at Lumby. Ever since returning to the Okanagan, in 1978, to spend summers at the cabin, I've felt that no place in the world was as meaningful to me as this valley.

The influence of my childhood home environment and the effect those memories left prompted a need for me to give my own children a feeling that they belonged to this area where home would be more than a location. It needed to have roots with history and endearment to my family's past.

———◆———

Grandma Helen Bickert was busy outside her home in Vernon trimming roses when we arrived that Sunday in July announcing we were now officially Okanagan residents and would be living nearby in Kelowna. Another purpose of the visit was to introduce Marlene's mother to my grandmother, knowing how she would enjoy the visit with her. Leonie Ibbotson had returned with me to inspect where we'd be making our home in the valley. We made the visit to Grandma Bickert after I picked up the family at the lake cabin. Being proud of my grandmother, I wanted to make the introduction to Marlene's mother while she was with us that summer feeling a little guilty in front of her for taking Marlene and the grandchildren away from Alberta and the attachment, they had to the Ibbotson side of family.

"My, you're just like Marlene, or should I say she's just like you," remarked my grandmother and then added, "Come in out of the heat." She took her right index finger from her mouth and used it to direct us to her home's entrance. Grandma would suck on the tip of her finger after working with roses as if a rose thorn had pricked her. She would smile and giggle after doing so, to advise that she hadn't really injured it. It was play to her. The same action accompanied when she'd cut bread or peeled vegetables in the kitchen while others watched nearby. The young girl in her had never left and it was amusement in her uncomplicated demure.

Subsequent to Grandpa's death she moved into a house she had purchased in Vernon. There she enjoyed the support of her daughters Gladys and Francis who both lived nearby with their families. Additional support and company to her were her brothers, Peter, who lived in Lumby and Bill, who resided in Vernon nearby. Her sister, Kay lived in Enderby.

My grandmother always kept her home orderly and it had the aroma of fresh garden vegetables or baking bread. Besides working in her garden and baking she would play the piano and visit on the phone with her daughters Gladys and Francis to busy herself. Youngest daughter, Jeanne would visit from out of town. By then, Grandma had given up the lap harp that, in the past she used to accompany Grandpa's fiddle when they'd perform together.

Her favourite flower was the rose and several varieties stood alongside her house where she'd trim them to pass time in the sun loving the wonders of nature for what enjoyment and food it provided her.

She was inclined to speak about the natural and upheld it in her conversation with others.

"Weather is only weather, it's all beautiful, however it arrives," she'd beam winter, summer, spring or fall." It was her response to anyone's complaint about it.

That day we had our short visit together and then we went on to show Marlene's mother Polson Park while gradually working our way to Kelowna after visiting other important landmarks in Vernon.

"See there's where my Dad bought his parents their first home and where Grandpa looked after the schoolyards, the irrigation ditches on the hillside and had his chicken pens. It was all to provide her with a sense of the Bickert family's history since the Bickert's arrived in Vernon during the Depression years.

We had a few days at our new home on Crawford Road with Marlene's mother before she departed back to Medicine Hat. Before leaving she helped Marlene unpack and organize the house. Meanwhile, I busied myself searching for a prospective practice location, although I wasn't in a hurry to commence my work again until I first had an opportunity to enjoy a long Okanagan summer break.

In September, Natalie entered eighth grade at Kelowna's KLO Secondary School. Taylor started fourth at Dorothea Walker Elementary along with Charity who was in first. Both schools were in the lower Mission area of Kelowna off Gordon Road.

My Irish mother used to say, "A son is a son until he takes a wife, but a daughter is a daughter all of her life." How descriptive those words were when she recited them as if they were intended for all her sons to understand the reason why she would spend hours caring for my disabled sister, Janice.

For a period, I had forgotten my mother's remark about daughters but was reminded of it when I saw how both my growing girls were so comfortable being at home with their mother for the balance of that summer. Taylor, on the other hand, was already off and exploring with other boys making it home only for his stomach's sake.

The new environment provided our girls with a sense of endearment to country living at the house on Crawford Road, but soon left. Natalie's entered KLO High School at summer's end and her affinity toward home life didn't return until she was nearing the completion of grade twelve. She fought a tug-of-war arguing for freedoms that we weren't prepared to impart on her even though those demands were no more than of any other youth. Our life with teenagers had begun and it seemed as though for the next twelve years the world had entered into our household and stolen peace as we warred with growing children and each other in a disruption that shattered the peace I had anticipated Kelowna would bring.

I should have known from experience that life would never cease imparting its lessons and raising teenagers would provide another opportunity to mature and learn. My faith was now testing my marriage along with the tests the children would provide as I introduced new components of my Catholicity and Marian devotion to my family. Initially, that seemed to complicate the whole matter of dealing with teenagers as they objected to my attempts that we pray the rosary together as family. Attempting to reduce their participation to a decade or two each day from five decades in order to appease them quickly resulted in no participation at all.

Initially, Marlene was quite prepared to sample the Mother Church's Marian affection, but that abruptly ended after I went off the deep end by pronouncing too much of my Marian devotion. She was going straight to Christ himself with her prayers, not wanting to exercise any fidelity to the Mother of the Christian family. I attempted to argue a defence of the Church's affection for Mother Mary but didn't succeed.

For the last few centuries, The Church of England has offered only a symbolic devotion to Mary. The devotion waned as the Protestant Reformation expanded and some tradition was abandoned, but as strains of disunity befell the Church of England expanding in the twentieth and twenty-first centuries, the more orthodox members again embraced their congregation's heritage and Marian icons reappeared along with Marian prayer.

The Catholic Church along with the Ukrainian Catholic and Eastern Orthodox Church, represent not just most of the Christians in the world, but the earliest remnants of Christian Churches dating back to the first century since Saints Peter and Paul travelled to Rome and Saint Paul went on to Greece. They've always held that Mary should be given the title Holy Mother of God and venerated, since Christ, the Eternal One and God, were one and the same God. The Marion devotion was re-affirmed as early as the General Council of Ephesus after Nestorius a heretic began to preach against Mary.

Catholics choose to elevate her by esteeming her as the Mother of God and Mother of the Church, which the Church goes on to describe as union of all the Saints in Heaven and abiding in Christ on Earth. The spiritual connection to Mary was affirmed by Jesus, who appointed her as our Spiritual Mother when at the foot of the cross he gave her to the Church, represented by the Apostle John, The Loved One. John, standing at the foot of the Cross with the Blessed Mother, was asked by Jesus to take Mary as his mother and Mary, to take John as her son. (John 19:26-27). Additionally, many of the earliest Christian writings affirm Mary as the mother of all Christians.

It wasn't until after Luther's Reformation that the practice of Marian devotion dwindled in the Protestant faith. Luther himself prayed to Mary and continued a Marian affection until death. Calvin like many early reformers after Luther believed in Marian devotion, but the practice of Marian devotion in the Reformation was lost over the years afterwards as the evangelical fervour developed in Protestantism and that fervour had little historical understanding or appreciation of tradition. A theologian from Trier named Andreas Heinz discovered a vita Christi Rosary that dated to 1300, suggesting the origin of the current rosary extends back at least to that time. The Christian victory at the Battle of Lepanto in 1571 was attributed to the praying of the Rosary by masses of Europeans based on the request of Pope Pius V and eventually resulted in the Feast of Our Lady of the Rosary. In 1569, the papal bull 'Consueverunt Romani Pontifices' established the devotion to the rosary in the Catholic Church.

In the Evangelical freedom of expression Christians ignored a lot of tradition as they educated themselves outside the Mother Church and many were devoid of direction of the apostolic heritage their predecessors had revered.

Like Luther, some Protestants today have a Marian devotion, particularly European Lutherans who not only pray for Mary's heavenly assistance as their Spiritual Mother but invoke the intercession of other saints. Recently, in Rome, Lutheran theologians from Sweden prayed to Saint Bridgett of Sweden for her intercessory guidance on a joint statement they wanted to prepare with Rome to rectify an error in Protestant teaching. Those who were present to sign the Justification Document, an ecumenical statement jointly formed with the Vatican that clarified to the Christian world, that the Lutheran Church is one with the Roman Catholic on the matter of what is required of those of faith. Some fundamentalists had been spreading that "... all you have to do is believe in Jesus to be saved" The new document known as The Justification Document, relied on the scriptural statement of James for its authority. "What doth it profit a man, if he says he has faith and does not doeth works? Can faith save him?" (James 2:14).

Mathew's writings further assisted in clarifying the recent Justification Document. "And every one that hears these sayings of mine and does not do them shall be likened to a fool who built his house upon sand." Matt: 7:26,

There has been a developing perspective of latter-day Evangelical Christians to accept the Bible that was first assembled by Saint Jerome under the request by Pope Damascus in 383 A.D. and further fully assembled by other Roman Catholic scholars before 600 A.D. Those same latter-day evangelicals feel The Roman Church has it all wrong in its very traditions it backs by The Bible for the meaning of the Church's sacraments and its authority under the seat of Peter. (the first pope)

In a less than scholarly leap, these very evangelicals often insert words like Rapture to replace Parousia for their modern interpretation of the book of Revelations meanings, when they are more appropriately described in the traditions of the Church over centuries. 'The Rapture' is a recent term that originates from a 19th Century American evangelical belief, that all Christian believers who are alive along with resurrected believers, that they will rise "in the clouds, to meet the Lord in the air." This idea has never been found in traditional Christianity. Parousia actually refers to the Second Coming of Christ, which Catholics and those in Communion with the Church get a sampling of in the Sacrament of Holy Communion, provided you are in the 'state of Grace' when you receive The Sacrament. When and how this 'rapture' will occur is entirely speculative and should not be a focus of Christians of which such focus should be to build his Kingdom through our good works and holy lives and not just by believing for 'faith without good works is dead.' (James 2:14-26)

It's a bold step to claim that such events as Rapture will occur. So, be careful not to make that mistake as millions of those early Roman Christians shed their blood for those traditional beliefs in order to get to Heaven. Even bolder to march off and claim to understand scripture without knowing the faith that assembled it.

Not only Lutherans, but Methodists, Episcopalians and Anglicans are reacquainting themselves today with early protestant devotion to Mary that followed them away from the Mother Church. Yes, Christians throughout the world are all guilty of picking and choosing devotions, but to disregard Mary is akin to disregarding the woman of a household that you may visit and then you attempt to reach her son without respecting his mother. Mary is the "Queen of All Saints," a title rightfully addressed to her by the Church.

In Luke, she affirms her own dignity to all nations of Israel (The Church) in what is referred to as her Magnificat.

"My soul doth magnify the Lord
And my spirit hath rejoiced in God my Saviour.
For He hath regarded the low estate of his handmaiden: for
Behold, henceforth all generations shall call me blessed.
For He that is mighty has done to me great things..."

Luke 1:46-49

St. Luke never did meet Christ nor likely, did he ever have the opportunity of meeting Mary. He was of a different generation of Christians and tells the story of Christ and the formation of the early church when later in life he wrote the Acts of the Apostles. This should give a clue to every Christian that the church came first and then later the New Testament was assembled as tradition and practices of faith by early Christians were paramount. Especially those teachings tested in time through tradition and practices of those appointed down through history since the apostles and those who have led the church up to the current day.

Mary is appropriately named, 'Star of the Sea' ever since Columbus's Santa Maria, Nina and Pinta made their voyage to the Americas with Spain's early explorers. Today, while having our own ocean of distress to navigate through in life as the faithful and living out our lives with Christ, we need the loving care of a mother in heaven who can protect and guide us on that pilgrimage to her son.

Families need to grow in charity and become skilled at the business of living together. It's often daunting and can be a humiliating experience, but in the process, we mature and enrich through the partnership as we share in family, if we endure together.

Being "one" in faith, as we journey and investigate our individual conviction is what Christ prayed for the night before he died when he asked his Father in heaven to make us one as He and the Father are one is easier. Tradition is what guided Christians in faith over history.

Faith always provides a provocation to the faithful and to those who put up with them. It's a test of conviction, but also a winepress of discovery. Christians, not just Catholics, carry a cross that is often born by the sword of division, where lessons must be learned about charity and respect of other members of the Christian family and the world. It's been a struggle since the early church when the apostles themselves fought over what was correct. Fortunately, today more Christians are working toward unity since Pope John XXIII`s Vatican Council in the Sixties. We should not beat each other over the heads with our heritage and practices but live in love and kindness towards each other. For if God wants us all to be one in faith, he wants even more that we learn to love first.

In Kelowna, for a period, our love was painfully chilled over a rancorous division through trial that would eventually result in the deepening of our individual convictions. Still a necessary forgiveness that would enrich our relationship began to transpire.

Chapter Thirty-seven

Her eyes have always offered a special intensity in the blue lustre that surrounds each pupil while portraying honesty of her conviction in glances that thwart any of my opposition to her intent.

I usually had difficulty opposing Marlene's stand on any matter. It's because she is so sincere, and her face depicts goodness. I guess that's why I continue to try so hard to convince her on my stand regarding matters and so easily end up sparring over what should be obvious. It frustrates me that her persuasion has been equally sincere as mine but has differed. How can two people be so right, but miles apart on various marriage issues with a religious fervour that needs to be ameliorated as well?

For each encounter over matters of faith and how we individually witnessed to our children meant searching deep to find something better than what was obvious. The apparent, repelled while the deep, was always sublime requiring something more of us that resulted in a respect for the other's conviction. The exercise always led us to discover more of our faith, as a gift, measured in whatever amount the Lord gave. For when we began to shine performing in charity, we grew. Particularly, through all the tumult of those early years in Kelowna we needed to discover a richer charity in our union and earn peace while we deepened our individual witness and relationship with the Lord.

In 1983 my brother, John, had left his teaching career with Edmonton's Catholic School Board and enrolled in Marietta, Georgia's Life University's Chiropractic College being the third Bickert to take an interest in the profession following Patrick and me. By then, John had a family of three children. Charmaine, being the oldest at fifteen, Michael was eleven and Careese, five. It was quite an undertaking for John who took over a curriculum note business to finance his studies there while Gail assisted in operating it.

Geoffrey continued to reside in Yellowknife working as Regional Director of Justice for the Federal Government. He made regular visits to see Mom and Dad at Edmonton, alone in the city with Janice after John and his family departed.

In June 1983 Patrick and Mary settled in Kelowna after Patrick had completed his degree at Canadian Memorial Chiropractic College in Toronto. By then, my youngest brother's family had grown to two children. Sean was six and Neale two.

Patrick had planned to open his own clinic but wanted a little time to figure out where in the community he'd do that, so initially started seeing patients at my office. Patrick and I have always been a good mix as brothers, but our decision not to make a permanent arrangement out of practicing together was to protect that relationship.

It's seldom that any emergency health event takes place at chiropractic clinics. Most patients present themselves with chronic disorders and cricks, sprains, back and neck pain making for a kind of a predictable environment for any health care provider to work. Otherwise, many will visit chiropractors with their families to maintain health as adjustments alleviate stress and maintain the integrity of the spine and nervous system.

My practice at 2640 Pandosy Street offered that extra bit of excitement, because I had two cardiologists at work in a clinic a few doors from mine. On occasion we'd have those patients arriving in our reception area invariably being confused while suffering coronary distress at the time they'd show up.

Some of the cardiologists' patients that mistakenly arrived in my office required the CPR procedure. My reception area was always full as I would fumble with the few patients mistaking my office as the cardiologist's clinic. They really should have gone to Kelowna General's Emergency, but they'd come into my office and collapse in front of the reception desk. On one occasion Patrick and I worked on an elderly man until an ambulance arrived at the scene and paramedics took over. Pat and I often chuckle over the fact that I had a new receptionist and she nearly had heart failure herself during the event.

In November 1983, Gladys Sasges advised the family that Grandma Bickert had passed quietly in her home at eighty-six years. Sherry told me that losing the grandmother who raised her as a child was painful. I recall Dad, at the internment site placing a hand on Sherry's shoulder being sensitive to the moment as she wept.

Grandma's death was just one of many sad events for my children that autumn. Just prior to it our pet Fox Terrier, Scooter, died after being run down by a car. The mishap occurred in front of the home on Crawford Road a couple of weeks after Chilly, a pet Budgie, was found dead in the bottom of its cage. Both pets had accompanied the family from our home in Calgary. Prior to that, our children were too young to have experienced the meaning of death. It was a sad time for them being the beginning of many more losses we'd have to endure while in Kelowna.

In family, we should discover something of the value of bereavement. In its emotional labour there is an effect that burnishes our souls enriching us in maturity while we discover value in one another. I suspect the process serves our faith, teaching us something of the personality of God whose goodness is exuded through each individual lifetime in gifts realized through each member's individual credit displayed in the process of living.

Chapter Thirty-eight

I've always credited my mother's conviction as the dominant component to the development of my conscience. She's affected me the most in life along with those standards provided by the nuns at St. Joseph's and later the offerings of the Franciscans of Edmonton. It was in my father's example that I would always endeavour to travel the course of my life while spurred by Mom's spontaneity and faith.

I've mused about what it would have been like to have had Dad's mannerism. Would it have helped with the rearing of my own children and in my relations with others? I've felt I needed more to hold my tongue and keep silent as he did by utilizing those valuable glances in expressing emotions rather than resorting to words. Dad's disposition may have fallen short though in other aspects of my life as mine was a different career calling and my children of a different culture and age. Perhaps in my circumstance I needed to be forthright and convicted as my mother who served that part of my nature. Strangely though, in faith, I felt like there was always a paradox operating in my being as I managed the two basic traits of my parental mannerisms.

It was how I approached faith with those I loved and lived thinking that salesmanship would impress. Of course, that trait came from Mom, but in the end, lessons proved for me that humility and example at times better served the witnessing of faith in the home. Evangelization is often best left for pulpits and preachers when it comes to family as Christ was often imparted in the food of charity not by lectures. It's a lesson I continue to learn repeatedly even today.

The 1980's were an interesting period and even more fascinating for Catholics that enjoyed a devotion to Mary. The effect of world events for the past three decades appeared to be reaching a pinnacle. Soviet leader, Nikita Khrushchev had been forced out of office in 1964 by Moscow's Communist elite, who then appointed Leonid Brezhnev the USSR's chief. He was a man of some degree of moderation providing the West hope that the Kremlin could befriend the West and the chill of the Cold War tension warmed. To the contrary, in 1968 Brezhnev ordered the invasion of Czechoslovakia resulting in even more distrust to follow for a couple of years before Detente occurred and the joint signing of the Strategic Arms Limitation Treaty (SALT) thawed relations all over again.

Unfortunately, in November 1982, Brezhnev died, and the Cold War reached new heights. Yuri Andropov, a long time KGB head for the Soviets, known also as a diehard Stalinist who organized the invasion of Hungary in 1956 and subsequently, commanded the overthrow of Czechoslovakia in 1968 was appointed head of the Soviet Presidium and successor.

Just prior to Andropov's appointment, in 1981, the Church and most of the world watched horrified at telecasts where Mehmet Ali Agca, shot Pope John Paul II in the middle of a St. Peter's Square General Audience almost fatally wounding the Pontiff. In due course, John Paul gave Our Lady of Fatima credit for his life being saved. His remarks were made when he visited Fatima after recovering from the ordeal. Our Lady of Fatima, also known as the Blessed Virgin Mary, was another title given to the Mother of the Church after her early twentieth century appearances to three children in Fatima, Portugal. In the 1980's Vatican press and other media published articles about the Soviets despising the Polish Pope's influence resulting from his connections with Poland's Lech Walesa's Solidarity movement. Walesa was challenging the Communist Polish Government installed by the Soviet Union.

Catholics, including myself, were spellbound as the crux of the Fatima messages came to fruition. In 1917, in the Fatima apparitions, Mary foretold of Russia spreading her errors throughout the world in the future.

It all seemed so plausible that this was the moment Mary spoke of when she appeared to the three peasant children in six-separate-apparitions at Fatima from May 13 to October 13th, 1917 warning that Communism would become the "Instrument of the Chastisement," spoken of in Sacred Scripture. Oddly, nobody in the world outside of Russia knew what a Communist was during that period of history.

Pope John Paul II's remark that the Virgin of Fatima had saved him and the subsequent Consecration of the World including Russia to the Immaculate Heart of Mary in springtime 1984 awoke the Catholic in me. I wondered, "Was this the consecration requested in 1917 by the Blessed Mother when she appeared to Lucy, Jacinta and Francisco, the visionary children at Fatima?"

From the time I was a child attending St. Joseph's School in Nelson, I had been aware of Mary's request, "...that the Pope in union with all of the Catholic bishops of the world must consecrate Russia to Mary." Mary had apparently stated to the visionaries to tell their local bishop that the Pope must make the consecration, "...so the Will of the God be appeased, and she be honoured by the world as "Mother of God and Mediatrix of Peace." Only then, would a period of peace be ushered into the world.

To demonstrate the authenticity of the apparitions, the greatest alleged public miracle in history occurred on October 13th, 1917 when the sun began to dance in the sky before seventy-thousand witnesses that had gathered in the Portuguese hilltop village of Fatima. The crowd was there as a result of Mary's promise to the children that apparitions would be proven to be more than "hoaxed," as suggested by local Fatima officials. The miracle apparently was God's stamp of approval on the apparitions at Fatima. The sun danced in the sky changing colors and then fell to the earth before retreating to the heavens again. Many Portuguese newspaper outlets witnessed the event reporting that the supernatural occurrence that had been promised did occur.

Some Christian denominations have difficulty with the title 'Mother of God' failing to tie the connection to Christ as the 'God Man,' and are repulsed by the thought of elevating Mary as their Mother. In life I was taught that the Gospel according to Saint John clarifies to us that Jesus is the Word of God made flesh. "In the beginning was the Word and the Word was with God and the Word was God." (John 1:1) "And the Word was made flesh and dwelt amongst us." (John1:14). So, Mary is the mother of God incarnate in Jesus Christ.

For me, it was an easy connection to honour Mary as Mother of the Christian family and Mother of God. Fatima made so much sense to me to pray for Mary's intercession for a troubled world.

This all disturbed Marlene while I became emphatic that the family should join me along with other Catholics who complied by praying the rosary for world peace.

On May 13, 1983, sixty-sixth anniversary date of the first apparition at Fatima, Pope John Paul II invited all the bishops of the world to jointly consecrate the world to the Immaculate Heart of Mary. In the next two decades remarkable events unfolded in front of the eyes of the world when Poland liberated itself from the Soviet Union. Shortly afterwards Czechoslovakia, Hungary and East Germany were liberated as well. Gorbachev, who replaced Andropov in Moscow, visited the Pope, proclaiming his own infant Orthodox Christian baptism.

There was a period Marlene and the children appeared equally mystified by the Fatima connection to world events; however, their interest was short lived. Russia`s conversion was occurring and Communism falling apart, but my own family was also falling apart. Marlene and I argued over the Church and home became so disrupted all because Mary's influence had complicated Jesus for us.

In retrospect, the upheaval was good. Faith had been challenged and in the process of arguing, forgiving and renewal, we lived as a family the complexity of a society that was diverse. The five of us eventually became one, beginning to celebrate Christ while each had individual uniqueness moving us, one by one, toward a deeper understanding of our transcendent God.

My parents moved to Kelowna in the springtime of 1986 providing more depth to my family's number in Kelowna. That same year Marlene's Grandma Margaret Manson (Ibbotson), mother of Alleyne Ibbotson along with my wife's Aunt Kay, sister of her father had also located in the city. Their move into the lower Mission area added warmth to my wife's feeling of belonging amongst all the Bickert's who had arrived around the same time.

I had always wanted to be closer to my father in his retirement years to watch as he aged and became enriched in wisdom. He was such a fine man. I don't know why I was more excited about Dad being near, because my feelings should have been the same toward my mother. I guess it was my hope to do things with a dad I had never done as a boy, to fish, golf and be a friend. His retirement should have afforded him time for that.

"What would he advise me about my relations?" I wondered. Life with my parents had always been so elusive for me as a result of my being apart from them since I was sixteen. Other than a couple of years in Edmonton after marriage where they lived nearby, I spent little time at home.

I admired how Dad had given so much of his life to family and to his own parents and their household. He had given up time from his daughter's childhood to serve overseas during the War. Music was always a passion of his, but he set it aside after providing guitar lessons to his younger brother, Edward. Dad's resignation toward playing an instrument emphasized the difference between him and his brother. Dad understood that music was something life would not allow him the luxury. The long hours that he spent working to assist in supporting the Harry Bickert household and the fact that music wouldn't provide for that, was enough to make it impractical for him to continue. Youth and age allowed his brother, Edward, the indulgence of time to develop the talent. Dad's childhood was interrupted by a Depression and then, his youth by war, divorcing Ethel and then, after finding love and marriage again, there were additional mouths to feed. He never felt cheated understanding the necessity of his contribution while priding himself in stability for his wife and family.

My parents found a level lot on Barnaby Road of the Upper Mission area in Kelowna after a month-long search. It was morning after they had purchased the retirement home site that Dad offered to take my car in to the shop for a tire rotation and drop me off at work. He sat beside me as we motored toward the city and I asked, "Dad, what are your plans for your life here in Kelowna?"

"Nothing, I just want to be with my boys," he replied placing his left hand on my shoulder as I drove.

I looked at him and he smiled giving me a feeling that his words meant more. Something was present deep in his eyes, but I didn't understand. Dad never explained himself, because he was always finest in his gesture and glance. It's unfortunate that I wasn't as acutely perceptive now as he was himself accurate with the 'nothing' remark.

Though spoken syllables in Dad's life were few they were ever faithfully declared with simplicity and reason where extra verbiage would never suffice, because too many words complicated what was best served by Dad's emotions or intent.

The next morning at five-thirty on April 29th, 1986, the day after Dad drove me to work and later took my car to the tire shop, Mom entered our bedroom startling us out of our sleep by announcing, "Paul, I think your Dad is dead." We didn't doubt what she meant. We leapt out of bed and went to the bonus room above our garage where the two and Janice had slept the night before.

Dad's body sat erect in a lounge chair with both his arms crossed and legs crossed, but his head was positioned backward against the back of the chair. Apparently, sensing something during his sleep, he had gotten out of bed and moved to the chair and then fallen back asleep never to awake again. It was as if he had always done in the past, slipped off for a nap unannounced. This time he wouldn't awake again.

In retrospect, Dad said it all to me in those thirty days before he died when he resided at our household on Crawford Road. I learned that being a good father and husband is a gift that words don't properly convey. It's in actions that should be full of charity, fostered in quiet respect that's most fruitful. Guidance and observation, with little necessity of correction or attempted disruption will enhance the calling. Before any husband or dad earns full respect, he needs to provide witness to it garnering admiration around himself. Then, once compliance postures in family members that are good, then a man can celebrate his calling.

Chapter Thirty-nine

That May, the renewal I expected from the Okanagan's springtime vibrancy was gone after Dad passed being replaced by concerns I felt over my mother's future without him. Everywhere I went I would observe men older than my father alive and seemingly healthy. I'd ask myself, "Why's he gone while men much older are still here?" It was all part of the adjustment I went through, but interior workings brought solace and thanks that his death was peaceful with Mom and Janice here in Kelowna where we could assist and comfort them.

Mom appeared to adjust quickly to the loss. She abruptly pronounced, "I'm going out tonight!" It was only two weeks after the funeral and she briskly went off to a social at the Canadian Legion; however, shortly afterwards she was back in a slump remaining quite sorrowful for the next couple of months.

Never the type to admit depression or to be down for long, she picked up again. Mom prided herself in faith that explained life and what the purpose death served, never considering that it would come so quickly for her partner. Fortunately, Janice anchored her, because she required Mom's attention and homemaking. Additionally, the new home construction on Barnaby road, at the site she and Dad purchased needed constructing to provide her a place to live.

During the upset over the loss of Dad, my brother Geoff, who in 1985 married a Halifax woman, Denise Harper, advised that his bride had left him. Denise had come to Kelowna to attend the funeral with Geoff and both seemed untroubled at the time, so we didn't suspect a problem. The two had met while each worked in the North. I don't know the specifics of the breakup; however, do recall that Denise returned to Eastern Canada shortly thereafter.

Geoff never did malign her, but explained she was not ready for marriage. All in all, my brother's hardship with the departure of his new wife was enough to take everyone else's mind off the loss of Dad as we shifted our attention toward that news.

I have always held Geoff in high esteem, mainly because of his controlled disposition and charity toward family. His care of his parents was unmatched in this family. He was genuinely involved with them in their old age. Both of my parents regarded him as special.

Geoff was a lawyer though and loved to debate and it could be annoying to be on the receiving end of those debates. He usually knew when to ease up on his opponents including his disagreements with my mother who would frequently tangle with him. Our closeness as brothers was reaffirmed when Geoff asked me to stand in as Best Man for his second marriage which was well attended by family and friends in Vancouver. He married Sarah Tosdevin, a fine lady that he met while doing work for the British Columbia Provincial Justice Department. Sarah and Geoff had two children Mathew and Emily. Several years later they moved to Ottawa where Geoffrey became an Assistant Deputy Minister of Aboriginal Justice and later Assistant Deputy Attorney General of Canada in the Litigation branch. He retired from that position in 2019 and they now plan to return West. Their children Mathew and Emily are in University in Ottawa and Montreal respectively.

I recall around the same time as my father's death that daughter, Natalie was experiencing difficulty in her grade twelve biology course, so the day after Marlene and my twentieth anniversary dinner I took Natalie off to Vancouver for some one-on-one time to see if I could assist in her catching up in her homework and preparation for midterm exams. We stayed in a Vancouver hotel for a study session where I prepared her for the test that was mostly about cellular physiology. The result was she received a high-test score and our father-daughter relationship improved that year.

In summer 1987 Mom's oldest brother, John Griffin, died of cancer. He had lived in the Toronto area of Richmond Hill with his wife Sally, a retired public health nurse, while he worked with the Ontario Government as a Standards Development Officer. John had left the Canadian Air Force in 1963. They raised their four children, Thad, Michael, Lyndon and daughter Elizabeth in Moose Jaw, Moncton and Richmond Hill prior to his own retirement from the Civil Service in 1983.

Mom travelled east to be at John's bedside spending a couple of weeks with him while he was still conscious enough to enjoy her visit. It was one of about four occasions that she had to visit with her brother since leaving Marquis during the war.

We all admired John's warm disposition. At Geoff and Denise's wedding in Halifax, I got to know Sally and John better. I transported them around Halifax and off to Peggy's Cove during the wedding weekend providing the opportunity to renew our acquaintance.

In August 1987 Mom suffered a dissecting aortic aneurism which put her in the hospital for three weeks. The ordeal would take her several more months to fully recover. It occurred after she moved a truck load of dirt in her back yard with a wheelbarrow while refurbishing her Iris beds. The phone rang at work late one afternoon and she screamed, "Paul I think I'm dying. I'm in such pain!"

It was the end of the workday and my office was empty when the call came. I immediately phoned for an ambulance and then ran out the door toward where I thought I had parked my car. I hadn't taken my car to work that day but walked that morning which required that I engage the nearest merchant to give me a ride home to my car.

After arriving home, I sped toward Mom's house arriving at the same time as the ambulance. She was in her basement bedroom lying in agony appearing very cyanosed and visibly in pain that appeared to radiate from her lumbar spine and abdomen. I suspected an aortic aneurism was tearing as I viewed her abdomen pulsate visibly. I knew what aneurisms were, having witnessed other patients with back pain that on examination revealed chiropractic was not what was required but emergency vascular surgery. None had been so serious as my mother's.

"It's likely an aneurism," I advised the paramedics who stood helplessly understanding that moving my mother could kill her.

"Paul, do something," she screamed while elevating her abdomen off the bed with her shoulders and legs.

All I could do was offer a gentle thoraco-lumbar chiropractic adjustment concluding it may assist in relaxing her. Immediately she relaxed and the pain subsided. The paramedics were speechless as I told them to take her to the hospital.

"Don't damage that light fixture," she ordered as the paramedics struggled to lift the ambulance gurney up stairs without dropping her on her head. The circumstance and her remark made everyone laugh, because, moments earlier she was near death and was now ordering the young medics' round.

Mom's CT scan revealed the aneurism had torn back into the vessel wall itself rather than splitting outward and bleeding into the abdominal cavity. Her aneurism had dissected, and I suspect that the fragile aortic wall had been better off with the adjustment and relaxed enough to prevent the external tearing. It was heart warming that I was able to help my mother at such a time. Chiropractic adjustments don't have to be forceful, but can be delivered with miniscule effort without hurting the patient. Adjustments are certainly not intended to stop aneurysms, but specifically intended assist the body in whatever recuperative ability it inherently possesses. Adjustments don't require much force. They can be performed with as little effort a dipping your finger into a bowl of water and the concentric waves ripple out to the edge of the bowl. Little more is needed than a minute directive correction and then the doctor let's the patient's nervous system do the rest.

It took a few months for her to fully recover, but by springtime 1988 she was back on the dance floor with a line-up of older gentlemen that competed for her affection. Eventually, she would dump all of them, stating, "I'm tired of dancing with old men! I liked it better when I danced with a younger man!"

In late summer that year Mom was served advance notice in her own abdomen along with a premonition before receiving official news that her twin sister, Mary Norman, had suffered serious stomach cramps while walking with my Uncle Jack Norman in Manhattan while they were on vacation and visiting daughter, Maureen and family. Mary was soon diagnosed with stomach cancer by the attending American doctors. She died on September 3rd that same year after her return to Crescent Beach, B.C., where she and Jack had resided for several years.

The twins had always been close in spirit, even if life's circumstances kept them at a distance. They would call or write one another, and Mom frequently spoke of how she missed her sister. Both Mom and Janice travelled with Marlene and me to Mary's funeral in Vancouver that was attended by my sister, Sherry and her husband, Len along with numerous other Norman relatives and friends.

Mary and her husband Jack Norman had moved over to the Marpole area of Vancouver in the mid fifties after leaving Prince George. Jack, the man we called 'Mr. Cheese,' because of his work with Kraft foods continued his sales career until retirement. They raised four children. David, the oldest, became a Franciscan Friar and theologian joining my friend, Father David Crosbie in Edmonton. Maureen and her husband Phil resided New York City with their children while Phil, a physicist worked for IBM. Brothers, Ron, an editor and Tom, a chef, live on Canada's West Coast.

That autumn I joined six others on a pilgrimage to Fatima, Portugal, Rome, Assisi, Medjugorje and Loreto and on the occasion, I attended my first Papal audience with John Paul II. It was one of the most impressive experiences of my life. The very popular Pope was loved worldwide and my affection for him led me to attend two other subsequent public audiences with him during his papacy.

Pilgrimages have one purpose and that is to enrich faith. I commenced the pilgrimage six months before the trip occurred with prayer and a daily Mass vigil. My trip to Europe that year coincided with the seventy-first anniversary of the Oct 13th Miracle of the Sun apparition at Fatima. We travelled to Rome and Medjugorje, a village in the mountains of Bosnia, across the Adriatic from Italy. Medjugorje has been the site of an alleged ongoing Marian apparition to six young adults that commenced when they were teenagers.

The supposed supernatural events that surrounded the Medjugorje apparitions have apparently been witnessed by millions of others who have visited the apparition location. One of the supernatural events frequently witnessed there is the 'Miracle of the Sun' as was once apparently seen by the Fatima visionaries in 1917 along with a crowd of seventy thousand that gathered in the Portuguese mountain village on October thirteenth that same year. I witnessed similar gyrations of the sun in Medjugorje and will attest to it as a strange phenomenon. I was in a crowd of over a thousand others who saw the sun change colours and twirl in the sky moving toward earth and away as we stood there in astonishment. I must have stared at the sun steadily for five to ten minutes without my eyesight being ruined. I didn't realize until later that I hadn't looked away from the sun for several minutes which would have been impossible under normal circumstances. I must admit that it was dimmer and appeared harmless but why? It was a clear day. It would have to have been something unusual that made it so in front of the crowd that day to not harm our eyesight.

All six members of the pilgrimage group witnessed the same. Medjugorje's apparitions still haven't been ruled on by the Catholic

Church, however Cardinal Joseph Ratzinger, prior to becoming the Pontiff, Benedict XVI, spoke favourably on the occurrence to the Catholic press stating many of these supernatural Marian events attest to God's grace and the times we live in requiring more prayer and attention to our faith to hold us firm.

What did the event do for me? I marvel at it from time to time but would have to state that what transpired in me after Medjugorje was more inspiring. I felt a deeper commitment to my family and was less inclined to be critical of where they were in faith trusting more in The Holy Spirit to move them individually. A greater work was being performed in me than in the sky over Bosnia that day.

Within a few months of my arrival back in Kelowna Mom was back in the hospital having suffered a serious a heart attack. The stress of the loss of Dad, her brother, John and sister, Mary was likely part of the strain on her. Following that setback more bad news came as Dad's sister, Gladys Sasges, Maid of Honour at my parents' wedding, passed from a brain tumour. Mom would complain of losing those closest to her but continued in her determination to recover for the sake of Janice.

"I just can't die, too; Janice needs me!" It was Mom's response to her own health problems.

Afterwards, my mother was on heavier medication as her chest began to congest from the effects of heart failure. She'd strain to climb stairs and keep up with the demands of homemaking for herself and Janice. She wasn't one to complain about it. Instead, she'd go with Janice to dances at the Legion and off to other socials that the Legion offered joining the ladies' auxiliary where she assisted with bake sales and so on.

Finally, a wedding day came and not a funeral to attend! In August 1989, Sherry and Leonard's oldest son, Dwayne, married Rita Shultz, a Langley girl. It was a happy reprieve for the family. My sister, Sherry hadn't looked so good in years. She explained that she had just completed a radical Chelation therapy program and at the time it seemed to be working. Three weeks later Sherry was admitted to hospital in Vancouver with a blood clot in her leg. That night, Leonard called and asked that I come to Vancouver and see my sister. I left immediately, but Sherry passed at five-thirty in the morning, just before my arrival. She was dead at forty-eight passing on September 3, 1989.

Sherry came into my life in 1947, when I was two and she was six. I don't recall that occasion, but the meeting occurred after the move we made to Lumby from Marquis. Subsequent impressions of Sherry's involvement did not form in my mind until my mother married John Bickert in 1949. By then, I had reached four years and Sherry was eight. I do recall how warm and sensitive a sister she was and how she took an interest in her new brothers reading storybooks, playing board games, colouring and cuddling with us.

Sherry was much like her dad, never conversing a lot, but possessing an uncomplicated calm disposition, chuckling her way through life with an ever-present crackle emitting from her chest which became more apparent when she was middle aged, likely an early sign of congestive heart failure.

When I consider the period when our families blended, I remember Sherry was a little taken aback by my mother who was more verbal than what my stepsister was accustomed to in the care given her by Grandma Helen Bickert. In contrast, the warmth my mother offered was overshadowed by an assertiveness that aroused distrust in Sherry as Mom attempted to direct her. It took time for my new sister to warm to Mom's role. Mom too, had a difficult time figuring Sherry out after she had endured two other mother figures, Ethel Nash and Helen Bickert.

I recall a similar struggle affecting my brother John, as our new father took over from Father Harrison in Lumby and our past association with Grandpa LaLonde. John too, seemed troubled by the parenting Dad offered in the early years. I think that I was too young to be as affected by those changes.

Sherry eventually became very close to our mother as daughters do. I recall an event where Mom once received a call from a distressed neighbour who claimed Sherry had brought a bundle of cigarettes over to her house to share with the daughter of the caller. My mother in her typical unalarmed response to the irate woman stated, "Well Sherry knows the cigarettes won't make her or your daughter pregnant, so don't be so troubled!"

Len met Sherry on a blind date when she was in her Psychiatric Nursing studies in Coquitlam. Their favourite pastime after marriage became fishing and camping. When at home, Sherry and Len would spend time putting up food, renovating the house and playing shuffleboard in their basement on a table Len built. Sherry became so competitive at the game and such a sore loser that when she lost, she sent Len off to work with peanut butter and mustard sandwiches! Their camping began early in the spring on weekends when they'd head toward Manning Park often to find in the mornings, a foot of snow had fallen on their tent which was collapsing under the weight. Fishing trips included several full coolers of food for the outing. On return trip the coolers were full of fish.

Since marriage, Sherry had occupied her life mothering her children, Dwayne, Stephen and Gary and homemaking while the family resided at 2920 Adanac Street in Vancouver, where Leonard reported to work from as a lumber grader. She had an early departure from psychiatric nursing after enduring several beatings from the mentally deranged at Essondale's Crease Clinic, a psychiatric hospital, renamed in 1966, Riverview Hospital. Her training had been a two-year Psychiatric Nursing degree offered in those days at Crease before the program was eventually moved to the British Columbia Institute of Technology. I attended Sherry's graduation during Easter break from St. Anthony's College in 1962.

From Vancouver, the Hackett's made annual trips to visit and stay alongside our cabin in their tent trailer where Sherry would sit on her lawn chair beside Leonard holding his hand and enjoying her summer's rest. She struggled while her failing heart strained with most of the demands placed on it. There she sat inactive and her weight gain became a further complication. Leonard would do most of the chores in managing the family catering to his ailing wife over the years of her illness.

I seemed to look past Sherry's physical struggles while attempting to examine the person who was my sister, but she was always protective about her feelings, expressing few emotions, except what appeared to be a joyous and content life. "How can a person be so positive in her circumstance?" I wondered.

Sherry left me with this distinct memory of herself and that's a content smiling face, outlined by chestnut hair and dark beaming brown eyes. The warmth that Sherry offered when she became my big sister remained all her life. Read the last few verses of Mom's poem,

'Earth's Angel'

Then after treating dolly's arm, with tact
She'd make her rounds among the rest
And not one dolly patient ever lacked

And oft' when little brother tripped and fell,
Or sadness struck his heart and made him cry,
She'd hurry to hug and make her brother well

And as she grew in years and love for others
She gave her care and comfort to the aged
And tho' she did not know, a plan of Mother's

Then soon from family and friends she parted
To study nursing of the mentally ill.
With faith and hope and charity she started.

She learned about the saddest of all ills
With tolerance and understanding kindness
That mental comfort does not come from pills,

She sees how healing truly makes its start
And strives for further skill in her profession
And ministers His love, to every heart and mind.

And so, replacing Daddy's hanky there,
A nurse's cap caresses chestnut hair.

Leonard remained in Vancouver for a couple of years with his sons Steve and Gary while the boys attended university and he finished his last couple of years in the sawmill. Then he retired from his lumber grader position moving to Peachland where he purchased a home by Deep Creek. Len remarried within two years, but that union failed. He remarried again and died in 2001 of cancer.

In 2002 son, Steven got involved in testifying against a Hell's Angel biker gang leader resulting in my nephew being placed into witness protection. He hasn't been seen since. Nephew, Dwayne became a chiropractor locating in Lumby with his wife, Rita and their children, Reid and Kyla. Gary married in 2000 and he and Nancy with their three children reside in Langley, BC. Gary is a Realtor and Nancy provides Early Childhood Education.

Chapter Forty

John lost the lower portion of a top front incisor as a result of a fight I started with older boys when I was thirteen and found myself unable to finish. John stepped in for me. From then on, he had to live with a filed tooth in the middle of his smile.

At thirteen I was working at the midway of a carnival that had come to Nelson. A man running his own enterprise in a booth at the carnival had asked how old I thought he was, and I told him, "Forty-one."

"You're dead on! How'd you do that?" he asked.

"I knew you weren't forty-two because you told the guy who just left that he had a year on you when you guessed he was forty-two," I responded.

"You got good ears, but can you guess a man's age and weight without your ears?" The science of the man's enterprise was he got paid a quarter to guess a customer's age or weight. If correct the customer lost the quarter. If he was wrong, the customer won a stuffed toy.

"If you can guess the correct age on the next five customers, I'll give you a job. Do you want a job?"

"Sure!" I said.

The next five customers all lost their quarters and had me to thank for it. I started in the booth half an hour later after the man showed me a few other tricks of the trade and we settled on a salary. Afterwards, I did well as a carnie, but my talent upset a couple of older boys that lost their only remaining change for rides by trying to outsmart me with their age. It ended up that when I was finished for the day and was making my way home, they were waiting for me. They wanted their quarters back and I wasn't going to let that happen. They demanded all that I was paid for the hour I spent covering the booth. John came along just in time.

"What's up, Paul?

"See, you guys are going to have to square this matter up with my big brother now," I chided.

John took over and apparently gave the two a licking while taking a fist in the mouth after I wandered off. I figured my brother had it all under control.

There's nothing like a brother that you grow up with. John's year advantage always meant that I needed to work a little at keeping up with him or at least that's how I thought I should conduct myself to prove I wasn't holding him up. I had to defend myself against both his verbal and physical assaults from time to time, too.

From when we were boys on the farm in Marquis, I recall toddling behind John as he would explain how chickens laid eggs, horses wore shoes and gasoline was like Kool-Aid and so on. Tasting farmyard Kool-Aid from a fuel depot almost killed him though. He was four then and the contents of Grandpa LaLonde's fuel drum had to be pumped from my unconscious brother's stomach that day.

Later, in Lumby, his faith had its influence on me as he'd explain the early chapters of the Catholic Baltimore Catechism or the Church's sacraments and pretend to hear my confessions prior to any formal preparation I had for that sacrament in second grade. John would prime me in his makeshift confessionals.

Early after our move from Lumby to Nelson, John was the one to encourage that I become an altar server and join cubs. But at seventeen he wasn't successful at talking me into following him into the Canadian Navy, nor later at twenty, did he succeed in having me climb out of a Cessna aircraft at ten thousand feet onto the strut of the wing to skydive to the ground behind him. My brother was eventually cited with the North Western Junior Skydiving Championship after competing against other free fallers. I was advised later that all plummeted to their deaths over time discouraging John from ever continuing the sport. I must confess though that I was at least temporarily envious of his championship win.

One day as I watched the team of my brother's brave young friends along with John repack their chutes. I was convinced the web of strings would entangle me if I took the responsibility to do what skydivers pride themselves on doing before each dive.

I did do a live broadcast from the aircraft for Trail's CJAT Radio station and attended one ground school session where I was asked afterwards, "So are you ready to jump, Paul?" Nothing, not even my big brother whom I revered, could convince me to follow any of the skydiving team out of the aircraft.

John worked in those days at Trail's daily newspaper operation while I broadcasted at CJAT Radio. I never was impressed by the town's local effort at journalism always feeling that The Nelson Daily News, operated by Managing Editor, C.W. Ramsden, was far superior. Even the Nelson newspaper's front page, was captioned by a bright red Old English newsprint which colour captioning was earned by Ramsden's efforts wandering in and out of Nelson's tyrannical business enterprises. The paper's advertising space was on account of that community's pride of Ramsden's editorship. The Queen City's store owners always had a monopoly on customers but offered little regard for the town's broadcast operation; however, Ramsden did successfully sell newspaper ads. The paper closed in 2010 when circulation dwindled to 2000.

In Trail, John sold advertising for a full year after he followed me to town. Later, I recall one of CJAT`s advertising salesmen remarking about John`s success in taking over some of the radio station's customer account business. Trail's newspaper was the Nelson equivalent of a daily advertising circular having very little news beyond the cover page. The Nelson Daily News seemed to manage a minimum six pages of News including international events.

After leaving Trail, John moved to Vancouver and began flight school. He eventually earned his instrument rating and commercial licence. I recall one evening going for a flight with John. Marlene was along while my brother took us up in a small aircraft over Edmonton. He wanted to demonstrate to us some of the incipient spins and stalls that training pilots rehearse. I sat frozen in my seat as the plane fell to the ground and Edmonton's night lights spun around below my inverted head while the seatbelt pressed on my lap. It was the only time my brother talked me into an aircraft with him.

Once he impressed our Grandparents who lived in Lavington, outside Lumby. They had a one-acre asparagus patch behind a couple of chicken coups on their property where Grandpa worked next door as custodian of the Lavington Elementary School. John successfully landed the aircraft in the patch to enjoy a short visit. Harry Bickert bragged for years afterwards of his grandson's heroic flight manoeuvrings.

John quit flying after he married in 1968. His family and other responsibilities likely were the distraction. He never lost interest in aircraft though. Visitors would have to endure as he'd show reams of his aircraft photos that were mixed in with a few family photographs.

Through the Eighties Canada was in recession with the rest of the world. The difficult economic times had some affect on the family. First, my parents made their decision to retire from their Edmonton real estate work which was no longer profitable. The Hackett's were experiencing labour unrest in Vancouver and threatened layoffs were always a concern. John and Gail's sideline tiling company went broke.

It was an enterprise started with the intention of supplementing his teaching income that wasn't providing for his expanding family. The bankruptcy prompted the decision for him to make the career change to Chiropractic.

While a student in Atlanta, Georgia, they adopted a six-year old Central American disabled girl, Maria Luisa Santores. Maria had arthrogryposis, a condition that froze her spine in hyperextension with hyper flexed extremities forcing her to spend her life in a recumbent position moving around with her stomach operating as legs. She'd shift from location to location by swinging her torso from the floor utilizing one elbow to steer herself. Eventually, they acquired a form of motorized wheelchair flatbed for her to operate. It was with generous hearts and a warm display of courage that John and Gail took on such a responsibility. Maria was orphaned after birth by her mother in war torn El Salvador during the early 1980's.

Our disabled niece learned to dress herself managing that and the rest of her life with remarkable dexterity, despite the disability. In her teens, she began to discover freedom from the boundaries of home. If she'd misbehave her parents would take away privileges. One measure would be for her parents to cut her off art supplies that they'd normally purchase to encourage her interest in art. Maria could draw phenomenally well and her special gift was an inspiration to everyone. It was incredible, the achievements she'd make with a physical framework so contorted and inflexible doing Pietas, nature studies and murals.

At fifteen, Maria's physical inflexibility extended to her disposition. In response to her parents' correction, she once drove her battery-operated flatbed along the highway three miles to Grand Centre from Cold Lake after announcing, "I'm going to look for work if you won't give me money to buy art supplies." Remarkably, she succeeded and found a job as a radio announcer in the local station. It was a demonstration in front of the whole family that her spirit was enlivened by something extraordinary. Today Maria lives independently in Calgary still utilizing her flat-bed motorized assist scooter.

John's brotherly friendship became closest after I followed him back to the Catholic Church from the concurrent lapses, we both went through from our late teens until we were into our thirties. Next to our mother he had the greatest influence on my willingness to investigate deeper the faith of my childhood.

We both went through a form of charismatic upheaval as curiosity seemed to move us to investigate other denominations. Once, we wandered off to a healing revival in Edmonton where we both responded to an altar call as the entrepreneurial evangelist seemed to have all the words to convince both of us that revival was what we needed. There I knelt in front of the smooth-talking preacher whose cologne sweetly penetrated the air along with his voice. "Be saved, young man. Jesus loves you!" Then he mouthed some words in gibberish convincing the audience behind to follow in what was supposed to be tongues. So, I did the same and mouthed a few syllables in Latin, remnants from my altar boy days, hoping the preacher would be impressed and not recognize the vernacular. After his benediction, he stopped speaking tongues and his two comrades who were now behind me with their hands on my shoulders, helped me to my feet and took me to the back of the meeting hall where they handed me a donation envelope and instructed that it was my duty to give. I declined the almsgiving.

For me, the Catholic Church appeared to have order and tradition. It stood the test of centuries, the faithful witnessing to it with many offering their blood over history to allow it to survive.

John's faith has continued with a missionary zeal to educate and inform. It's like he's defending his younger brother at the carnival when defending the Church. He's all in for the fight and usually trumps the best with his theological efforts as opponents meet with unmatchable knowledge and spirit, albeit John sometimes has been known to come out of those events with more than just a chipped tooth, as do his opponents.

Once he lost a teaching assignment over his zeal. John had explained to a student that had joined Demo lay of that organization's Masonic affiliation which the Church objected to for its secretive and anti-Catholic history. He didn't take the statement any further feeling his pronouncement was his responsibility as a Catholic educator and that the student should act on the advice and reconsider his affiliation. Well that angered the boy's parents. Eventually, both the parents and the school's principal sided together, and John's teaching contract was not renewed for the next school term. The posture of the principal became typical of some Catholic leaders of the day that were uncomfortable with anything that could provoke others, whether that stand was justified or not. John had the support of Calgary's Archbishop Henry, who was known in his day as a contrarian toward modern culture's views that collided with Christian beliefs.

For CFTW

Go to:

cftw.org

Catholics had begun to secularize with the rest of the country and the strains of a Christian differentiating oneself from the mainstream began to show as government and laws became sensitive to Canada's invading minorities having other beliefs. Laws were enacted to protect the minorities as the social norm was to remain neutral to other viewpoints. Certain immigrants coming to Canada would appear to broaden and paganise a society that attracted those from homelands with narrower religious standards in the first place.

Once, John asked me to speak to his tenth-grade science class about chiropractic. I spent forty minutes describing the relevance of the Central and Peripheral nervous systems to structure, function and health describing how chiropractic corrects nerve rootlet interference. I inquired at the end of the class if students had any questions. Only one question came from the class. It was a young girl who stared at her manicured fingernails asking, "Would I have to cut my fingernails if I wanted to become a chiropractor, Dr. Bickert?" It is obvious, teachers have something I've never quite had a handle on and that is perception of youth. Since John himself was a young boy, I recall his play with others while he'd direct, interrogate, compel, investigate and listen with peers and younger children too. He is gifted in an appropriate way for a man who has spent most of his life teaching.

John quit teaching after the Masonic episode and at sixty-five resumed practicing chiropractic in Northeast Calgary and remains practicing at age seventy-six. He makes several trips each year to India to care for patients there while he chairs Chiropractic for the World Foundation that I founded with Dr. Robert Champagne of Calgary. His wife, Gail, the girl he married a year after Marlene and I married, became a wonderful match for my brother. They raised five children, Charmaine, Michael, Maria, Careese and Andrea all except Andrea remained in Alberta. She married and resided in Arlington Virginia. Careese passed suddenly in 2019 at age forty-one of undetermined cause.

Chapter Forty-one

Prior to my sister's death in 1988, I travelled to Toronto in search of Carl Ellis, my natural father. I was forty-two years and had always wondered about his wellbeing from his years of drug abuse and incarceration for various offences related to supporting the habit. It seemed an ominous venture to search for the man who had traded his expectant wife and young son, John, for narcotics and an uncontrolled life that led to crime and several years behind bars, but I had to find out about him. The inner need to ameliorate that part of my being that wanted reconciliation with the man who never was there troubled me more after my dad's death. It was as if I needed to extend a healing to the man's conscience that likely had some sense of culpability for his life lacking self discipline. To tell him that it all worked out for us, without him, seemed important at the time and I wanted to say that I wished him well. All my life I had prayed for his recovery as Mom had always suggested that.

In the process of preparing for the trip I phoned my mother and asked if she would like to come East and see her mother hoping that she might be able to fill in the many gaps I had of Carl's life. I figured she could help with the contact of his family and she agreed.

When we arrived in Toronto Mom became elusive regarding my inquiries into his life. She didn't seem to want to assist me. At first, that was troubling and then I realized she was worried. The forty-three-year absence of an older woman now having to face her twenties and a difficult time in her early adulthood could be reopening old wounds

I phoned the Ontario corrections people who told me prisoners' records were confidential and could not be released. After spending a couple of days attempting to contact every Carl Ellis in Ontario, my search was unsuccessful.

Reassuring Mom, I said, "Don't worry I have the best parent right here, so Carl Ellis could never convince me otherwise about your reason for leaving him."

"Try Don and Klara Ellis in Trent River, Paul," was her response to my comforting her.

It was the clue I needed. Don Ellis was Carl's only brother. He was a couple of years older than Carl, seventy-two at the time. Aunt Klara, his wife, answered the phone warming the line with her friendly voice reassuring me that I had found someone who would lead me to my natural father.

"Paul, Carl died twelve years ago at fifty-seven years of age from a heart attack."

I had no idea that I could be so upset, but the news created unexplained grief and filled me with disappointment. I wanted to believe that my visit would be important to him, but it was too late.

Klara had us over for dinner the next day where we met Uncle Don and Aunt Thelma Innes, Carl's siblings. They had continued to reside in Trent River, a small community northeast of Peterborough. The visit was warm providing news on Carl's recovery from narcotics during his later years. Apparently, the heroin addiction led to alcoholism which persisted. He had spent twenty-two years in prison and fathered a total of eleven children by three different partners in his short adult life of freedom from incarceration. Klara spoke of his frequent mention and wish to see his boys, John and Paul. They claimed that Carl was well liked by children. He had healed the best he could with the alcohol remaining until his death. Carl's remorse for his past misdeeds was accompanied with faith that remained since his childhood. His last ten years were spent living with Don and Klara, where he did work assisting the minister brother doing property maintenance on lake cabins that Uncle Don owned. Carl also performed church maintenance for him.

There's a wonderful story in the Book of Genesis about Noah's Ark and the Flood. It raises many questions for any reader who doesn't understand the significance of why it's told and for whom, but for those that have been told the story's meaning, it provides insight to the covenant God makes with mankind in the cleansing action of Christ dying on the cross and our partnership in offering our own sufferings along with Christ's to the Father.

For generations after Eden, humankind had become more and more disassociated with what was required of God's people and their omission of acknowledging Him in their lives during that period of ancient history which led to an apparent chastisement. The story tells us that the Lord told Noah to build an ark and upon completing it to round up the few good people that lived on earth along with a pair of all the creatures in existence placing them in the ark. Apparently, the rains came and brought a great flood destroying everything that was not in the ark.

It's hard to imagine such an event taking place or that it would be possible for anyone to be capable of building such a huge ark to place a pair of every living creature in the structure; however, there's a more important parallel discovered when one does not give the story a literal interpretation. That is not to say that such an event couldn't take place if the creator willed it.

The apostle Peter, tells us in Peter 3:18-22, that the flood spoken of in Genesis saved eight people who lived in union with God's laws and that the flood prefigured what it means today to be baptized in Christ; that Noah's flood waters are a type of baptism where only eight were saved and how today, many more are saved by their baptism in Christ.

In the parallel we can understand that man is not washed of physical dirt in baptism with Christ but washed spiritually and through the pledge of the good conscience of God (the covenant) and by Christ's Death and

Resurrection, we're saved and inherit eternal life. After this discussion, the apostle goes on to say that anyone who suffers in Christ during life on earth is not dominated by human passions but by God. The apostle gives us a lesson that by suffering we become detached from always wanting to experience pleasure, something that is supposed to be good for the soul, cleansing us.

Apparently, God doesn't want us always to have it our own way and His covenant is to give all people who seek Him and live in harmony with His ways an additional gift of grace to enhance their willingness to suffer or practice self denial.

Another parallel is given when for forty days after baptism by John the Baptist, Jesus went out into the desert and fasted while praying for forty days. (1 Mark12-13) It was another example for Christians to learn about self denial rather than having their own way. What may appear to be a stranger requirement of the people of God goes back even earlier in Genesis where in the Garden of Eden our ancestral parents, Adam and Eve, were told not to eat the fruit from the tree.

It's an incredible task to find a balance in life and to be a person of faith, too. Saint Paul speaks in his letter to Romans of a frustration he endured with the inward struggle to avoid sin, "I fail to carry out the things I want to do, and I find myself doing the very things I hate." (Romans 7:15-16). He goes on to explain that it's the predicament of being enslaved to sin and with Christ we are freed, so to speak, from sins consequences, but we still have to fight to act as good people in the face of a tempting world. So, by Paul's own life we find even Christian believers continue to struggle with self denial and sin but persevere to participate in the victory.

It's unfortunate that people do so much to avoid God's calling to discipline wanting so much of the world while simultaneously yearning to be close to God, too. Fortunately, most of us grow and discover something of self denial being an important part of human order. It's the first requisite of charitable acts extending oneself to loving others rather than living for self. I believe all good intentioned people have learned something of the calling to self discipline. When members of society are self serving, others suffer from that. It happens in families too. Both can have serious consequences. We each teach one another more of the benefit of self denial and how it is a prerequisite to becoming more charitable and ordered in life.

Carl Ellis eventually learned what was required of him in life and he lived it the best he could under the circumstance of addictions that were formed at a time of his life when he was young, weak and vulnerable. He paid a price with incarceration, loss of families and deteriorating personal health. He likely suffered a good deal with internal conflict throughout his life, but in the end, succeeded in repairing what relationships he could with those that would still have him. I expect that Carl's baptism and faith saved him as it does all of those who cling to the cross of Christ and to the work of self denial, charity and love of those closest to them. Those latter efforts are crosses too, that could be the most difficult ones to bear. They offer the weary soul as much recompense on that pilgrimage to God and one's eternity as the one as distant as Calvary does. That is not to say we can reduce Calvary's work, but that our own acts identify us with it and work as a form of expiation for our souls too.

Carl's misdemeanours had a toll. Of the thirteen children he fathered, one committed suicide, another attributed her lesbian life to several rapes from male friends that would take heroin with Carl in his home, one had a mental breakdown and three others became alcoholics. For all their endurance in family, faith and suffering a refuge was discovered teaching them that pain was an important contribution to life's enrichment providing depth in perspective for their souls.

I've since met all the surviving siblings Carl fathered. Robert Ellis remained closest of the two other Carl Ellis families. When I took Robert to meet my mother after I had found him in Costa Mesa, California, she told Robert that she never stopped loving Carl Ellis; however, life was too dangerous with him and that Robert reminded her most of him. It was interesting that her remark meant as much to

Robert as it did to me at the time, for love is what every child wants in his parents, whether they remain together or not. It was obvious that some of the hurt had healed over the years and that feelings lingered for the man she once married. My trip to search out Carl Ellis helped my mother, too! She reconciled with his sister and brother her sudden departure from Carl. They all embraced one another.

Robert is the next youngest sibling to me. A couple of years separate us. In 1987, when we first met, he worked as a practicing naturopath and massage therapist along with a chiropractor who shared his office, His work in the health field, regardless of the separated lives we lived and having never met before, offered a strange parallel to the work John, Patrick and I were involved in at the time. Robert died in 2013 of esophageal cancer.

I also met Carl's two other wives, Audrey Ellis and Ruby Ellis. They were both lovely ladies that had endured struggles with Carl, but still found good to say about the man, too, providing a comfortable completion of the search I went on to find my natural father.

Chapter Forty-two

In 1984, Coke, a Welsh terrier, replaced Scooter the dog run over in front of our house a year earlier. Coke was shipped to us air freight from Sault Saint Marie. We selected the breed from a dog book that suggested his pedigree offered "no known disadvantages as a family pet." For the next eleven years he would favour me by lying or sitting by my side. In later life, he panted his approval for the joyful life he led full of affection from the family. The dog's breath was a constant reminder that he needed walks. Those kept me from gaining weight by dispelling any resistance I would otherwise have to daily exercise.

Natalie had taught both dogs a repertoire of tricks to perform on command for treats. Coke moved in when the kids were teenagers and he seemed a better reason than any, for them to come home as he was entertainment and ameliorated any chill from disagreements they'd experience with their parents.

Our youngest daughter, Charity seemed so controlled in her teens. Her containment didn't necessarily represent self restraint as much as a cautious survey of the world around her. Exteriorly, our youngest child gnawed on her fingernails and continues to do so to this day displaying my boldness only as a form of defence. She likes dogs but is easily annoyed by them.

At twelve, Charity was quiet and exhibited few emotions, something that was quite disturbing to me. The silence lasted until she was fourteen when her face began to shine again, but by then the glow was through a mild case of adolescent acne. She had become more open, or at least that's what we thought.

Her parents had grown to ignore teen escapades and it wasn't until much later that Charity divulged to us about her regular flights out her bedroom window. While we slept, our youngest enjoyed an inventiveness and expanded horizons that otherwise would have been trimmed had we have been more observant.

"I saw what Natalie and Taylor went through with you guys, so didn't let you in on my social life," she quipped.

Natalie and Taylor were more open about their intentions asking for or overtly stealing liberty. For us, it became a learning process. In the beginning we'd be shocked at their rebellion and exist in a state of emotional anguish over the insults they'd hurl in defiance, before we toughened up.

Taylor never responded to discipline and laughed it off. Once, I broke a bone in my right foot over a frustrated attempt to correct him as he made his flight out the front door. It was the same type of management my dad used on our pet dogs at home when I was a boy. On crutches, I paid for attempting to physically manage my son's belligerence, all a reflection on my deficient parenting preparation.

Natalie threw tantrums screaming and hollering the typical, "I hate you," and then attempted to extort consent out of us with threats like, "I'm leaving then!" Taylor would just ignore us or utter some vulgarity that would infuriate me.

Although raising teens was difficult, it was predictable. The period had boundaries. Then, we prevented them from harming themselves. Later, their leaving home was capricious. We had no control and that made us insecure over what was out there with them. Then, we resorted to talking to the dog more, over the frustration of the emptying nest.

"So, Coke, when are they coming home to see us?" We were lamenting the loss of teenagers. Who could have believed it?

After graduating in 1987, Natalie worked a year for The Bay Portrait Studio in Kelowna and then grew frustrated with the hours and pay there, so took over office management of a second chiropractic clinic I had acquired and operated in West Kelowna, staffed by two of three doctors that joined me in practice between Kelowna's Pandosy Street clinic and the Westbank clinic. She did an excellent job; however, I had grown frustrated with directing the other doctors and soon chose to sell out to one of the doctors. She continued working with the new owner.

One afternoon, we received a call from Kelowna's General Hospital advising that Natalie had been admitted to Emergency after her vehicle was broadsided on the West side of the original Okanagan Lake Bridge which was subsequently demolished and replaced in 2008. The neck injuries she sustained continued to affect her health for years afterwards. Spinal nerves serving her larynx and vocal cords were damaged leading to a permanent recurring dysphonia that rattled her voice box when she'd speak. The annoying condition was most noticeable when our oldest daughter became fatigued or stressed and continues to this day at fifty years.

Subsequently, Natalie left home in 1989 and attended a two-year photographic arts program at Edmonton's Northern Alberta Institute of Technology. After graduating from NAIT, she lived in Edmonton working as an Assistant District Manager for Photographic Impressions of Canada which had operated The Bay Portrait Studios branch where she worked here in Kelowna after high school graduation. In 1993, she was promoted and transferred to Vancouver to work as District Manager.

A high school boyfriend followed her to Edmonton and then on to Vancouver becoming the father of her only child, Caeleb. Our grandson was born August 1st, 1997. Any efforts to advise our daughter during the emotional entanglement throughout high school and afterwards, were fruitless. She needed to discover the mismatch on her own. Brent was drinking and the negative co-dependency that had been going on for far too long already, resulted in a pregnancy. They had planned to marry in 1995, but broke up just before the wedding date, just to re-commence dating again months later.

No parent would want their child to be exposed to such detrimental circumstances, but I suppose in God's own design he makes the best of a situation by giving people the wherewithal to discover new avenues away from their individual mistakes. I presume it's how I found correction in my own life and Natalie would eventually be emancipated from her own predicament, too. Work had to be done though. We had a single parent daughter and a new grandson. The grandson part was wonderful, and we loved what was to be the reward for our concerning over our daughter. Through all the tumult over our first child, our parental leash on Taylor was slipping as we fought a tug of war to get him through school. During High School he had about as much regard for his formal education as his own father did when he was young, seldom showing up for classes. Taylor was brilliant enough to pass exams and receive above average marks, regardless of his lack of enthusiasm. He graduated in 1991 and then took a break before going on to university, first moving to Richmond to live and work in various jobs including the odd motion picture industry position acting. Eventually, he managed my company's Globus X-ray division for two years. Taylor returned to university at Simon Fraser in Burnaby and attended California State in San Bernardino and UCLA in Los Angeles completing his Bachelor's degree. He then did some graduate studies in business and later in psychology at Adlerian School of Psychology.

Meanwhile in the autumn of 1991 the United Nations authorized sanctions against the nation of Iraq whose leader, Saddam Hussein, had forcefully annexed the small country of Kuwait a year earlier. A thirty-four-nation coalition of military forces gathered in neighbouring Turkey and Saudi Arabia led mostly by United States and British troops to invade Iraq in support of the American led Operation Desert Storm for the purpose of evicting the Iraqi forces out of Kuwait and to defeat the Iraqi army which threatened its neighbours with its army of 1.4 million.

The enormous military effort was viewed by the horrified world mostly on CNN Television News a newly formed and relatively unnoticed American network that made its mark during the war. CNN's telecasts carried live images of Iraq's Soviet manufactured Scud missiles being lobbed into Israel and Riyadh, Saudi Arabia in retaliation against the sophisticated cruise missiles that the Americans used to obliterate much of Bagdad's central core along with the Iraqi army and most of the nation's strategic military sites positioned throughout Iraq. The fear was that the conflict would trigger a world war while Iraq enjoyed the support of the Soviets who ultimately capitulated on any pre-war threats it made against the Americans; however, it continued to supply Iraq with military advisors and armaments throughout the conflict.

In the end, after an additional conflict with Iraq ten years later, the devastation and future occupation of Iraq that would take yet another two decades to resolve and for Hussein and his henchmen to be rounded up jailed or executed. It cost an estimated one hundred thousand Iraqi troops and more than thirty-five thousand civilians lives. Israel suffered only two civilian deaths. Later peace was again broken when fundamentalists captured most of Iraq to force America and her allies to fight the spread of an Islamic state, ISIS.

In the first military conflict that was of a non-peacekeeping nature for Canada to become involved in, Canada's Prime Minister Jean Chretien ordered the Canadian Armed forces to send a contingent of CF18 fighter aircraft and a couple of naval ships to support the Americans. There were fewer than 300 coalition fatalities sustained in the Gulf War, mostly sustained by the USA and Britain. Canada's forces suffered no loss of life. Iraqi loss of life was restricted as the Americans attempted to hit military targets over civilian.

In 1997 Charity married Christian Pender who fathered her two sons Kiran, born March 1, 1998 and Jonah Paul, born February 14, 2001, before Christian revealed a cocaine dependency ending the marriage in 2002, just after Jonah's birth.

Life became a whirlwind in our home as our adult children moved to and from home with furnishings and their children, all as our three adult children encountered the world and discovered their limitations. Through it all our faith and lives would be gifted with three grandsons by 2001 cementing our sanity.

In 1992 we celebrated our twenty-fifth wedding anniversary. My mother and brother, Patrick, organized the surprise celebration for us occurring one week after the actual anniversary date taking us by complete surprise. It was attended by forty or so friends and family including Best Man, Steve Serenas. The moment prompted a great deal of gratitude and emotions for my life, family and marriage partner. My mother was strong during the period having recovered for a time from her health issues. She was seventy years old and back to her normal self.

In January 1993 Marlene and I travelled to Armstrong to visit Judy Weir, the youngest daughter of Bill (Wilhelm) Dyck, brother to my Dad's mother. Visits to my second cousin, her family and Uncle Bill and Aunt Jean were frequent over the years since we re-acquainted back in 1979 after purchasing the summer cabin. The Weir's lived on wonderful Armstrong area farms, the first being east of Armstrong and then later they moved to a hillside above Otter Lake overlooking the scenic valley and district of Spallumcheen, four kilometres south of Armstrong.

Doug Weir worked his farmland to grow vegetables and feed a small herd of cattle. It was more as a hobby for him while he managed a tree falling operation in the forest industry for regular employment. From the first spring thaw until autumn's end he enjoyed the farm and was seldom inside. His incredible generosity toward friends and family with the vegetable crops he'd harvest were a departing gift to every visitor. Judy fed my cravings for her cooking and huckleberry desserts. It was country hospitality at its best along with the familiarity of Dyck family roots and mannerisms that endeared me to them. Judy displayed the prominent Dyck forehead, eyes and nose of my Dad along with his quiet disposition to match. Their boys Keith and Kallum were hardy country product that our children enjoyed the company of as well. Judy's sister, Sherry was a childhood playmate of mine in Lumby. Sherry and her brother, Alan along with his family will frequently join in on our visits with Judy and Doug.

As we drove to see them, a news story aired on the car radio about cellular phones having been blamed for brain tumours in several people throughout North America. We had given Natalie one of the new devices as a graduation gift a couple of years earlier and immediately became concerned for her health.

"I should rig something up to protect her from the electromagnetic radiation," I told Marlene.

"If you can do it for her you should do it for the world," she replied.

"I'll have to give that some thought," I responded.

That was the end of the conversation for a couple of days and the beginning of an experience that would take me to new discoveries about myself and others. For the next six years, every second of my existence would become absorbed at the centre of a technological industry and debate over public health concerns about electromagnetic radiation emitting off wireless phones. My life would be immersed in a monumental undertaking to convince the wireless industry and regulators of a patented product I soon co-invented being a solution to industry woes and public health fears. Those years would be incredibly complicated having their effect mostly on my own health.

Chapter Forty-three

Good healers need to actively contemplate and to contemplate actively. By that they discover the depth of life and the worth of healthy thought through action, thus becoming more compliant with the true self in harmony with God. I'm referring to body, mind and soul that require purging for one to become contemplatively active as a healthy doctor. Most doctors never become true healers and I probably only got halfway there myself. I'm referring to the "Doctor heal thyself statement." In life, I had become somewhat contemplative, but faults in my makeup overshadowed that.

It's human to relish the comfortable by circumventing the mundane, but as Christians we're instructed to live uncomplicated lives and be frugal. For me its ambition that derails my Christian will while self gratification overpowers my sense of direction.

At forty-eight I remained unhealed of past failures, or simply continued to be too motivated with the glory of success to ever become satisfied. I should have rested and left myself alone as a chiropractor, but when thought inspired me, I became easy prey to vanity.

The suggestion that I assist the world with an invention that would reduce the dangers of electromagnetic radiation emitting from wireless phones was the marauder that would steal from me more of my airs.

Coke always stayed in the entrance doorway when I'd signal my planned departures by packing bags to leave for the many weeks, I'd spend on the road fundraising for my company or to market the invention. Unfortunately, by 1995 he was put down by a veterinarian after a bout with lung cancer. Afterwards, Marlene was home alone. Charity had graduated and gone off to Australia for six months before eventually settling into her own basement apartment in Kelowna where she'd do clerical work for my company at 1955 Moss Court. I had sold my chiropractic practice in autumn of 1993 and immersed myself with the new enterprise, that seldom allowed me home time with family.

During the year, I was reminded of Charity's high school graduation exercise when she faxed to Toronto a transmission of her face with the question captioned below reading, "Remember me? That was followed by the statement, "I'm graduating this year!"

Charity had grown confident at eighteen making us proud. Nothing seemed to hold her back. While travelling in Australia with a graduation companion, who had a history of Fetal Alcohol Syndrome, the companion went missing on the Aussie continent's Gold Coast. They partied enjoying freedom away influencing the health of Charity's friend. Australia's beach communities encouraged a lifestyle that resulted in the occurrence of delusion and delirium to 'kick in' resulting in a four-day period of the girl's wandering off missing. Our youngest phoned home distraught after receiving no police co-operation in her search for her friend. The popular region had grown insensitive to panicking international youth whose friends went missing and provided police no apparent good reason to respond with alerts.

I made telephone contact with Chiropractic colleagues there, in order to have them assist our daughter in impressing upon the region's media and police that her concerns were real and to "get with it and find my daughter's missing companion." Fortunately, on the fourth day, her friend wandered by a police station, barefoot and delirious. She was recognized from a police poster that was pasted on a pole by the police station. She was apprehended and hospitalized and spent several days recovering on anti-psychotic medications.

Afterwards, the event didn't curtail Charity's travel abroad. She went off to Europe with other girlfriends and toured again the next year. Taylor joined them for part of the trip but stayed in Greece where beaches offered a good deal more 'Eye Candy' than the rest of southern Europe.

Leonard Hackett had remarried in 1995 after settling in Peachland, outside Kelowna. Nephew, Dwayne was in Chiropractic studies, at Palmer West in Santa Clara, California, with his wife, Rita who worked at the Palmer Campus. Len's marriage to his new wife, Elaine lasted less than a year after she announced her major motivation for marrying was financial. The woman seemed a little bonkers. My mother never liked her making it known when she was first introduced. Mom had Elaine pegged from the beginning stating, "You, lady, will never measure up in life to my daughter." My mother had become a very direct and vocal person in her old age. Something nobody really liked about her that I find quite prevalent in me. Leonard had rebounded in loneliness with his choice to replace my deceased sister.

In 1993, three years after divorcing Elaine, he married Anne Collett, a good wife and the two continued to reside in Peachland. The marriage to Anne occurred after quite a list of female suitors attached themselves to my widowed and subsequently divorced brother-in-law. They were a handful for him. First, one lady was perturbed after being ignored on the dance floor and resorted to overturning his flowerpots on his deck during the night while he slept. Another stripped all his home's wallpaper while he was away. Len was a quiet man and rather than telling a lady he wasn't interested in her advances, he would just date another before finding Anne and marrying.

My mother's congestive heart failure required more attention while the BC government cut back on support services required for the infirmed including those necessary for my disabled sister, Janice. I would spend time with them when I was back in Kelowna but recognized that that effort was inadequate. Mom was lonely as outings became infrequent and burdensome as a result of fatigue due to lack of oxygen in her blood over the heart failure.

In 1997, for a seventy-fifth birthday to cheer her, the siblings sent her off with a Nelson girlfriend for an Alaskan cruise with a suite that had a deck requiring little movement around the ship. It provided a temporary lift for her spirit. She talked about the trip for months afterwards.

Sometime during the period, her brother, Patrick who resided in Thunder Bay, died and that took her down again. Patrick would visit every few years in Kelowna when travelling to see his daughter, Jan and her husband, Richard Monaghan of Calgary. She always looked forward to those occasions when Patrick would stay with her in Kelowna.

Then, our lives had the additional distraction of Natalie's new toddler, Caeleb who was midway through his first year. They'd moved into our home after her breakup with Brent Lindores. Just prior to that, in October 1996, Marlene's mother had relocated to Kelowna after showing early signs of Alzheimer's, so Marlene was occupied with answering upwards of thirty telephone calls per day from her mother in addition to daily visits to her mom's condo and providing for her banking, grocery shopping and personal needs.

"Mom, you just phoned me about that," she'd remind her mother, but the calls came repeatedly as Leonie fretted over one thing or another at the seniors' complex she moved into. It wasn't long before delusions started and the telephone calls continued all night long.

By spring 1998, Natalie moved out of our home into a Kelowna apartment complex allowing Marlene some space to deal with her mother. Previously, her mother had settled in Medicine Hat, Alberta, just prior to our departure from Calgary. There she had the company of oldest son, Rupert and his family. Rupert commenced managing a Ford dealership there, but eventually went into the pet store business a few years prior to Leonie's leaving The Hat. By then, Rupert had raised his children, daughter, Tracie and son, Ryan.

Marlene's brother had sent over distress signals regarding his mother's failing memory and his own life being pre-occupied by a mental illness of his wife and our nephew who were both in emotional turmoil. That and the pre-occupation of operating a busy pet business were such that Leonie's repeated telephone interruptions were daunting. Initially, we thought Rupert was exaggerating his remarks about his mother; nevertheless, we soon discovered his concerns real after she moved to Kelowna. At the same time a dear friend of Marlene's succumbed to a brain tumour.

Another friend, Father Dave Crosbie O.F.M., who married us, was fighting a battle with cancer at the time. I visited Father Dave at Mount Saint Francis Retreat House in Cochrane, when I'd be in Calgary. He and I always enjoyed a close friendship, since St. Anthony's. He succumbed to the illness on August 16, 2003.

———◆———

In response to Marlene's suggestion that I do what I intended to do for Natalie's cellphone for the world. I came up with the idea of utilizing heavy metals to displace the radiation emitted. That led to the concept of a shielding device.

Curiously, I had disassembled the lead apron in my clinics x-ray room for an experiment, to see what would happen if a smaller portion was placed on the antenna. I calculated that perhaps the signal was displaced from the phone because it still worked, obviously not interfering with the wireless transmission. I realized that research needed to be done.

"What do you think?" I asked Kelowna Patent Lawyer, Tony Edwards.

He swung a complete circle on his chair and said, "I'll be darned; a chiropractor came up with this?" In the past, he was obviously unimpressed with chiropractors.

I didn't disagree. I expected that I was a little out of my field of expertise as I studied his wall murals, all being jet aircraft that he had either worked on at Boeing or diplomas citing his Patent law credential.

"Can you get some support on this at the university to back you up?" he asked.

"I can try." I wasn't afraid of asking someone to scrutinize my invention. Edwards stopped me, "Hold on we should at least file a patent claim first. Time is a factor."

I left his office that day after handing over a cheque for one thousand dollars to commence his work on my behalf. It was the beginning of a silent period that would last until March 12th nearly two months later, in the spring when the US Patent Office advised that the field was clear of other inventions and issued the Patent Pending.

I required a lot of funds for scientific development of my invention. A broadcasting background gave me the confidence to issue a press release to the Canadian Press about the invention with hopes that the announcement would bring forth interested parties, both investors and manufacturers. It did and fast!

Within days of receiving investor response disturbing mail from cranky wireless industry regulators came from Ottawa. The intimidating threats of legal action didn't affect me long. I answered them by responding to a placating telephone message left on my answering machine by Okanagan College's Physicist, Dr. Dan Murray. He would help defend me. That college eventually became the University of British Columbia - Okanagan in Kelowna.

One letter, from the radiation protection branch in Ottawa, suggested they would impose penalties, or worse, prison terms, for perpetrating a fraud. Their defence was that wireless devices posed no risk to the public. I wasn't that upset, as my thick skin had grown over defending the Science of Chiropractic, and by working in the past as broadcaster, I could understand they were posturing. Those provided the armour necessary to carry my project forward, but the scientific costs would soon escalate.

Murray was a skinny, unravelled young academic type that wore his pants too short, glasses crooked and his hair uncombed, but for an intellectual he had an amazing personality. He was Guelph University's premier quantum physicist. Students loved him and I immediately grew fond of his character which appeared to respond well to my taunts about his background being that of a man parented by two medical doctors that would hate him to become involved with a charlatan. "That, I won't hold against you!" He told me.

"Nor will I, hold that against you!" I retorted.

His constant use of the word plausible about my invention provided only marginal encouragement.

"A lot of work needs to be done to survey this, Paul, but you have something here and I think it's unfair to judge it as worthless. It's plausible that you've discovered something very worthwhile."

I told the man that I would like to hire a research team and wondered if he could assist. "Yes, I can and in fact, there would be research money available. On a project such as this, The National Research Council will pay fifty percent of any employee's salary. I can start preparing an application for the grant."

Murray was hired and by the end of summer 1993, I had spent over thirty thousand dollars plus grant money on research that only scratched the surface. By that time the company had partners and was evolving. I had appointed a Board of Directors, one of the directors being a colleague and personal friend, Dr. Ron Armstrong from Calgary, an early investor. By mid September 1994, I was so involved in the project, I sold my practice and with considerable savings felt confident that I could afford to take the chance and move my company forward without the added business income of chiropractic practice. The next spring, we had over one hundred shareholders after raising one and a half million dollars. Unfortunately, we were burning through the money as fast as it was coming in.

Shareholders demanded an exit strategy, and some discussed the option of taking the company public with the directors who agreed it was time. We were all encouraged by the 'Nineties Technological Boom' taking place in the world while Globus grew as an organization. Listing opportunities on the NASDAQ Stock Exchange through its starter exchange the Electronic OTC (over the counter) Bulletin Board became available. First, there were several hurdles to overcome, but after the acquisition of a public shell and preparing listing documents, which were voluminous, we commenced trading on September 15, 1995, on NASDAQ – OTC Bulletin Board just two years after my first investors came on board.

I was already beginning to resent the time involvement and felt my life out of control as public company pressure and the demands of investors grew overwhelming. I had no time to myself or family, but my net worth and the company were growing rapidly.

Marlene's support was incredible as she managed investors' telephone calls from home where I had originally placed the office in Taylor's former basement bedroom. There she supervised packaging of the first twenty-five thousand manufactured antenna shields.

Cellular phone models were changing faster than we could design and make new ones, so we decided to forget exploiting the device any further. The invention moved to a new phase. My head physicist and Director of Research, Murray, was working on the original idea of refraction and his work didn't seem to be going anywhere as the lab he directed burned through money at such a pace that my fundraising attempts were barely sufficient to keep up with his needs to employ researchers investigating how to make the invention more practical.

"They're just atoms and molecules, Dan, you should be able to make the antenna do anything you want, even the Two-step!"

"Electrons!"

"Say, what?"

"Just atoms and electrons," he retorted.

I was so frustrated with the man's vague hypothecating that I wanted something conclusive.

"What do you want from me, I'm a physicist?" The skinny scientist objected while rubbing his hands through the disorganized curly mass of hair at his forehead with his eyes revealing frustration written all over his face. It didn't help the man that the entrepreneur ordering him around was a chiropractor and his medical bias feigned that.

One night I was sitting at our dining room table at home examining my wedding ring.

"Boy, I certainly need to clean my diamond band, there's no lustre in the diamonds with too much crud behind."

"They look good from over here," Marlene responded from the other side of the dinner table."

I though, "Hmm, refraction, that's why she sees the lustre more over there!"

The next morning at 5:30, I awoke, thinking cellphone signals are light rays, why are we not refracting them away from users' heads?"

The inspiration resulted from earlier physics class discussions in chiropractic studies regarding refraction of light rays. In this case I was thinking of refraction of light off diamonds. "Perhaps, heavy metals could do it?"

"What I want from you is to make that antenna dance!" I pointed to a phone I was holding that had been strapped to the side of a road kill's brains. Murray had been doing electromagnetic field testing to measure the signal coming from the phone and its effect on the dead animal's cranium.

"I want the signal at the end of the antenna, not at the user's head. Can't you make that refract like diamonds?" I read once, where all matter is resonating atoms. Why can't an antenna resonate at a different pitch, like a guitar string, by moving something up and down the antenna, just as a musician does on the fret when he plays a guitar?" Perhaps you should contort your mouth like my Uncle Ed Bickert does when he needs to improve his performance," I added.

I thought he was shocked and disgusted "...and this comes from the mouth of a chiropractor?" he asked.

I had hit on something that made him go into full gear; however, he both resented the musician quip and the order originating from the practical scientist who stood in front of him objecting to his theoretical mind.

There was a Hollywood motion picture out at the time called, "Clueless." Its poster was positioned in the lab above a photo of Albert Einstein prompting the laboratory physicist to hang it to remind the head of the company and all his student physicists that inspiring investors about an invention has little or nothing to do with science. I always enjoyed the looks on the faces of the students of Murray, as they'd ponder the corporate management revealing cracks in the company's genesis.

My proclamation requiring practical investigation, instead of endless wandering though the universe of thought by a theoretical physicist was a continuous frustration to the physicist who directed the students. "Put a device on the end of the antenna. Please!" I pleaded. They complied and the result was astonishing. The equipment Murray designed and developed to measure the changes and invention proved the signal could be moved by placing the device on the end of the antenna away from the user's head. That improved the performance of every phone it was tested on afterward. Heavy metal coils on the end of the antenna replicated the dielectric properties of diamonds. The stocks opened at two dollars a share and within eighteen months the market crashed, and Globus stock traded at sixteen cents. We had blown through most of our resources and needed money to go on, but now we had the solution to drive us forward.

In August 1997, I suffered an atrial fibrillation incident becoming hospitalized for twenty-four hours and then released with medications. The episode set me back enough that I came close to resigning but mustered enough enthusiasm and strength to move forward with the company. I had trips to London, New York, and Taipei that autumn enough to kill any CEO that endured health issues. I would get adjusted by my chiropractor who'd often remind me that I wasn't living the rules and was endangering myself. I questioned myself, "Who would die first, Mom or me?" The adjustments assisted in coping with the lifestyle.

Twenty-hour flight crews to the Orient fed passengers only noodle soup and cashews as the airlines moved to austere cutbacks and customer food service was curtailed. In London, the food was equally troubling. They were going through a Mad Cow Disease outbreak and beef was not recommended. I was so bloody hungry that the first restaurant I found was a Black Angus Steak House in the Oxford district.

"What the heck, I'm going for it!" I told myself. It was a steak that only the British could ruin, but I was nourished enough to get back to Toronto where I over ate at the expense of the Vice President of Toronto Dominion Bank's Evergreen Investment Division who offered me lunch, a game of golf and dinner on the same day.

Chapter Forty-four

Charles Dickens wrote of a young Pip in Great Expectations intrigued while standing in the lobby of a posh London hotel viewing a group of successful investment bankers discussing with one another their affairs. The bankers' prosperity and what comforts they appeared to provide moved Pip to aspire toward the same in life. I read the story when I was a young man and for years envied such men not aware of what scoundrels they had likely worked past in order to become esteemed. Nor, did I consider that most successful bankers could be cunning and deceitful men.

By 1996 the investment communities of Toronto and New York had discovered the story of Globus. My corporation's publicly traded share value climbed after both the Toronto Dominion and the Canadian Imperial Bank of Commerce investment divisions began to encourage clients to invest. The stock moved rapidly out of record lows from the 1997 crash. Meanwhile, I continued to make the circuit every six months between Las Vegas investor forums, Los Angeles television interviews, New York, Miami, Chicago and Denver radio talk shows as well as to the Toronto brokerage houses to promote my high-tech business for the purpose of financing our operations that required cash infusion from the sale of equity to shareholders. Those trips were mixed with excursions to London, Hong Kong, Taipei, Seoul, Dallas and Chicago where I had opened dialogue with prospective manufacturers that expressed interest in licensing our technologies.

Unfortunately, the double-edged sword of promoting to inflate share value lasted only temporarily and that would be tested regularly in market fluctuations as discerning investors' attention spans were always short during the volatile High-Tech period. There was little loyalty or staying conviction in any stock. Technological companies took years to develop into income earners and the fickle markets placed them in precarious circumstances during the 1990's.

By 1999 the company had scarcely made a dollar, while its worth in market capitalization had risen to nearly a billion Canadian dollars. One year the company sold sixteen million worth of cellular product but earned less than a million on the technology itself as licensing dawdled. The tedious process of developing additional technologies to prove the patents required extensive research and more time to develop them.

As a distraction, in 1996 I was named co-defendant in a twenty-million-dollar lawsuit against Globus. A New York investment banker who had invested a quarter of a million dollars to acquire a dilapidated chemical company in Toronto claimed that he purchased the business in the hopes of supplying our Globus X-ray division with his company's x-ray developing chemicals. Globus management had expressed an interest in the IDEX Corporation and discussed the purchase of it; however, we backed out prior to any deal feeling it was too risky and overvalued. The man proceeded with the purchase himself, but his newly acquired investment failed and closed its doors in less than one year. It was a spurious suit but required considerable attention. I was then engaged making additional trips to New York, the jurisdiction of the complaint and paid Empire State Building lawyers to clean up a mess which absorbed thousands in additional cash to cover the costs of the legal proceedings.

Earlier that same year while making a return trip from Miami where I was interviewed by a business circular, I had a layover in Toronto and was greeted by a Wall Street investment banker having Canadian citizenship. The meeting resulted from telephone conversations with the promoter regarding his firm handling our investor relations and

US stock promotions work. The man seemed to have the savvy for the work which encouraged Globus management, so we contracted him to look after all brokerage firm contact with the added commitment that he'd provide investor relations support services to our shareholders. The man was given stock options as well as tradable shares for his services.

Not long after that, he and one of his firm's employees, were arrested with fifty-three others who had become involved in a New York Attorney General's sting operation where undercover officers posing as brokers entrapped both promoters and some corporate managers in illegal activity. Those arrested had attempted to bribe undercover officers posing as brokers to invest resources from various pension funds into publicly traded companies that the promoters and CEOs represented. Globus was named as one of the corporations indirectly involved resulting in a Halt Trading Order being placed on our corporation's shares. Consequently, The New York District Attorney requisitioned every document our company had ever produced including receipts, cheques, share certificates and so on. We had seven days to comply with the order. Feeling our management was innocent, rather than hiring lawyers to mediate and provide extra time to sort out the mess, I decided that full co-operation was the best solution. For seven days, twenty-four hours a day, my employees generated over one hundred kilograms of documents for the authorities and produced a complete diary of our dealings with the promoter. In the middle of the preparation of the voluminous documents, the photocopier quit costing the company twenty-five thousand dollars to replace it.

Fortunately, none of the Globus corporate officers traded out any shares during the involved promoter's illegal debacle and that was convincing enough to demonstrate that we were not benefiting from the man's misdemeanour. Unfortunately, the same could not be said for himself. He had sold fifty thousand of his own Globus shares during the debacle, enough to enforce the conviction.

I received a phone call from the State of New York District Attorney extending his compliments for the way the matter was handled on our end. He was thoroughly impressed with our record keeping. Apparently, it was customary for American lawyers to stonewall such an investigation, in defence of their clients and for them to present documents in a disorderly fashion requiring investigators to search for documents that were difficult to assemble coherently. I had hired an Executive Director of Globus Operations. He had a talent for organizing our corporate chaos. His work was a reward to our company in the end.

We never heard about the matter again but did read news of several other company officers and their stock promoters going off to jail along with our company's newly contracted promoter. He properly fully vindicated Globus management of any wrongdoing with him. Globus management's biggest error was in trusting an outsider to look after the promotions of the company.

My son, Taylor had come to work with Globus in 1994 to assist with the x-ray film and chemistry supply division that I wanted to build. He was twenty-one and anxious to help. I established a relationship with a film manufacturer to supply an un-labelled film product to my company which in turn I decided that my company would label the product with the GLOBUS GOLD brand name. Sales were off to a great start as a result of my son's enthusiasm for the work of managing the division that I appointed him in charge. Within a few months he had studied up on x-ray developing and exposure technique and become more proficient on the subject of film developing and quality control than most x-ray room technicians that the company would service. As a result of his efforts the division became the lead supplier of clinical imaging throughout Western Canada over the course of three years. Eventually we sold off franchises in Calgary, Montreal, Toronto and Halifax along with one American franchise in Louisiana.

In 1995, while travelling over the Roger's Pass, Taylor's vehicle had a blowout of the front driver's side tire and careened over a two-hundred and-fifty-foot embankment. The BMW's mid-air flight was slowed by only the tips of a couple of spruce trees before it landed less than six feet from the raging waters of a swollen creek. My son's heavy-duty

European sedan was totalled; however, he survived with what appeared at the time to be a slight neck injury, head concussion and sprained thumb. We received the telephone call from the Royal Canadian Mounted Police division in Revelstoke where Taylor was hospitalized. Prior to the mishap, Taylor had been at a trade show in Banff exhibiting Globus X-ray film. The heavy cartons of film that were carried in the backseat of his vehicle hit him on the back of the neck and head as he soared to the bottom of the cliff. The resultant effect of the injuries, continued to trouble him affecting his concentration, vision and stamina as well may have been a contributing factor to his lengthy mental health issues that followed for years afterwards. Eventually he did complete his undergraduate degree and did complete graduate studies at UCLA in Film Finance, prior to his mental health issues disabling him. He has resided with his mom and dad since.

After I stepped down as CEO of Globus and sold out my position, the remaining board of directors for Globus had expressed disapproval of my hanging on to the patent that I had contracted to Globus when I formed the company. It had obligated the company to pay license fees to me. Insisting that the license was the beginning of the company and that all that proceeded from it was to the benefit of the shareholders was my position. All those transactions were fully disclosed to investors annually in our Company's financial statements. Unfortunately, the increasing obligation that the company owed to me as I waved salaries and patent payments, in lieu of accepting stock options grew my position while other's positions shrank. It was a source of frustration and I presume jealousy for the board.

Over the last two years that I ran the company, I wore myself out. The politics of being a public company officer living on the perilous and emotional rollercoaster was daunting contradicting everything I had come to believe in, both as a healthcare practitioner and Christian person.

In May 1999, I travelled with a delegation of four other Globus employees to Taipei and Seoul. The purpose of the trip was to meet with five Asian manufactures who had expressed interest in licensing the Globus Patents. One day after arriving in Taipei, I experienced chest pains and then went into atrial fibrillation at Taipei's Crown Plaza Hotel. Afterwards, I didn't leave my room for four days having attended only one meeting at the beginning of our stay there. On the fifth day, still exhausted, I forced myself to fly on to Seoul where I attended a couple of meetings and dinners with the Korean hosts, Hyundai and Daewoo. I had invited the corporate vice president, Bernie Penner as one of the delegates from Globus. He was quite capable of assisting with negotiations and discussions on tooling the antenna. When in Taipei I asked him up to my hotel room and posed a question to him. I knew he'd want the position, but he was pensive and asked that I allow him time to consider. We had struck two license agreements on that trip, one with Auden, a Chinese antenna and wireless phone accessory manufacture, the other with a small Korean manufacturer. I didn't care anymore. The company wasn't worth dying over, so when I returned to Kelowna, I resigned. Penner accepted the appointment as CEO. It was intimidating to strike balance for investors while satisfying the brokerage firms that prodded for insider tips all being analogous to the joke I once heard told.

A mathematician, an accountant and a public company officer, each were being interviewed about what two plus two equals. The mathematician emphatically stated, "Four!" The accountant stated, "Four, give or take ten percent." The public company officer got up off his chair, closed the curtains, sat down and lowered his voice whispering in the ear of the interviewer, "What would you like two plus two to equal, sir?" Everyone wants to hear something different from you, but they all want to profit from what you give them.

Within two weeks the locks had been changed on the door of my Moss Court building that had been leased by me to Globus for one year already and management instructed all employees not to communicate with me.

Dr. Ron Armstrong phoned, "Paul, they've removed me from the Board of Directors."

It was the beginning of a two-year legal challenge instigated by the board of directors to challenge the company's indebtedness to me for the patents and money owing me for loans I had given to the company. I hired lawyers and accountants and over the next two years convinced Globus management to sign an agreement settling the matter. The agreement admitted to my ownership of the patents and required that the company pay its indebtedness to me as well, albeit a reduced amount was agreed to. In the end Globus defaulted after running out of cash and couldn't pay to satisfy the terms of the agreement. I kept the Patent and by 2002 the company closed its doors.

I sold most of my Globus shares within six months of quitting the company. The lawsuits succeeded only in any licensee or potential licensee questioning ownership of the patents; hence, not wanting to pay or to license. Additionally, the lawsuits deteriorated market support, I knew both would be disastrous for the company I built.

A year later, during the clean-up of the company's belongings at the Moss Court building, Globus management found computer files of Director of Engineering, who had taken over after Dr. Dan Murray left the company. Emails revealed a sinister plot the newly appointed director had with Motorola Corporation Management to steal Globus patents.

I attended a meet where it was disclosed by Penner that company physicist, was working to subvert Globus management while at the same time diverting Globus intellectual property over to Motorola. Apparently, the physicist had been successful at not only convincing Globus management that patents were not useful, but he had in fact, disseminated them over to Motorola for his own gain and resulting in Motorola benefiting from them.

Globus filed a complaint with the Royal Canadian Mounted Police and initiated a Class Action lawsuit planning to in turn conjoin Motorola. I joined the Class Action. Police were successful in convincing the Crown Prosecutor to proceed with criminal charges, but the matter was plea bargained to a lesser charge of mischief. All decided that the mischief matter would be insufficient to convince any court to award the millions in damages Globus investors sustained with the shenanigans.

The Director of Research had been introduced to Motorola management in 1988 when we attended their Plantation Florida research facility together being flown there by Motorola to investigate my company's antenna. The activity was typical of the day when High Tech companies routinely stole from one another both intellectual property and staff.

The invention was something the world needed, but the course of taking it to the world pilfered my peace. Leaving my chiropractic practice to become an entrepreneur meant leaving the predictability and comforts I enjoyed within the confines of my life as a doctor and family man.

Chapter Forty-five

"I looked for my God, my God I could not see.
I looked for my soul, my soul eluded me.
I looked for a friend and then I found all three."
Ralph Waldo Emerson

It's no small wonder that a philosopher such as Emerson would coin a statement such as the one above. It's in God's 'crowning glory,' mankind, that we discover Him. Friends seem most significant to our finding God, probably equally as important as family in that discovery.

Since becoming an adult, I realize that there have been three apparent reasons for friendships in my life. They could be categorized according to my faith, work and emotional needs. All have had a profound effect in reminding me of life's pilgrimage that we all share in journeying to the face God. I can bounce my thoughts off friends, expand my thinking through them, find protection in them, be myself or hide from others around them, play with or pray with them, but most important be a fool or make mistakes and be forgiven by them.

No friend has been as valuable to me as my wife Marlene. I guess it's a given that that would be so after over fifty-three years of marriage. We've talked about everything, disagreed about some but agreed about most. We've found comfort in one another and certainly enjoyed being together. Most of all we've grown together.

If I was to choose a second-best friend, it may surprise those closest to me that I would make this selection, because they'd know that the two of us have often been farthest apart. I've probably felt the most hurt from this friend and have also felt the most love. When I required his friendship most he was sometimes there, but not always. I suppose he could say the same about me. He's my son, Taylor. There's been a special loss I felt when he was distant, absorbed by his own life and what his lengthy mental illness since his accident in Revelstoke has done to him.

It seems fathers need to be close to their sons just as mothers require that of their daughters. It's an expectation, men have of sons and women of daughters that they are near us as we hope and pray for them and want them to find in us what we feel for them. I often wonder if my dad ever felt that of me when I'd forget and was so absorbed in self.

I felt closest to Taylor, when he and I worked together. We'd laugh and enjoy one another more than I did any other man. We fit well together always enjoying one another's opinions. I was very proud of his effort and felt he was of mine. That closeness was enjoyed travelling together, either on holidays or when doing business, it was always good to share experience with him.

Later, I began to understand more of a refined closeness with my son in the love I felt for his just being Taylor. He didn't have to be near me or in contact with home. That love and friendship came then from the parent part of me. Taylor will always be most important to me just being a son, even though I realize the days of father/son have parted and he is now a man; however, I'm thankful he is nearby living with us. Since a child there has been a special bond to him.

Early in life friends taught me of society and all the connections we share in one another and how we needed friendships to discover and search out Truth. There was the play, the prayer, the fights and the required forgiving, necessary for me to discover more of the goodness that would come out from each of us. I never selected my friends, life directed that.

Throughout life some friends have disappeared; however, closeness passes as lives change. Those that I don't see, I continue to value as if they were still in my life today. What friends I've enjoyed I am thankful for. They know who they are and the times we've enjoyed one another together. Good has always come from knowing them.

My daughters' friendship means so much to me.

There's a contemporary John Mayer song that I hear on the radio, Daughters and its verse goes something like this:

> "Fathers, be good to your daughters
> Daughters will love like you do
> Girls become lovers who turn into mothers
> So, mothers be good to your daughters too."

In my girls, who are grown and mothers now, there is something that reminds me even more of where I have a gift in a wife and mother of my children. It's where family is completed, mothers and daughters providing that special softness and hominess to the family unit living in love and friendship dependent on us men for respect and endearment.

Natalie came at a time in our marriage when both Marlene and I needed something to exemplify the 'us' in our union. I wasn't prepared for how taken I would be by my first child. Having to re-admit her to the hospital only a week after she arrived home was terribly upsetting. She was so, reliant on her parents as we were on her. The love in our thirty-month marriage had grown immensely since Natalie arrived home. We had become 'three' making me feel my family was so threatened when her life was at risk over an umbilical infection. We re-admitted her to Edmonton's Royal Alexandra hospital when she was less than ten days old feeling lost without her.

Charity was coy as a child and in other ways seemed soft and vulnerable, too. She spent many hours on my lap, quite different from son, Taylor. Where sons are close, they don't melt in your arms like daughters. I knew from early in raising girls that I would have to shelter them from predators and insincere approaches that would harm them. It was so important that I prepare them, but my words became only noise from an overbearing father.

I feel I have something to share in their lives being partially spoiled by men that were insincere as I once was. Society may have been better off with one less scoundrel in my youth. Mayer's song goes on to remind me of that,

> "On behalf of every man
> Looking out for every girl
> You are the god and the weight of her world."

I suppose there are lessons to be learned in every encounter. In daughters I've worried that they could have missed the joy of finding a little bit of God in a good man; however, I wonder too, if I could have fallen short in what was necessary to direct them to a man. I hurt with my daughters and pray their hurts become allayed. In Charity, who has a husband for nine years now, Peter is a great joy to this family in his love and respect of our youngest daughter and two grandsons. He's also a good friend with his help in our old age and the love we feel from him.

Grandchildren offer something special in friendship too! I see myself when I was a boy in my grandsons, their play, talk and questions and the perspective of the world seen through their youthful eyes.

"Grandma, are you calling Grandpa a worn-out bum?" Twenty-year old Kiran asked when at eleven, he saw a note left by Marlene on my trousers that had a hole in them, and the note was left to advise me not to go out wearing them.

And then there's Kiran's younger brother, nineteen-year old Jonah Paul's carefree and athletic ability that adds something new to this family. He's a real athlete where any other member of the family had to work at that.

A year prior to the marriage Charity had completed the process of annulment of her first marriage. The marriage was blessed in the Roman

Catholic Church in Kelowna where the original wedding was planned; however, the sudden change of venue was on account of Peter's mother being very ill with cancer. The Marvin's are Guelph natives. Both Charity and Peter arc happily married and have resided in Kelowna since their marriage.

Caeleb, my oldest grandson is now twenty-two but when he came into my life I was so taken by his joy. I like it most when Caeleb laughs, sings and dances. He's infectious! As he's matured, he's become a good conversationalist and sensible man. I like that!

Echoing my mother's need to evangelize my friends and family, I've perhaps been overbearing as a friend by social norm; nevertheless, it is a constant compulsion that I feel. I need to provoke a faith response in those I encounter. I expect it's been received as superfluous, even though vocal reminders have epitomized my life and to announce what I am here for? My Catholic Catechism taught me, "...to know, to love and to serve God, in order to be happy with Him in the next life," is the purpose of my life.

I can honestly state that at moments I have been embarrassed to be Catholic with the scandals that have rocked the church, but with that said I know that Christ always did associate with disgraceful company.

Over the course of my life much has changed in the world, particularly with respect to the reverence society has for the Roman Catholic Church within and out. Of course, modern day Judases do not control the Church or what the faithful hold and teach, nor should anyone find it excusable not to practice their faith because of the scandals that rock the Church. Just as when Jesus died, his followers fell apart, so will the Church over the centuries falter when one or groups of its members scandalize it. The Resurrection followed as more than a corpse coming to life on the first Easter Sunday, but as a triumph over the destruction of Christ's community when the followers were reborn. Each new resurrection in the faithful is a constant witness to non-practicing faithful. I share that enthusiasm in front of my friends who are not Catholics for them to find some truth in the power of faith.

Christians today are constantly being reborn sharing in the Body of Christ and continuing to exude the deepest respect for other faithful that inspire us despite scandals that surround us. We live a religion of incarnation garnished in truth.

History books will likely have much to say about the events that played out during and after John Paul II's pontificate including his involvement with emancipating Eastern Europeans from Communism. His unification gestures were well received by Eastern Orthodox Christians, Anglicans and Lutherans. Overtures were also made to reconcile centuries-old wounds between Catholics, Muslims and Jews. Nevertheless, more will likely be written about John Paul II's successor, Benedict XVI and what transpired during that pontificate. Further, Pope Francis today is reforming thought in the Church daily.

A paradox exists between secular and Christian values to the extent that the two often conflict. For the most part, where civil law seeks justice for individuals, it often represents the majority and ignores minorities, favouring public opinion to initiate law and administer it. In contrast, the Church attempts to teach and minister Christ's standards within the Church which protect individual confidentiality and dignity; however, in the process, these standards often fail social norms of justice. Such was the case where certain Roman Catholic clergy were not publicly exposed for their sexually abusive acts that occurred throughout the 20th century.

Disappointedly, public airing of victims of sexual abuse through courts and media reached a crisis point during 2010 in Benedict XVI's pontificate. The faithful stood with him in solidarity understanding the norms of the faith in contrast to those which the world offers. While Benedict XVI underwent the torrent of media and public criticism for what were admitted as Church blunders in the handling of clerical sex abuse cases, faithful Catholics endured a bit of that criticism too. Communion or solidarity requires something from the faithful when the Church is attacked. We become what we always pray for, 'to be bread blessed and broken' as food for those who do not believe nor forgive.

One explanation for a delay in airing these might be that Christian conscience and Roman Catholic confidentiality practices made exposing the sins of penitent clergy a difficult matter. Undoubtedly, publicizing clerical and parishioner confessions would make confessional line-ups even shorter than they'd already become in modern times. Everyone including priests shared the right to privacy in the confessional while confessing sins, otherwise the sacrament would be made a sham. Unfortunately, that is where social justice and Christ's justice clashed.

In a New Testament narration, we are told of Christ providing an example of how He dealt with a woman adulterer when she was brought in front of Him. While writing on the ground He asked that anyone who had not sinned cast the first stone. The accusers left him alone with the woman. He then told the woman that her sins were forgiven. In other words, Christ didn't agree with the accusers that she be publicly punished. Subsequently, what should be central to the Christian is forgiveness as Christ practiced. While His standard of justice may clash with social norms it is something that the Church has an obligation to minister. That is not to say that it should hide those who perpetrate criminal atrocities; nevertheless, we need to protect our sacraments and exercise charity, particularly when penitents confess. Some would argue that the Church should have required more of the penitent by way of restitution just as it has always required forgiveness by victims! Perhaps yes?

As for the victims their hurt can never be disregarded. It will take years for those wounds to heal requiring a sensitive, sympathetic and faithful ministry of Christ's love and compassion. Just as the wounds of the Middle Ages took time to heal. The workings of the Holy Spirit will certainly bring healing.

With friends and family that don't practice the Catholic faith I've stood defending the Church. I believe that those were opportunities to shine for the Church Christ instituted through his Apostles and not for me to cower.

The Church offers us the sacraments and no doubt that is where the most vulnerable of our faithful could be attacked easiest, in the confessionals while receiving the Sacrament of Reconciliation. There, Satan was certain to provide predators! Sad is the state of our world and not surprising as sex has been exploited to the extent that it has affected the clergy like others. Still the Church grows and faithful continue to find the truth of Christ in the Church and the sacraments.

Fortunately, in Christ, resurrection occurs after death! In November 2009, several Anglican bishops and clergy that embraced early Church of England traditional theological values asked to re-unify with Rome. They had grown frustrated with contemporary Anglican changes. These actions resulted in a petition to Rome by those disenfranchised Traditionalist Anglicans who requested permission to re-enter full communion with the Roman Catholic Church. Rome, in a welcoming gesture opened the door, re-establishing full communion between these Anglicans and the Roman Catholic Church while encouraging them to continue to embrace their early Anglican traditions. Married Anglican Bishops and priests were welcomed too. It was both a charitable gesture by the Anglicans to ask and for Rome to welcome them which signalled that a major wound was beginning to heal the division, which took place in the Middle Ages under King Henry VIII.

The result of the Anglican re-entry presented an opportunity for my wife to come to full communion with the Catholic Church. In winter 2010 she accompanied other Traditional Anglicans to unify with the Church of Rome on Benedict XIV's invitation. You can imagine how reconciling that was for both of us. See, God has His way of delivering us!

Friendship should embrace loyalty. My greatest friendships are because of the Church, in the marriage I've enjoyed and the parents, the family and friends whom have shared the faith with me. I am thankful to all friends as we are Church, the vehicle that inspires me, '...to see more of the God I cannot see.'

Front row: Grandsons Jonah, Charity's youngest on the left, daughter, Natalie (center) with our grandson Caeleb on right. Back row: (Lt.-Rt.), daughter, Charity and Son-in-law, Peter with grandson Kiran, granddaughter, Tiann with a boyfriend, Tammy and my son, Tad (Tiann's Parents and then our son, Taylor beside Marlene and me (circa 2013)

Front row: Janice, John, Back Row: Lt. to Rt. Geoffrey, Patrick and Paul 2015

Chapter Forty-Six

In 1996 the British Columbia Adoption Act was amended as a result of shifting societal attitudes requiring openness and easier access to birth records. As a result of much consideration over the years, I felt it time to encounter my past. In the spring of 2000, I wrote the adoption reunion agency and asked if they would put me into contact with my son, born in December 1964. Initially, the attempt to make contact was declined by the agency as they had no records that indicated I was the father. Regardless, in a written response it was suggested that I could be noted in my son's file of the attempt I made to contact him through the agency and if he decided that he wanted to meet me they would advise of my whereabouts. I was disappointed.

The decision to offer the son I had fathered an explanation of why he had been left to Social Services at birth seemed a responsible and timely move now that records were supposed to be open. I drove one day to Savona, the town west of Kamloops where her family once lived, and I inquired of the family's whereabouts. My ex-girlfriend's sister's ex-husband was the only family member identified by locals as still residing in the small community. That day we met, and he informed me that he had driven my son's mother to the hospital in Kamloops the night the baby was born in 1964 recalling having met me earlier that same year. He then provided the mother's last known Vancouver Island address, stating, "She's not been well. She had a stroke."

I wrote describing my interest in contacting the child I had fathered, unaware of whether she had made contact herself. I was unsure about the process knowing I was opening old wounds. I attempted to explain that I was proceeding based on feeling a need to inform a young man that may need to know why. I never received a response from her.

Meanwhile, in November that same year Marlene received a telephone call from family in Alberta that her brother Rupert had died. In 2000 Rupert was going through a marriage breakup with his second wife, Linda and had moved into the basement of the family home in Medicine Hat. Linda had her own mental health concerns that apparently existed sub-clinically since she was a child, requiring she receive psychotherapy for several years.

For five years Rupert was prescribed Prozac an anti-depression medication that eventually became labelled by critics as the 'Suicide Pill.' Patients taking the drug experienced super depressive episodes, a serious side effect of the medication which frequently was overprescribed during the period. In the end the drug obtained the ultimate from Rupert.

It was a painful period for Marlene who hurt for both her mother and herself over Rupert's demise. Leonie Ibbotson's failing mind was still lucid enough to understand her firstborn son was gone. Marlene had lost a brother who for years was her best friend. Rupert's widowed wife, Linda continues to reside in Medicine Hat while Tracy and Ryan are married and living in Calgary.

By then, we had moved into another home at 4234 Hobson Road in Kelowna. Charity, whose husband, Christian had left over his drug addiction, had her hands full with her two sons, so, our decision was to renovate an area of the home and make it into a two-bedroom suite providing both a home and support to Charity and her family. It was an endearing time for all of us as our daughter healed from her marriage breakup and we in turn benefitted with the enjoyment of having our two grandsons, Kiran and Jonah Paul nearby. At the time, Kiran was three and Jonah Paul, one.

More than six months passed and in July 2001, after my original contact with the Adoption Reunion Agency, I received a short letter from that agency again. Without any other explanation it asked that I contact the agency immediately. I phoned and was told by the officer that I spoke to that another file had arrived at her desk wherein she had proof that I was the father of a son whose name was Tad, born December 14th, 1964, in Kamloops. The Adoption Reunion Agency worker had just spoken to my son and he advised her that he would like to talk to me.

There is only one way that I can describe what I felt at that moment. It was as if I had found a child that had been missing for thirty-seven years. No other word can express the feeling except, joy!

I made the call and we had our first conversation together. That day, Tad expressed his delight with the occasion in an emotional telephone visit we shared together. The connection resulted in Tad, his wife, Tami and daughter, Tiann coming to Kelowna being welcomed warmly at our home by my whole family on the August 1st long weekend, three weeks after we had our first conversation together. We gathered again that Christmas and since have enjoyed a very close relationship

Tad was never adopted but taken into a foster home by Vera May and Robert Francis Goddard of Kamloops. There the couple foster parented for thirty years two hundred and fifty other children along with Tad who remained since his birth until age eighteen as a member of the Goddard family. Goddard family members continue to provide him the sibling attention that grounds him. Tad is a professional singer, writer and recording musician. He has scored music for motion pictures, recorded albums and performed in many successful bands winning a gold record with the band Prism.

I met my son's foster mother, Vera a couple of years prior to her death at eighty-nine, on February 24, 2004. She was a gracious woman who exuded love for Tad and life itself. I continue to feel a great deal of gratitude for the Goddard's and their work in Tad's life and the willingness of his mother to have shared her son with me during her final years.

Finding Tad has filled a vacant chapter in my life. I understand that I could never be a replacement for Robert Goddard, a Kamloops carpenter and his wife, Vera. Their capacity to unselfishly share their lives and home with Tad and so many other children was what was required for my son. The Goddard's taught each child they cared for about the importance of the human heart and the greatness of its capacity to give and love. Something most of the children they foster parented would otherwise never have had the opportunity to understand before leaving the Goddard home.

My own mother was troubled for years over the secret that I thought I held between myself and my wife, since sharing it with my bride prior to marrying. Mom never liked that I had withheld discussing the matter and grumbled about it in a vague sort of way on one occasion when angry with me. I guess I owed being open to her, but it was too painful for me to discuss the subject as my mother always seemed severe in her reaction toward me. It was reflected in a disharmony that remained between us for years, something I never understood, but that surfaced from time to time.

I brought Tad to her and from that moment on she was healed of it. After meeting Tad, she boasted of the grandchildren she had, "Twenty-one!" Tad had been added to the count after the meeting.

2013 Son, Tad Goddard shows his Gold Record Award

Chapter Forty-Seven

N ever had I spent time in Mom's Kelowna home alone, but that summer I felt the finality of closing of her affairs quite moving. We had the burial at Coldstream cemetery where Dad, my sister, Sherry and her husband, Leonard had been laid to rest in the cemetery where Dyck, Bickert and Sasges deceased rested. Afterwards, Marlene stayed with Janice for a couple of months prior to Mary Bickert asking if the brothers would object to her caring for Janice. It was a generous and wonderful offer that was well received. Janice continues under Mary's care for eighteen years now. Today Janice is sixty-six years.

Patrick and I were named executors and the disposition of the effects was handled by the two us. There were years of mail and paperwork to sort through collected in closets, cupboards and drawers. Each letter or document revealed events, attesting to births, baptisms, marriages, friendships and lives lived, but one, a family tree arranged by LaLonde family historian, Ken Cannon, told a story I had not known. It revealed the date of Mom's marriage to Carl Ellis. It seems that their wedding would have been considered a matter of necessity during the time it occurred, October 25, 1943. If accurate, Mom would have been expecting my brother, John, who was born in May 1944. In disbelief, I studied the family tree document reviewing in my mind the sequence of dates and events that would have led to her marriage to my natural father. But why had she written Ken Cannon and been specific about the date that would be recorded in his historical tree document and not have beforehand discussed the circumstance with family?

Many papers that I studied in her home had inconsistencies with dates or errors in names recorded. Some were handwritten documents assembled over the years by various registries and churches. I recall when Ken asked family members to provide him with the dates while he was doing his tree. He provided forms for each to fill in. Perhaps the date was incorrect or perhaps not. Mom had become a little forgetful by then. If the date was correct, it was because the two, Mom and Carl, wanted to honour the circumstance and save the embarrassment in a day when it would have been considered inappropriate not to marry. Letters between the two, left with her possessions after her departure back to Marquis indicated the endearment of Ellis to my mother.

What troubled me more was that I had failed to entrust to my parents a discussion on the matter of my predicament after Kamloops when I was a young man and that my mother had done nothing to ease me into the conversation that she seemed to want to engage in years later. If her dates were accurate then, we both denied the openness and trust that society for years had since begun to enjoy.

Mom's own past likely had enlightened her of youths' vulnerability where entrapment from error required years to recover. She was as much of a character as any of her past or future family could ever become themselves and spirited enough to be saintly, while vexatious and at times cunning enough to be avoided. Every family member that knew my mother understood that she possessed that required Light in her life to deliver her soul to a peaceful eternity. She had a rich faith and trust in Calvary!

Imperfect humans as we are, every event we live out together can be part of growth and when shared within the community of family is better. Entrusting detail about individual lives grows us to become whole people. That's why I write, and I expect my mother did as well. Her recording of the marriage date in the family tree document could have been intentional.

The years that followed her death on June 30th, 2002, provided many reasons for the Bickert family to gather, but none were more compelling than the memories of the mother she had been, who frequently insisted we love one another and be family together.

Once again, I was asked by my siblings to deliver another eulogy, my mother's. I tried to describe her legacy, but no words could describe the reason for it better than what was penned in her poem:

'I write.'

I write to tell of many things I love
Children, friendship, blessings from above.
I write for laughter and for heart's content
For every written word's a message sent.

I write of April rain, of grain fields, flowers,
The warmth of home, our books, the joy of hours
Spent with parents, listening to their gems
Of wisdom, from which our courage stems.

I write to keep the spring I must remember
I write to halt my speeding through September.
I write to warm the winter that will come
For summer was so brief, so 'on the run.'

I write of all the hours God was near
Through summers lively walk with six to rear.
And as a parent, pen my love and trust
And so, I know I write because I must.

My pen must pulsate with an eager beat
To strike out malice, ignorance and deceit
To teach them of the flow of Holy Light,
Point out the dangers of despair and fright.

To foster strength in all they will endure,
Encourage talent, gentleness and more;
To teach them love of God and fellow man
And so, my words require careful plan

I write for I have reached no worldly goal.
I write to calm disquiet in mine own soul.
Then I, a humble poet, gratefully
Thank poets fine and famed, who write for me!

Hence, I have written you about her and others and the life they've inspired me to live.

Paul Francis Bickert
November 2020

Paul Francis Bickert's Family Lineage

Michael Griffin from Doosheen, Ireland, born March 28,1875 and Mary Anne Foerster of Hesson, Ontario born August 19, 1881 marry in Regina, Saskatchewan on June 19, 1917 and Mary Anne gives birth to John and then Patrick and then on February 27, 1922 to twins, Kathleen and Mary. Mary Anne Foerster dies ten days later. Kay was then adopted by John LaLonde, born May 18, 1892 and wife, Gladys (Naylor) 1898-1993. The other twin is adopted by the neighbouring Kennedy family in Marquis. Michael lived another nine years and married housekeeper, Gertie Hanlan who was stepmother to Michael`s sons, John and Patrick Griffin.

Kathleen Helen Bickert, born Kathleen Helen Griffin 2/27/1922 (registered in error Catherine Helen Griffin) to Mary Anne Foerster and Michael Griffin February 27, 1922 adopted as an infant by John LaLonde and Gladys LaLonde (Naylor).

John LaLonde born May 18, 1892 was the son of James LaLonde and his wife, Anna (Zoller) who married on July 22, 1887. He married Gladys Naylor and the couple adopted Kathleen LaLonde

Herman and Helena Dyck Mennonite immigrants via Russia come to Canada with son Johan Dyck who marries Agatha Hilde and give birth to Helen Dyck + brothers, Jacob, John, Peter, William and Sisters, Agatha, Lizzie, Mary, Kay, Susanna and Agnes.

Helen Dyck (oldest daughter) marries Harry Bueckert giving birth to John Irvin, Frances, Gladys, Edward and Jeanne.

John Irven Bickert, born John Irven Bueckert, born April 4, 1919 to Harry Bueckert and Helen Bueckert (Dyck). Their names changed to Bickert. He marries Kathleen Helen Ellis (LaLonde/Griffin at birth) on October 17, 1949, after his failed marriage to Ethel Nash and Kathleen`s failed marriage to Carl Ellis. Kathleen had given birth to Carl`s sons, John George and Paul Francis. John Irvine Bickert had custody of his daughter, Sherry, born to Ethel Bickert (Nash).

Kathleen LaLonde + Carl Ellis >> John George Ellis May 7, 1946 & Paul Francis Ellis b. May 29, 1945

John I. Bickert + Ethel Nash >> Sherry Anne Bickert b. June 12, 1941

John I. Bickert + Kathleen Bickert married Oct 17, 1949. The resultant blended family consisted of children, Sherry, John and Paul. Children of the marriage were: Irvine Joseph Bickert b. July 7,1951 Geoffrey Michael Bickert b. Aug. 15, 1952, Kathleen Mary Bickert b. Sept. 18, 1953, Janice Mary Bickert b. Sept 8, 1954, Patrick Gerard Bickert b. Feb. 11, 1956

Paul Francis Bickert, was born Paul Francis Ellis, May 29, 1945 in Moose Jaw, Saskatchewan. His natural father was Carl Ellis, first husband of Kathleen LaLonde. He married Marlene Margaret Ibbotson on February 4, 1967

Marlene Margaret Ibbotson was born March 3, 1946 in North Battleford, Saskatchewan, the daughter of Alleyne Charles Ibbotson and Leonie Melina Ibbotson (L'Heireux).

Marlene Margaret (Ibbotson) Bickert and Paul Francis Bickert give birth to Natalie Carmen Bickert September 24, 1969 and Taylor Christian Bickert January 27, 1973 and Charity Marie Bickert May 1, 1976.

Paul Bickert has a son from his relationship with Karen Olson giving birth to Tad Conrad (Olson) Goddard born Dec 14, 1964. Tad Goddard.

About the Author

Paul F. Bickert D.C.

The author's childhood was marred with sickness and injury. In his matriculation year of high school, he took an interest in broadcasting and after the school term ended was hired as a news broadcaster earning the title 'Golden Throat.' Eventually he worked with both Capitol and Columbia records working in association with numerous celebrities while they toured. He earned a Doctor of Chiropractic degree (Cum Laude) at Palmer Chiropractic in Iowa, and practiced for 20 years before inventing a wireless antenna that resulted in him taking his company public during the technological bubble.

His oblique direction in life led to financial success, so he formed the Chiropractic for the World Foundation (CFTW) funding African projects. His brother runs the foundation today.

His Catholic faith and marriage to an Anglican, along with being raised in a blended family have led him to a tolerant and ecumenical Christian approach to conciliation with others along his life's journey.

CPSIA information can be obtained
at www.ICGtesting.com
Printed in the USA
BVHW030358100221
599415BV00001B/4